Mortgage Management For Dur
by Eric Tyson and Robert Grisw

Eric and Robert's Top Tips for Borrowers

- *Before* you get a mortgage, be sure you understand your personal financial situation. The amount of money a banker is willing to lend you isn't necessarily the amount you can "afford" to borrow given your financial goals and current situation. See Chapter 1.
- Maximize your chances for getting the mortgage you want the first time you apply by understanding how lenders evaluate your creditworthiness. Don't waste time and money on loans that end up rejected. Most obstacles to mortgage qualification can and should be overcome prior to submitting a loan application. See Chapters 2 and 3.
- Because the ocean of mortgage programs is bordered with reefs of jargon, learn loan lingo before you begin your mortgage-shopping voyage. This will enable you to hook the best loan and avoid being taken in by loan sharks. See Chapter 4 and Appendix C, the Glossary.
- To select the best type of fixed-rate or adjustable-rate mortgage for your situation, clarify two important issues. How long do you expect to keep the loan? How much financial risk are you able to accept? See Chapter 5.
- Special situation loans — such as a home equity loan or 80-10-10 financing — could be just what you need. However, some "special" loans, such as 100 percent loans and balloon loans, can be toxic. See Chapter 6.
- Whether you do it yourself or hire a mortgage broker to shop for you, canvas a variety of lenders when seeking the best mortgage. Be sure to shop not only for a low-cost loan but also for lenders that provide a high level of service. See Chapter 7.
- Investigate when shopping for a mortgage on the Internet. Be cautious. You may save time and money. Or you could end up with aggravation and a worse loan. See Chapter 8.
- Compare various lenders' mortgage programs and understand the myriad costs and features associated with each loan. To help you keep score and do a fair comparison, we provide helpful worksheets. See Chapter 9.
- Just as you must prepare a compelling résumé as the first step to securing a job you want, craft a positive, truthful mortgage application as a key to getting the loan you want. See Chapter 10.
- After you get a mortgage to purchase a home, stay informed about interest rates, because a drop in rates could provide a money-saving opportunity.

Refinancing — that is, obtaining a new mortgage to replace an existing one — can save you big money. Assess how long it will take you to recoup your out-of-pocket refinance costs. See Chapter 11.

- You may benefit from paying off your mortgage faster than is required. But before you do, examine what else you could do with that extra cash and what may be best for your situation. See Chapter 12.
- If you're among the increasing number of homeowners who reach retirement with insufficient assets for their golden years, carefully consider a reverse mortgage, which enables older homeowners to tap their home's equity. Reverse mortgages are more complicated to understand than traditional mortgages. See Chapter 13.
- If you fall on tough economic times and get behind on your housing payments, don't resign yourself to foreclosure. Take stock of the situation. Review your spending and debts and begin a dialogue with your lender to find a solution. Make use of low-cost counseling approved by the U.S. Department of Housing and Urban Development. See Chapter 14.
- Use the Loan Amortization Tables in Appendix A to determine your monthly payment after you know a loan's interest rate and term (number of years until final payoff).
- After you've had a loan awhile, see the Remaining Balance Tables in Appendix B to know how much of your original loan balance remains to be paid.

Mortgage Payment Calculator*

To calculate your monthly mortgage payment, simply multiply the relevant number from the following table by the size of your mortgage expressed in (divided by) thousands of dollars. For example, on a 30-year mortgage of $125,000 at 7.5 percent, you multiply 125 by 7.00 (from the table) to come up with an $875 monthly payment.

Interest Rate (%)	Term of Mortgage	
	15 years	**30 years**
4	7.40	4.77
4⅛	7.46	4.85
4¼	7.52	4.92
4⅜	7.59	4.99
4½	7.65	5.07
4⅝	7.71	5.14
4¾	7.78	5.22

Interest Rate (%)	Term of Mortgage	
	15 years	30 years
4⅞	7.84	5.29
5	7.91	5.37
5⅛	7.98	5.45
5¼	8.04	5.53
5⅜	8.11	5.60
5½	8.18	5.68
5⅝	8.24	5.76
5¾	8.31	5.84
5⅞	8.38	5.92
6	8.44	6.00
6⅛	8.51	6.08
6¼	8.58	6.16
6⅜	8.65	6.24
6½	8.72	6.33
6⅝	8.78	6.41
6¾	8.85	6.49
6⅞	8.92	6.57
7	8.99	6.66
7⅛	9.06	6.74
7¼	9.13	6.83
7⅜	9.20	6.91
7½	9.28	7.00
7⅝	9.35	7.08
7¾	9.42	7.17
7⅞	9.49	7.26
8	9.56	7.34
8⅛	9.63	7.43
8¼	9.71	7.52
8⅜	9.78	7.61
8½	9.85	7.69
8⅝	9.93	7.78

Interest Rate (%)	Term of Mortgage	
	15 years	30 years
8¾	10.00	7.87
8⅞	10.07	7.96
9	10.15	8.05
9⅛	10.22	8.14
9¼	10.30	8.23
9⅜	10.37	8.32
9½	10.45	8.41
9⅝	10.52	8.50
9¾	10.60	8.60
9⅞	10.67	8.69
10	10.75	8.78
10⅛	10.83	8.87
10¼	10.90	8.97
10⅜	10.98	9.06
10½	11.06	9.15
10⅝	11.14	9.25
10¾	11.21	9.34
10⅞	11.29	9.43
11	11.37	9.53
11¼	11.53	9.72
11½	11.69	9.91
11¾	11.85	10.10
12	12.01	10.29
12¼	12.17	10.48
12½	12.17	10.48

Warning: Mortgage payments are only a portion of the costs of owning a home. See Chapter 1 for figuring out your total costs and fitting them into your personal finances.

Mortgage Management

Mortgage Management

by Eric Tyson, MBA, and
Robert S. Griswold, MSBA,
with Ray Brown

Mortgage Management For Dummies®

Published by: John Wiley & Sons, Inc., 111 River Street, Hoboken, NJ 07030-5774, www.wiley.com

For general information on our other products and services, please contact our Customer Care Department within the U.S. at 877-762-2974, outside the U.S. at 317-572-3993, or fax 317-572-4002. For technical support, please visit https://hub.wiley.com/community/support/dummies.

Wiley publishes in a variety of print and electronic formats and by print-on-demand. Some material included with standard print versions of this book may not be included in e-books or in print-on-demand. If this book refers to media such as a CD or DVD that is not included in the version you purchased, you may download this material at http://booksupport.wiley.com. For more information about Wiley products, visit www.wiley.com.

Library of Congress Control Number: 2017942339

ISBN 978-1-119-38779-4 (pbk); ISBN 978-1-119-38780-0 (ebk); ISBN 978-1-119-38781-7 (ebk)

Manufactured in the United States of America

10 9 8 7 6 5 4 3 2 1

Contents at a Glance

Table of Contents

Introduction

Welcome to *Mortgage Management For Dummies!* If you own or want to own real estate, you need to understand mortgages. Whether you need a loan to buy your first home, want to refinance an existing mortgage, seek to finance investment properties, or are interested in tapping some of the value you've built up in your home over the years, you've found the right book.

Unfortunately for most of us, the mortgage field is jammed with jargon and fraught with fiscal pitfalls. Choose the wrong mortgage and you could end up squandering money better saved for important financial goals, such as covering higher education tuition for your adorable little gremlins, buying that second home you've always wanted, or simply having more resources for your retirement. In the worst cases, you could end up losing your home to foreclosure and end up in personal bankruptcy. Just look at what happened in the late 2000s when the real estate market declined in many parts of the country. Folks who overextended themselves with risky mortgages ended up in foreclosure.

For typical homeowners, the monthly mortgage payment is either their largest or, after income taxes, second largest expense. When you're shopping for a mortgage, you could easily waste many hours and suffer financial losses by not getting the best loan that you can based on your specific needs and financial situation.

Because so much is at stake, we want to help you make the best decisions possible. That's where we come in.

How This Book is Different

How is this book different and better than competing mortgage books, you ask? Let us count the ways. Our book is

- **Objective:** Our goal is to make you as knowledgeable as possible *before* you commit to a particular mortgage. Most mortgage books are written by mortgage brokers or lenders who loathe to share the secrets of the mortgage business. Typically, they're more interested in promoting their own business by convincing you to use a particular mortgage broker or lender. We're not here to promote any specific brokers or lenders — we wrote this book to help you. Consider us your independent advisors.

- **Holistic:** When you obtain a mortgage, that decision affects your ability to save money and accomplish other important financial goals. We help you understand how best to fit your mortgage into the rest of your personal-finance puzzle. We also offer tips on strategies to pay off your mortgage debt efficiently or use it creatively to build overall wealth. Other mortgage books don't help you consider these bigger-picture issues of personal finance before you buy.
- **Jargon-free:** One of the hallmarks of books intended to confuse and impress the reader, rather than to convey practical information and advice, is the use of all sorts of insider terms that make things sound more mysterious and complicated than they really are. We, on the other hand, pride ourselves on simplifying the complex. Between the two of us, we have more than seven decades of practical experience explaining things to real people just like you. Eric has worked as a financial counselor, teacher, and syndicated columnist. For over 15 years, Robert hosted a real estate radio program; he was the live, on-air real estate expert for NBC-TV, and he has written several real estate books. Our combined experience can put you firmly in control of the mortgage-decision-making process.
- **User-friendly:** You can read our book piecemeal to address your specific questions and immediate concerns. But if you want a crash course on the world of mortgages, read it cover to cover. In addition to being organized to help you quickly find the information you're seeking, each portion of the book stands on its own.

Foolish Assumptions

Yes, we know that making assumptions is foolish, but we just can't help ourselves. We assume that you, dear reader, fit into one of these categories:

- You're preparing to purchase your first home.
- You want to refinance your current mortgage.
- You desire to explore real estate as an investment.
- You're interested in tapping into the equity you've built up in your home.
- You want to find realistic, legitimate ways to pay off or significantly reduce your mortgage early.

Icons Used in This Book

Sprinkled throughout this book are cute little icons to help reinforce and draw attention to key points or to flag stuff that you can skip over.

TIP

This icon flags key strategies that can improve your mortgage decisions and, in some cases, save you thousands of dollars. Think of these little light bulbs as highlighting words of wisdom that we would whisper in your ear if we were close enough to do so.

REMEMBER

This icon designates something important we don't want you to forget when you're researching, applying for, and finalizing your mortgage.

WARNING

Numerous pitfalls await prospective mortgage borrowers. This symbol denotes mistakes committed by those who have come before you. Heed these warnings and save yourself a lot of heartache.

TECHNICAL STUFF

This icon marks stuff that you don't really have to know but that may come in handy at cocktail parties thrown by people in the mortgage industry.

Beyond the Book

In addition to the material in the print or e-book you're reading right now, this product also comes with a free access-anywhere Cheat Sheet that can help you think about the best and most cost-effective ways to select, use, and manage mortgages. To get this Cheat Sheet, simply go to `www.dummies.com` and search for "Mortgage Management For Dummies Cheat Sheet" in the Search box.

Where to Go from Here

If you're not quite sure where to start, flip to the table of contents or index and find a subject that piques your interest. Feel free to dive in wherever you find chapters that apply to your circumstances. If you're more conventional, start at the beginning and trust us to guide you safely through the mortgage maze. By the time you finish the book, you'll be a mortgage master.

1

Getting Started with Mortgages

IN THIS PART . . .

Determine how much mortgage debt you can *really* afford.

Find out how to qualify for a mortgage and why getting preapproved is a smart move.

Discover the importance of your credit score, the secrets your credit report holds, and how to get both in top-notch shape.

» Estimating your likely homeownership expenses

» Considering your other financial goals

Chapter 1
Determining Your Borrowing Power

If you're like most folks, the single biggest purchase you'll make during your lifetime will be when you buy a home. And, to make that purchase, you'll likely have to borrow money by using a loan called a mortgage. The cumulative payments on that mortgage will far exceed the sticker price on your home due to the interest you'll pay.

Most people thinking of purchasing a home focus solely on the price of the home. If you're in the enviable position of being able to pay all cash, then the price is really all you need to consider in determining whether you can afford a given home. But the vast majority of people purchase real estate with financing. So although the purchase price is important, the reality is that the mortgage terms that you're able to secure and negotiate will determine the monthly payment that you can afford and will dictate the maximum price you can pay for your new home.

In this chapter, we help you tackle this first vital subject to consider when the time comes to take out a mortgage — how much mortgage can you really afford? ***Note:*** We intend this chapter primarily to help people who are buying a home (first or not) determine what size mortgage fits their financial situation. If you're in the mortgage market for purposes of refinancing, please also see Chapter 11.

Only You Can Determine the Mortgage Debt You Can Afford

Sit down and talk in person or by phone, or use a website to gather information and then meet face to face with a reputable mortgage lender, and you'll be asked about your income and debts. Assuming that you have a good credit history and an adequate cash down payment, the lender can quickly estimate the amount of mortgage debt you can obtain.

Suppose a mortgage lender says that you qualify to borrow, for example, $200,000. In this case, the lender is basically telling you that, based on the assessment of your financial situation, $200,000 is the *maximum* amount that this lender thinks you can borrow on a mortgage before putting yourself at significantly increased risk of default. Don't assume that the lender is saying that you can *afford* to carry that much mortgage debt given your other financial goals.

Your overall personal financial situation — most of which lenders, mortgage brokers, and real estate agents won't inquire into or care about — should help you decide how much you borrow. For example, have you considered and planned for your retirement goals? Do you know how much you're spending per month now and how much slack, if any, you have for additional housing expenses, including a larger mortgage? How much of a reserve or rainy day savings fund do you have? How are you going to pay for college expenses for your kids? Are you or will you soon be helping to care for elderly relatives?

In the following sections, we start you on the path to answering these questions.

Acknowledge your need to save

Unless you have generous parents, grandparents, or in-laws, if you want to buy a home, you need to save money. The same may be true if you desire to trade up to a more costly property. In either case, you can find yourself taking on more mortgage debt than you ever dreamed possible.

After you trade up or buy your first home, your total monthly housing expenditures and housing-related spending (such as furnishings, insurance, and utilities) will surely increase. So be forewarned that if you had trouble saving before the purchase, your finances are truly going to be squeezed after the purchase. This pinch will further handicap your ability to accomplish other important financial goals, such as saving for retirement, starting your own business, or helping to pay for your own or your children's college education.

Because you can't manage the unknown, the first step in assessing your ability to afford a given mortgage amount is to collect data about your monthly spending (see the following section). If you already track such data — whether by pencil and paper or on your computer — you have a head start. But *don't* think you're finished. Having your spending data is only half the battle. You also need to know how to analyze your spending data (which we explain how to do in this chapter) to help decide how much you can afford to borrow comfortably.

Collect your spending data

What could be more dreadful than sitting at home on a beautiful sunny day — or staying in at night while your friends and family are out on the town — and cozying up to your calculator, banking and credit card transactions, pay stubs, and most recent tax return?

Examining where and how much you spend on various items is almost no one's definition of a good time (except, perhaps, for some accountants, IRS agents, actuaries, and other bean counters who crunch numbers for a living). However, if you don't endure some pain and agony now, you could end up suffering long-term pain and agony when you get in over your head with a mortgage you can't afford.

Now some good news: You don't need to detail to the penny where your money goes. That simply isn't realistic. What you're interested in here is capturing the bulk of your expenditures and allowing for some margin for unanticipated expenses, plus savings for an emergency fund. Ideally, you should collect spending data for a three- to six-month period to determine how much you spend in a typical month on taxes, clothing, transportation, entertainment, meals out, and so forth. If your expenditures fluctuate greatly throughout the year, you may need to examine a full 12 months of your spending to get an accurate monthly average. You also want to include any known changes in upcoming expenses. Maybe your child will be starting preschool next year at a private institution or your car is getting old and you know you'll soon want to get a new vehicle.

Later in this chapter, we provide a handy table that you can use to categorize and add up all your spending. First, however, we need to talk you through the specific and often large expenses of owning a home so you can intelligently plug those numbers into your current budget.

Determine Your Potential Homeownership Expenses

If you're in the market to buy your first home, you probably don't have a clear sense about the costs of homeownership. Even people who presently own a home and are considering trading up often don't have a great grasp on their current or likely future homeownership expenses. So we include this section to help you assess your likely homeownership costs.

Making your mortgage payments

A *mortgage* is a loan you take out to finance the purchase of a home. Mortgage loans are generally paid in monthly installments typically over either a 15- or 30-year time span. Chapter 4 provides greater detail about how mortgages work.

In the early years of repaying your mortgage, nearly all your mortgage payment goes toward paying interest on the money that you borrowed. Not until the later years of your mortgage term do you rapidly begin to pay down your loan balance (the *principal*).

As we say earlier in this chapter, all that mortgage lenders can do is tell you their own criteria for approving and denying mortgage applications and calculating the maximum that you're eligible to borrow. A mortgage lender tallies up your monthly *housing expense*, the components of which the lender considers to be the mortgage payment, property taxes, and homeowners insurance.

Understanding lenders' ratios

For a given property that you're considering buying, a mortgage lender calculates the housing expense and normally requires that it not exceed 40 percent or so of your monthly before-tax *(gross)* income. So, for example, if your monthly gross income is $5,000, your lender may not allow your expected monthly housing expense to exceed $2,000. If you're self-employed and complete IRS Form 1040, Schedule C, mortgage lenders use your after-expenses *(net)* income, from the bottom line of Schedule C (and, in fact, add back noncash expenses for items such as real estate and equipment depreciation, which increases a self-employed person's net income for qualification purposes).

This housing expense ratio completely ignores almost all your other financial goals, needs, and obligations. It also ignores property maintenance and remodeling expenses, which can suck up a lot of a homeowner's dough. Never assume that the amount a lender is willing to lend you is the amount you can truly afford.

In addition to your income, the only other financial considerations a lender takes into account are your debts or ongoing monthly obligations. Specifically, mortgage lenders examine the required monthly payments for other debts you may have, such as student loans, auto loans, and credit card bills. They also deduct for alimony, child support, or any other required payments. In addition to the percentage of your income that lenders allow for housing expenses, they typically allow an additional 5 percent of your monthly income to go toward other debt repayments.

Calculating your mortgage payment amount

After you know the amount you want to borrow, calculating the size of your mortgage payment is straightforward. The challenge is figuring out how much you can comfortably afford to borrow given your other financial goals. This chapter should assist you in this regard, especially the previous section on analyzing your spending and goals.

SO YOU THINK YOU CAN HANDLE EXCESS BORROWING?

Some people we know believe they can handle more mortgage debt than lenders allow using their handy-dandy ratios. Such borrowers may seek to borrow additional money from family, or they may fib about their income when filling out their mortgage applications.

Although some homeowners who stretch themselves financially do just fine, others end up in financial and emotional trouble. You should also know that because lenders usually cross-check the information on your mortgage application with IRS Form 4506T (the lender receives your actual tax return you filed, which certainly didn't overstate your income), borrowers who fib on their mortgage applications are caught and their applications denied.

So although we say that the lender's word isn't the gospel as to how much home you can truly afford, telling the truth on your mortgage application is the only way to go. It may be painful to learn that you don't qualify for the loan you need to purchase that home of your dreams, but you're likely better off in the long run not overextending yourself with mortgage debt.

We should also note that telling the truth prevents you from committing perjury and fraud, troubles that catch even officials elected to high office. Bankers don't want you to get in over your head financially and default on your loan, and we don't want you to either.

Suppose you work through your budget and determine that you can afford to spend $2,000 per month on housing. Determining the exact size of a mortgage that allows you to stay within this boundary may seem daunting, because your overall housing cost is comprised of several components: mortgage payments, property taxes, insurance, and maintenance (and association dues if the property is a condominium or has community assets like a swimming pool).

Using Appendix A, you can calculate the size of your mortgage payments based on the amount you want to borrow, the loan's interest rate, and whether you want a 15- or 30-year mortgage. Alternatively, you can do the same calculations by using many of the best financial calculators available for less than $50 from companies like HP and Texas Instruments. (In Chapter 8, we discuss the ubiquitous online mortgage calculators, which are often highly simplistic.)

Paying property taxes

As you're already painfully aware if you're a homeowner now, you must pay property taxes to your local government. The taxes are generally paid to a division typically called the County or Town Tax Collector.

Property taxes are typically based on the value of a property. Because property taxes vary from one locality to another, call the relevant local tax collector's office to determine the exact rate in your area. (Check the government section of your local phone directory to find the phone number or search for the name of the municipality and "property tax" online.) In addition to inquiring about the property tax rate in the town where you're contemplating buying a home, also ask what additional fees and assessments may apply. In California, many recently developed areas have special assessments (such as *Mello-Roos* districts), which are additional property taxes to pay for enhanced infrastructure and amenities, such as parks, police/fire stations, golf courses, and landscaped medians.

If you make a smaller down payment — less than 20 percent of the home's purchase price — your lender is likely to require you to have an *impound account* (also called an *escrow account* or *reserve account*). Such an account requires you to pay a monthly pro-rata portion of your annual property taxes, and often your homeowners insurance, to the lender each month along with your mortgage payment. The lender is responsible for making the necessary property tax and insurance payments to the appropriate agencies on your behalf. An impound account keeps the homeowner from getting hit with a large annual property tax bill.

WARNING

As you shop for a home, be aware that real estate listings frequently contain information regarding the amount the current property owner is currently paying in taxes. These taxes are often based on an outdated, much lower property valuation. If you purchase the home, your property taxes may be significantly higher based on the price that you pay for the property. Conversely, if you happen to buy a home that has decreased in value since it was purchased, you could find that your property taxes are actually lower.

Tracking your tax write-offs

Now is a good point to pause, recognize, and give thanks for the tax benefits of homeownership. The federal tax authorities at the Internal Revenue Service (IRS) and most state governments allow you to deduct, within certain limits, mortgage interest and property taxes when you file your annual income tax return.

You may deduct the interest on the first $1 million of mortgage debt as well as all the property taxes. (This mortgage interest deductibility covers debt on both your primary residence *and* a second residence.) The IRS also allows you to deduct the interest costs on additional borrowing known as home equity loans or home equity lines of credit (HELOCs, see Chapter 6) to a maximum of $100,000 borrowed.

To keep things simple and get a reliable estimate of the tax savings from your mortgage interest and property tax write-off, multiply your mortgage payment and property taxes by your *federal* income tax rate in Table 1-1. This approximation method works fine as long as you're in the earlier years of paying off your mortgage, because the small portion of your mortgage payment that isn't deductible (because it's for the repayment of the principal amount of your loan) approximately offsets the overlooked state tax savings.

TABLE 1-1 **2017 Federal Income Tax Brackets and Rates**

Singles Taxable Income	Married-Filing-Jointly Taxable Income	Federal Tax Rate (Bracket)
Less than $9,325	Less than $18,650	10%
$9,325 to $37,950	$18,650 to $75,900	15%
$37,950 to $91,900	$75,900 to $153,100	25%
$91,900 to $191,650	$153,100 to $233,350	28%
$191,650 to $416,700	$233,350 to $416,700	33%
$416,700 to $418,400	$416,700 to $470,700	35%
More than $418,400	More than $470,700	39.6%

Investing in insurance

When you own a home with a mortgage, your mortgage lender will insist as a condition of funding your loan that you have adequate homeowners insurance, which includes both casualty and liability coverage. The cost of your insurance policy is largely derived from the estimated cost of rebuilding your home. Although land has value, it doesn't need to be insured, because it wouldn't be destroyed in a fire. Buy the most comprehensive homeowners insurance coverage you can and take the highest deductible you can afford, to help minimize the cost.

TIP

As a homeowner, you'd also be wise to obtain insurance coverage against possible damage, destruction, or theft of personal property, such as clothing, furniture, kitchen appliances, audiovisual equipment, and your collection of vintage fire hydrants. Personal property goodies can cost big bucks to replace. Some prized possessions like jewelry, antiques, and collectibles are often excluded from your base policy and can require a special added coverage policy with limits that need to be set based on the replacement value of the items.

In years past, various lenders learned the hard way that some homeowners with little financial stake in the property and insufficient insurance coverage simply walked away from homes that were total losses and left the lender with the loss. Thus, in addition to sufficient casualty and liability insurance, lenders require you to purchase *private mortgage insurance* if you put down less than 20 percent of the purchase price when you buy. This is risk insurance that protects the lender by making the mortgage payments to the lender if you're unable to. This could be because you have a loss of income whether from a job loss or an injury/illness.

REMEMBER

Private mortgage insurance is an extra cost that will factor into the calculation for the amount of your loan and reduce your ability to borrow. You may be able to avoid paying private mortgage insurance by using 80-10-10 financing. We cover this technique in Chapter 6.

Budgeting for closing costs

As you budget for a given home purchase, don't forget to budget for the inevitable laundry list of one-time *closing costs*. In a typical home purchase, closing costs amount to about 2 to 5 percent of the purchase price of the property. Thus, you shouldn't ignore them when you figure the amount of money you need to close the deal. Having enough to pay the down payment on your loan just isn't sufficient.

TIP

Some sellers may be willing to assist buyers by paying a portion of the closing costs. This is particularly true with new home subdivisions by major builders but is always negotiable with any seller. However, expect to pay a higher interest rate for a mortgage with few or no upfront fees.

Here are the major closing costs and our guidance as to how much to budget for each:

- **Loan-origination fees and charges:** Lenders generally levy fees for appraising the property, obtaining a copy of your credit report, preparing your loan documents, and processing your loan. They'll also whack you 1 to 2 percent of the loan amount for a *loan-origination fee.* Another term for this prepaid interest charge, as we explain in Chapter 9, is *points.* If you're strapped for cash, you can get a loan that has few or no fees; however, such loans have higher interest rates over their lifetimes. You may be able to negotiate having the seller pay these loan-closing costs. The total loan-origination fees and other charges may add up to as much as 3 percent of the mortgage amount.
- **Escrow fees:** These costs cover the preparation and transmission of all home-purchase-related documents and funds. Escrow fees range from several hundred to over a thousand dollars, based on the purchase price of your home.
- **Homeowners insurance:** Lenders generally require that you pay the first year's premium on your homeowners insurance policy at the time of closing. Such insurance typically costs from several hundred to several thousand dollars, depending on the value of your home and the extent of coverage you desire.
- **Title insurance:** *Title insurance* protects you and the lender against the risk that the person selling you the home doesn't legally own it. This insurance typically costs from several hundred to a few thousand dollars, depending on your home's purchase price. Happily, the premium you pay at close of escrow is the only title insurance premium you'll ever have to pay *unless you subsequently decide to refinance your mortgage.* Oddly, there are places like Northern California where the seller (not the buyer) pays for the "main" title policy. This is purely a matter of "local custom." Ask your agent what the custom is where you are buying.
- **Property taxes:** At the closing of your home purchase, you may have to reimburse the sellers for property taxes that they paid in advance. Here's how it works. Suppose you close on your home purchase on October 15, and the sellers have already paid their property taxes through December 31. You have to reimburse the sellers for property taxes they paid from October 15 through the end of the year. The prorated property taxes you end up paying in your actual transaction are based on the home's taxes and the date that escrow actually closes and cost from several hundred to a couple of thousand dollars. In some parts of the country, if you paid more than the prior owner for the property, you may also receive a supplemental property tax bill from your tax collector, after you close escrow, seeking payment for the incremental increase in the property taxes for your prorated period of ownership.

» **Attorney fees:** In some eastern states, lawyers are involved (unfortunately from some participants' perspectives) in real estate purchases. In most states, however, lawyers aren't needed for home purchases as long as the real estate agents use standard, fill-in-the-blank contracts. If you do hire an attorney, expect to pay at least several hundred dollars.

» **Property inspections:** As advocated in *Home Buying For Dummies* (Wiley), you should always have a home professionally inspected before you buy it. Inspection fees usually cost at least several hundred dollars (larger homes cost more to inspect of course). Be sure to carefully review this report and ask for additional information or hire a specialized contractor to conduct further investigation for any noted item of concern. If you are able, accompany the inspector when he inspects the property.

» **Private mortgage insurance (PMI):** If you make a down payment of less than 20 percent of the purchase price of the home, mortgage lenders generally require that you take out private mortgage insurance that protects the lender in case you default on your mortgage. You may need to pay up to a year's worth of premium for this coverage at closing, which can amount to as much as several hundred dollars. One terrific way to avoid this extra cost is to make a 20 percent down payment.

» **Prepaid loan interest:** At closing, the lender charges interest on your mortgage to cover the interest that accrues from the date your loan is funded — generally one business day before the closing — up to the day of your first scheduled loan payment. How much interest you actually have to pay depends on the timing of your first loan payment.

If you're strapped for cash at closing, try the following tricks to minimize the prepaid loan interest you owe at closing:

- First, ask your lender which day of the month your payment will be due and schedule to close on the loan as few days in advance of that day as possible. (Payments are usually due on the first of the month, so closing on the last day of the month or a few days before is generally best.)
- Or ask whether your lender is willing to adjust your monthly due date closer to the date you desire to close on your loan.
- Also, never schedule a closing to occur on a Monday because the lender will generally have to put your mortgage funds into escrow the preceding Friday, causing you to pay interest for Friday, Saturday, and Sunday. (Some lenders may be able to accommodate a Monday closing by same-day wiring the funds for an afternoon closing.)

» **Other fees:** Recording fees (to record the deed and mortgage), courier and express mailing fees, notary fees — you name it. These extra expenses usually total about $200 to $300. ***Note:*** Ask your mortgage lender for a complete listing of all fees and charges.

Managing maintenance costs

In addition to costing you a monthly mortgage payment, homes also need flooring, window treatments, painting, plumbing, electrical and roof repairs, and other types of maintenance over time. Of course, some homeowners defer maintenance and even put their houses on the market for sale with lots of deferred maintenance (which, of course, will be reflected in a reduced sales price that is often much greater than the cost to have made those simple repairs).

For budgeting purposes, we suggest that you allocate about 1 percent of the purchase price of your home each year for normal maintenance expenses. So, for example, if you spend $240,000 on a home, you should budget about $2,400 per year (or about $200 per month) for maintenance.

With some types of housing, such as condominiums or planned unit developments (PUD), you pay monthly dues into a common interest development (often referred to as a homeowners association), which takes care of the maintenance for the community. In that case, you're responsible for maintaining only the interior of your unit. Check with the association to see how much the dues are currently running, anticipated future monthly or quarterly dues increases or special assessments, what services are included, and how they've changed over the years.

Financing home improvements and such

In addition to necessary maintenance and furnishings, also be aware of how much you may spend on nonessential home improvements, such as adding a deck, remodeling your kitchen, and so on. Budget for these nonessentials unless you're the rare person who is a super saver, can easily accomplish your savings goals, and have lots of slack in your budget.

The amount you expect to spend on improvements is just an estimate. It depends on how *finished* a home you buy and your personal tastes and desires. Consider your previous spending behavior and the types of projects you expect to do as you examine potential homes for purchase.

Consider the Impact of a New House on Your Financial Future

As you collect your spending data, think about how your proposed home purchase will affect and change your spending habits and ability to save. For example, as a homeowner, if you live farther away from your job than you did when you rented, how much will your transportation expenses increase? If you currently don't live in a common interest development (that is, a community with a homeowners association), you'll quickly learn about dues and sometimes special assessments, which are rarely anticipated and included in your budget.

Table 1-2 can help you total all your current expenses and estimate future expected spending.

TABLE 1-2 **Your Spending, Now and After Your Home Purchase**

Item	Current Monthly Income Average ($)	Expected Monthly Income Average with Home Purchase ($)
Income		
Gross salary	______	______
Bonuses/overtime	______	______
Interest/dividend	______	______
Miscellaneous	______	______
Total Income	______	______
Taxes		
Social Security	______	______
Federal	______	______
State and local	______	______
Housing Expenses		
Rent	______	______
Mortgage	______	______
Property taxes	______	______
Homeowners association dues	______	______
Gas/electric/oil	______	______
Homeowners/renter insurance	______	______
Water/sewer/garbage	______	______
Phone (landline and/or cellphone)	______	______
Cable TV/Internet	______	______
Furnishings/appliances	______	______

Item	Current Monthly Income Average ($)	Expected Monthly Income Average with Home Purchase ($)
Improvements	______	______
Maintenance/repairs	______	______
Food and Eating		
Groceries	______	______
Restaurants and takeout	______	______
Transportation		
Fuel/gasoline	______	______
Maintenance/repairs	______	______
State registration fees	______	______
Tolls and parking	______	______
Bus/train/ subway fares	______	______
Appearance		
Clothing	______	______
Footwear	______	______
Jewelry (watches, earrings)	______	______
Laundry/dry cleaning	______	______
Hair	______	______
Makeup	______	______
Other	______	______
Debt Repayments		
Credit/charge cards	______	______
Home equity/installment loans	______	______
Vehicle loans	______	______
Educational loans	______	______
Other	______	______
Fun Stuff		
Entertainment (movies, concerts)	______	______
Vacation and travel	______	______

(continued)

TABLE 1-2 ***(continued)***

Item	Current Monthly Income Average ($)	Expected Monthly Income Average with Home Purchase ($)
Gifts	______	______
Hobbies	______	______
Pets	______	______
Health club or gym	______	______
Youth sports	______	______
Other	______	______
Advisors		
Accountant	______	______
Attorney	______	______
Financial advisor	______	______
Healthcare		
Physicians and hospitals	______	______
Prescriptions	______	______
Dental and vision care	______	______
Therapy/counseling	______	______
Insurance		
Vehicle	______	______
Health	______	______
Life	______	______
Disability/long-term care	______	______
Educational Expenses		
Courses	______	______
Books	______	______
Supplies	______	______
Kids		
Child care	______	______
Diapers/formula	______	______

Item	Current Monthly Income Average ($)	Expected Monthly Income Average with Home Purchase ($)
Toys	______	______
Child support	______	______
Other		
Charitable donations	______	______
Alimony	______	______
______________	______	______
______________	______	______
______________	______	______
______________	______	______
______________	______	______
Total Spending	______	______
Amount Saved	______	______
(subtract from Total Income)		

Acting upon your spending analysis

Tabulating your spending is only half the battle on the path to fiscal fitness and a financially successful home purchase. After all, many government entities know where they spend our tax dollars, but they still run up massive levels of debt! You must do something with the personal spending information you collect.

When most Americans examine their spending, especially if it's the first time, they may be surprised and dismayed at the amount of their overall spending and how little they're saving. How much is enough to save? The answer depends on your goals and how good your investing skills are. For most people to reach their financial goals, they must annually save at least 10 percent of their gross (pretax) income.

From Eric's experience as a personal financial counselor and lecturer, he knows that most people don't know how much they're currently saving, and even more people don't know how much they should be saving. You should know these amounts before you buy your first home or trade up to a more costly property.

If you're like most people planning to buy a first home, you need to reduce your spending to accumulate enough money to pay for the down payment and closing costs and create enough slack in your budget to afford the extra costs of homeownership. Trade-up buyers may have some of the same issues as well. Where you decide to make cuts in your budget is a matter of personal preference. Here are some proven ways to cut your spending now and in the future:

- **Purge consumer debt.** Debt on credit cards, vehicle loans, and the like is detrimental to your long-term financial health. Borrowing through consumer loans encourages you to live beyond your means, and the interest rates on consumer debt are high *and not tax deductible.* If you have accessible savings to pay down your consumer debts, do so as long as you have access to sufficient emergency money from family or other avenues.
- **Trim nonessential spending.** Although everyone needs food, shelter, clothing, and healthcare, most Americans spend a great deal of additional money on luxuries and nonessentials. Even some of what people spend on the "necessity" categories is partly for luxury.
- **Purchase products and services that offer value.** High quality doesn't have to cost more. In fact, higher priced products and services are sometimes inferior to lower cost alternatives. With so many products available online these days, and local bricks-and-mortar stores willing to price match, a little research can go a long way to finding real savings.
- **Buy in bulk.** Most items are cheaper per unit when you buy them in larger sizes or volumes. Superstores such as Costco, BJ's Wholesale Club, Sam's Club, Target, and Walmart offer family sizes and competitive pricing.

Establishing financial goals

Most people find it enlightening to see how much they need to save to accomplish particular goals. For example, wanting to retire while you still have good health is a common goal. And the good news is that you can take advantage of tax incentives while you save toward retirement.

Money that you contribute to an employer-based retirement plan — for example, a 401(k) — or to a self-employed plan — for example, a SEP-IRA — is typically tax deductible at both the federal and state levels. Also, after you contribute money into a retirement account, the gains on that money compound over time without taxation.

WARNING

If you're accumulating down-payment money for the purchase of a home, putting that money into a retirement account is generally a bad idea. When you withdraw money prematurely from a retirement account, you owe not only current income taxes but also hefty penalties — 10 percent of the amount withdrawn for the IRS plus whatever penalty your state collects.

If you're trying to save for a real estate purchase and save toward retirement and reduce your taxes, you have a dilemma — assuming that, like most people, you have limited funds with which to work. The dilemma is that you can save outside of retirement accounts and have access to your down-payment money but pay much more in taxes. Or you can fund your retirement accounts and gain tax benefits, but lack access to the money for your home purchase.

You have two ways to skirt this dilemma:

- **Borrow against your employer's retirement plan.** Some employers' retirement plans, especially those in larger companies, allow borrowing against retirement savings plan balances. Some companies offer first-time homebuyers a little financial assistance, so make sure you ask. Because you are borrowing your own money, the monthly payment (including interest) all goes back to your account. Also, monthly payments back to your retirement account do not count against your debt ratios.
- **Implement a first-time home-buyer IRA withdrawal.** If you have an Individual Retirement Account (either a standard IRA or a newer Roth IRA), you're allowed to withdraw up to $10,000 (lifetime maximum) per individual IRA account (so a married couple can access $20,000) toward a home purchase as long as you haven't owned a home for the past two years. Tapping into a Roth IRA is a better deal because the withdrawal is free from income tax as long as the Roth account is at least five years old. Although a standard IRA has no such time restriction, withdrawals are taxed as income, so you'll net only the after-tax amount of the withdrawal toward your down payment.

Because most people have limited discretionary dollars, you must decide what your priorities are. Saving for retirement and reducing your taxes are important goals; but when you're trying to save to purchase a home, some or most of your savings needs to be outside a tax-sheltered retirement account. Putting your retirement savings on the back burner for a short time to build up your down-payment cushion is fine. However, be sure to purchase a home that offers enough slack in your budget to fund your retirement accounts after the purchase.

Making down-payment decisions

Most people borrow money for a simple reason: They want to buy something they can't afford to pay for in a lump sum. How many 18-year-olds and their parents have the extra cash to pay for the full cost of a college education? Or prospective homebuyers to pay for the full purchase price of a home? So people borrow.

When used properly, debt can help you accomplish your financial goals and make you more money in the long run. But if your financial situation allows you to make a larger than necessary down payment, consider how much debt you need or want. With most lenders, as we discuss in Chapter 5, you'll get access to the best rates on mortgage loans by making a down payment of at least 20 percent. Whether or not making a larger down payment makes sense for you depends on a number of factors, such as your other options and goals.

The potential rate of return that you expect or hope to earn on investments is a critical factor when you decide whether to make a larger down payment or make other investments. Psychologically, however, some people feel uncomfortable making a larger down payment because it diminishes their savings and investments.

You probably don't want to make a larger down payment if it depletes your emergency financial cushion. But don't be tripped up by the misconception that somehow you'll be harmed more by a real estate market crash if you pay down your mortgage. Your home is worth what it's worth — its value has nothing to do with the size of your mortgage.

Financially, what matters in deciding to make a larger down payment is the rate of interest you're paying on your mortgage versus the rate of return your investments are generating. Suppose that you get a fixed-rate mortgage at 6 percent. To come out financially ahead making investments instead of making a larger down payment, your investments need to produce an average annual rate of return, before taxes, of about 6 percent.

Although it's true that mortgage interest is usually tax deductible, don't forget that you must also pay taxes on investments held outside of retirement accounts. You could purchase tax-free investments, such as municipal bonds, but over the long haul, you probably won't be able to earn a high enough rate of return on such bonds versus the cost of the mortgage. Other types of fixed-income investments, such as bank savings accounts, CDs, and other bonds, are also highly unlikely to pay a high enough return.

To have a reasonable chance of earning more on your investments than it's costing you to borrow on a mortgage, you must be willing to invest in more growth-oriented, volatile investments such as stocks and rental/investment real estate. Over the past two centuries, stocks and real estate have produced annual average rates of return of about 9 percent. On the other hand, there are no guarantees that you'll earn these returns in the future. Growth-type investments can easily drop 20 percent or more in value over short time periods (such as one to three years).

» Understanding how lenders size up borrowers

» Solving typical mortgage problems

Chapter 2
Qualifying for a Mortgage

We love a good thriller. If you're looking for a spine-tingling mystery, however, *Mortgage Management For Dummies* isn't it.

Qualifying for a mortgage shouldn't be the least bit mystifying. And after you understand how lenders play the game, it won't be. This chapter removes nearly every bit of puzzlement from the process. We show you exactly how to get started, tell you what lenders look for when evaluating your creditworthiness, and help you solve your mortgage problems — whether you're looking for a loan as a first-time homebuyer or trying to refinance or pay off your mortgage faster.

Getting Preapproved for a Loan

Everyone knows that time is money, so we decided to begin this section with a timesaving tip. If you're a homeowner who wants to refinance an existing mortgage, you have our permission to proceed directly to the next section, which discloses how lenders evaluate your credit. This segment applies only to folks who haven't bought a house yet. (Don't feel slighted. We devote Chapter 11 entirely to the fine art of refinancing.)

Now, for all you wannabe homeowners, be advised that there's a right way and a wrong way to start the home-buying process. The wrong way, astonishingly, is rushing out helter-skelter to gawk at houses you think you may want to buy.

Don't get us wrong; knowing what's on the market is important. It's even more crucial to educate yourself so you can distinguish between houses that are priced to sell and ridiculously overpriced turkeys. If you don't know the difference between price and value, you could end up paying waaaaaaaaaay too much for the home you ultimately purchase. (To find out everything you need to know about buying a home, check out *Home Buying For Dummies*, by Ray Brown and Eric Tyson [Wiley].)

But . . . first things first: If you can't pay, you shouldn't play.

The worst-case scenario

Suppose you've been looking at open houses from dawn to dusk every Saturday and Sunday for the past seven weeks. Just when you begin to think you'll never find your dream home, it miraculously appears on the market.

You immediately make an offer to buy *casa magnífico*, conditioned upon your approval of the property inspections and obtaining satisfactory financing. When the sellers accept your generous offer, the bluebird of happiness sings joyously.

Three weeks later, the bird croaks. The loan officer calls to regretfully advise you that the bank has rejected your loan application. The reason isn't because you offered too much for the house. On the contrary, the appraisal confirmed that the property is worth every penny you're willing to pay.

The problem, dear reader, could be you. Unfortunately, your present income and projected expenses may be out of whack. You may not earn enough money to make the monthly mortgage payments plus pay the property taxes and homeowners insurance without pauperizing yourself. Adding insult to injury, this depressing discovery is delivered to you *after* you've blown hundreds of dollars on property inspections and loan fees and put yourself through an emotional wringer for three weeks.

Now the good news: It doesn't have to be this way. After you establish how much you can *prudently* spend for your dream home, which we cover in Chapter 1, the next logical step is to get yourself preapproved for a mortgage. Then you're properly prepared to begin your house hunt.

Loan prequalification usually isn't good enough

You can use two techniques to get a lender's opinion of your creditworthiness as a borrower. One is the better way to go. The other is potentially a waste of your time and money and may even be grossly misleading.

We start by critiquing the second-rate method. Loan *prequalification* is nothing more than a casual conversation with a loan officer. After quickly quizzing you about obvious financial matters, such as your present income, expenses, and cash savings for a down payment, the loan officer renders a down-and-dirty guesstimate of *approximately* how much money he *might* lend you at current mortgage interest rates *assuming* that everything you've said is accurate. Most lenders graciously provide a prequalification letter suitable for framing or swatting mosquitoes.

Prequalification is fast and cheap. It rarely takes more than 15 minutes unless you're the type who has trouble parallel parking.

WARNING

Because the lender doesn't substantiate anything you say, the lender isn't bound by the prequalification process to make a loan when you're ready to buy. When your finances are scrutinized during the formal mortgage approval process, the lender may discover additional financial liabilities or negative credit information that reduces your borrowing power. In that case, you end up squandering precious time and money looking at property you aren't qualified to buy.

Loan preapproval is the way to go

After you read this section, you'll understand why formally evaluating your creditworthiness is such a protracted process. Loan *preapproval* is significantly more involved than mere loan prequalification.

Preapproval involves a thorough investigation of your credit history. In addition, the lender independently documents and verifies your present income and expenses, the amount of cash you have on hand, assets and liabilities, and even your prospects for continued employment. If you're self-employed, the lender conducts a diligent analysis of your federal tax returns for the past couple of years.

Obtaining the credit report, verifications of income and employment, bank statements, and other necessary documentation usually takes at least a week or two. That's time well spent. Getting preapproved for a mortgage gives you two huge advantages:

- **You know how much you can borrow.** Being preapproved for a loan is almost as good as having a line of credit when you start house hunting. The only thing the lender can't preapprove is the house you buy. Because you haven't begun looking at property yet, your dream home is still only a twinkle in your eye.

TIP

Be sure to stay in touch with your lender during your house hunt. The amount you've been preapproved to borrow is written on paper, not carved in stone. Lenders won't give you a firm commitment on your loan's interest rate until you actually have a signed contract to buy your dream home. If interest rates increase (or your employment income declines) after you're preapproved for a mortgage, the loan amount decreases accordingly. By the same token, you can borrow even more if interest rates happen to decline (or you get a well-deserved pay raise).

- **You have an advantage in multiple-offer situations.** In a hot real estate market, you may end up competing with other buyers for the same property. Being preapproved is proof positive to sellers that you're a real buyer. Your offer will be given far more serious consideration than offers from buyers who haven't bothered to prove that they're creditworthy.

WARNING

Some lenders offer free loan preapprovals to prospective homebuyers as a marketing ploy to endear themselves to borrowers. However, others charge for loan preapproval. Don't choose a lender only because you can get a freebie preapproval. Such a lender may not offer the most competitive rates, which could cost you far more in the long run. In Chapter 7, we take the mystery out of selecting a lender.

Evaluating Your Creditworthiness: The Underwriting Process

Suppose your best friend hits you up for a loan. If your pal wants to borrow five or ten bucks until payday, that's no big deal. But if your acquaintance needs five or ten *thousand* dollars for a decade or so, you'll probably analyze the odds of getting repaid six ways to Sunday before parting with a nickel!

Good lending institutions are even more careful with their depositors' funds. They employ professional *underwriters,* who evaluate the degree of risk involved in loans that the lenders have been asked to make to prospective borrowers. In other words, underwriters tell the lender how much risk is involved in lending money to *you.* If they determine that you're too risky, chances are you won't get the loan. Underwriting standards are quite similar but do vary somewhat from lender to lender.

- Most lenders comply with underwriting guidelines of two institutions, the *Federal Home Loan Mortgage Corporation (Freddie Mac)* and the *Federal National Mortgage Association (Fannie Mae).* These lenders sell their loans on the *secondary mortgage market* to Freddie Mac or Fannie Mae, who then resell the loans to investors such as insurance companies and pension funds.

» *Portfolio lenders,* who keep loans they originate instead of selling them in the secondary mortgage market, may have more flexible underwriting standards, but they may have higher rates or only offer adjustable rate mortgages.

TIP

Just because one lender turns you down doesn't mean that all lenders will. If you're having trouble getting a loan approved, head for a portfolio lender in your area. In addition to your own interviewing of lenders, a good mortgage broker can help you identify more flexible (portfolio) lenders; see Chapter 7. This section helps you navigate the underwriting process.

Traditional underwriting guidelines

Underwriting standards can vary from lender to lender, because the underwriters who examine loan applications are flesh-and-blood human beings, not machines. Two underwriters can evaluate the exact same loan application and reach different conclusions (regarding the degree of risk involved in making the loan), because each interprets the traditional underwriting guidelines differently.

To get a mortgage, you must give a lender the right to take your home away from you and sell it to pay the balance due on your loan if you:

» Don't make your loan payments

» Fail to pay your property taxes

» Let your homeowners insurance policy lapse

The legal action taken by a lender to repossess property and sell it to satisfy mortgage debt is called a *foreclosure.* Lenders detest foreclosures. They're typically financially detrimental and emotionally debilitating for everyone involved in the transaction, and they generate awful public relations for the lender. And, if a lending institution has too many foreclosures, state and federal bank regulators begin questioning the lender's judgment.

Lenders constantly fine-tune the way they evaluate mortgage applications in search of better screening techniques to keep borrowers — and themselves — out of foreclosure. The sections that follow explain the primary factors that lenders have traditionally used to assess prospective borrowers' creditworthiness.

Integrity

Lenders look closely at you when deciding whether to approve your loan request. They want to know whether you're a good risk. Will you keep your word? How great an effort will you make to repay the loan?

One of the first things a loan processor does after you submit a loan application is order a credit report. Surprisingly, blemishes on your credit record aren't always the kiss of death. Contrary to what you may have heard, lenders are human. They understand that financial difficulties related to one-time situations such as a divorce, job loss, or serious medical problems can smite even the best of us.

As we discuss in Chapter 10, all loan applications contain a "Declarations" section that's chock-full of red-flag questions. For instance, this section asks whether you've ever had a property foreclosed upon.

WARNING

As a result of the late 2000s housing market slump and mortgage meltdown, Freddie Mac and Fannie Mae issued extremely stringent underwriting guidelines for loan applicants who've had a foreclosure. In such cases, the application is manually scrutinized by underwriters probing for all facts related to the foreclosure. Check out Chapter 13 for more info on foreclosures.

If you answer yes to any of these red-flag questions, lenders want *all* the details. Even with the blemish of a bankruptcy or foreclosure in your credit history, however, you'll get favorable consideration from lenders if you established a repayment plan for your creditors. That commitment demonstrates integrity.

Conversely, people who've skipped out on their financial obligations are treated like roadkill. Lenders figure that if borrowers have cut and run once, they'll probably do it again.

Income and job stability

From 2000 to 2006 during the peak of the residential lending frenzy, *no doc* or *stated income* loans were, regrettably, far too easy to get. No doc loans are loans made without written documentation for such things as the borrowers' income, assets, and liabilities. Some borrowers claimed as much income as they needed to get their loan approved without having to substantiate their income. Lenders disparagingly referred to these mortgages as *liar loans* or *pulse loans.* If you had a pulse, you got a loan.

Fortunately, those reckless ways are mostly long gone. Now you have to not only have a job, but you also had better be able to prove it.

Lenders don't want you to overextend yourself. They know from past experience that the number-one cause of foreclosures is borrowers spreading themselves too thin financially. Most lenders ask for your two most recent IRS W-2 forms to establish your gross annual income plus the last 30 days of pay stubs as proof that you're still employed.

If a lender can't qualify you by using W-2s and pay stubs, the loan processor sends your employer a verification of employment (VOE) letter to independently confirm the employment information on your loan application, including your income, how long you've had your present job, and your prospects for continued employment.

Some lenders are more lenient than others are when they see that a prospective borrower has a history of job-hopping. All lenders, however, must be certain that you have a high likelihood of uninterrupted income. If you don't get paid, how will they?

Debt-to-income ratio

Lenders aren't as concerned about short-term loans that you'll pay off in fewer than ten months. They will, however, add 5 percent of any unpaid revolving credit charges to your monthly debt load.

For example, suppose you earn $4,000 per month. If your current monthly long-term debt plus the projected homeownership expenses total $1,200 a month, your debt-to-income ratio is 30 percent ($1,200 divided by $4,000).

If your debt-to-income ratio is on the high side, a lender puts your loan application under a microscope. Even if all your credit cards are current, the lender may insist as a condition of making the loan that you pay off and cancel some of your credit cards to reduce your potential borrowing power. Doing so reduces the risk of future default on your loan.

TIP

If you want to increase the odds of having your loan approved and accomplishing your financial goals, lower your debt-to-income ratio by paying off small loans and credit card debt and closing any unused open credit accounts *prior* to applying for a mortgage. An excessive number of open accounts reduces your credit rating.

Property appraisal

Lenders must find out what the house you want to mortgage is currently worth, because the property is used to secure your loan. They do this by getting an *appraisal*, a written report prepared by an *appraiser* (the person who evaluates property for lenders) that contains an estimate or opinion of fair market value. The reliability of an appraisal depends on the competence and integrity of the appraiser. Equally important is having an appraiser with significant current market knowledge of the area and type of property being valued.

Loan-to-value ratio

A loan-to-value (LTV) ratio is a quick way for lenders to guesstimate how risky a mortgage may be. LTV ratio is simply the loan amount divided by the property's appraised value. For instance, if you're borrowing $150,000 to buy a home with an appraised value of $200,000, the loan-to-value ratio is 75 percent (your $150,000 loan divided by the $200,000 appraised value).

The more cash you put down, the lower your loan-to-value ratio and, from a lender's perspective, the lower the odds that you'll default on your loan. It stands to reason that you're less likely to default on a mortgage if you have a lot of money invested in your property.

Conversely, the higher the LTV ratio, the greater a lender's risk if problems arise later with your loan. That's why most lenders charge higher interest rates and loan fees or require private mortgage insurance (see Chapter 4) whenever the amount borrowed pushes the loan-to-value ratio (as determined by appraisal) above 80 percent.

Underwriting standards for loan-to-value ratios vary from lender to lender. A portfolio lender, for example, may feel comfortable with a higher debt-to-income ratio if your LTV ratio is low because you made a big cash down payment.

Cash reserves

As a condition of making your loan, some lenders insist that you have enough cash or other liquid assets, such as bonds, to provide a two- or three-month reserve to cover all your living expenses in the event of an emergency. Other lenders reduce their cash reserve requirements if you have a low debt-to-income ratio or a low LTV ratio. Some credit unions and savings and loan associations require that you have another account (checking or savings) with them to apply for a loan.

New underwriting technology

The mortgage finance industry has undergone sweeping technological changes that profoundly transformed the way lenders make loans. The two big innovations have been automated underwriting and credit scores.

Automated underwriting

Decades ago, the mortgage origination process used to be a torturously slow, hideously expensive, ridiculously redundant paper shuffle designed by the devil to drive miserable mortals stark raving mad. Not anymore.

Now automated underwriting programs objectively and accurately evaluate the multitude of risk factors present in most loan applications. Although these computerized programs will never completely eliminate human judgment, they've reduced the volume of paperwork involved in the traditional underwriting process.

Reduced paperwork has cut borrower's loan-origination costs by hundreds of dollars per mortgage. And that's not all. Thanks to automated underwriting programs, mortgages that used to require weeks or, worse, months to process and approve can be handled from start to finish in, gasp, minutes. Hence, the tremendous increase in the number of options at various mortgage websites.

Increasing use of credit scores

According to information provided by Freddie Mac (the Federal Home Loan Mortgage Corporation), credit scores developed by analyzing borrowers' credit histories served as a bridge between traditional underwriting and automated underwriting systems. However, studies conducted by Freddie Mac have proven that credit scores are excellent predictors of mortgage-loan performance. As we discuss in Chapter 3, most lenders use them.

Credit scores are calculated in a neutral manner and have nothing to do with a borrower's age, race, color, gender, sexual orientation, religion, national origin, citizenship, disability, or marital status. Your credit score is determined by objectively analyzing your record of paying debts. The following factors are considered:

- **Public records pertaining to credit:** A search of public records in the county recorder's office shows whether you've ever declared bankruptcy. It also indicates whether legal claims have ever been filed against property you own to secure payment of money owed for delinquent loans, lawsuits, or judgments.
- **Outstanding balances against available credit limits:** What is the balance due on mortgages and consumer installment debt such as car loans, charge accounts, and credit cards? Outstanding balances that exceed 80 percent of your available credit limits put you in the category of a higher-risk borrower.
- **The age of delinquent accounts:** Another indicator of higher risk is whether you have been or are currently 60 or more days delinquent on your credit card or charge account debt or other loan payments.
- **Recent inquiries generated by a borrower seeking credit:** Having four or more applicant-generated credit inquiries in the past year indicates that you may need a slew of new loans or credit cards because you've maxed out your current ones. From a lender's perspective, that's an alarming development.

The credit scoring methodology most lenders use today was developed by Fair Isaac Corporation and is called a *FICO score.* FICO scores range from a low of 300 to a maximum of 850. If you're just itching to discover much, *much* more about credit scoring, Chapter 3 can scratch that itch.

Freddie Mac analyzed a broad sampling of 25,000 loans made by the *Federal Housing Administration* (FHA). It found that borrowers with FICO scores of 680 or more are highly unlikely to default on their mortgages. These creditworthy borrowers are rewarded with lower loan-origination fees and mortgage interest rates. Conversely, a FICO score of 620 or less is a strong indication that a borrower's credit reputation isn't acceptable. As a result, borrowers with low FICO scores are charged higher loan-origination fees and mortgage interest rates to compensate for their loans' higher risk of default.

TIP

Risk and the lender's required return are always related. Seek ways to demonstrate that you're a better risk and you can likely get lower interest rates and better terms for your loan.

Eyeing Predicament-Solving Strategies

If you need proof positive that perfection is an admirable but ultimately unattainable quality, let a lender investigate your creditworthiness. Your financial flaws will be exposed to harsh scrutiny like a mess of worms wiggling when a rock is first turned over.

Mighty few folks have flawless credit and unlimited cash. Run-of-the-mill ordinary mortals have a plethora of extremely human imperfections. Most individuals need a bit of assistance to surmount their shortcomings. The following sections are chock-full of suggestions you can use to solve the most common mortgage problems.

Insufficient cash for a down payment

When subprime lending was at its height, getting 100 percent financing for home purchases was easy. Not anymore. Now most loan programs insist that you have "skin in the game." That's their catchy way of saying you must put some of your own money into the transaction. Even if you make only a modest 5 or 10 percent cash down payment, they figure you'll be less likely to walk away from the loan because you also have money at stake. There are a few exceptions though; the Veterans Affairs and USDA Rural Development loan programs both allow for $0 down.

Some things, like the exquisite hue of your baby blue eyes, are permanent and can't be changed no matter what you do. Fortunately, a shortage of legal tender (that's cold, hard cash for the less sophisticated) can be nothing more than a temporary inconvenience if you're sufficiently resourceful, motivated, and disciplined.

TIP

Plenty of people have respectable incomes. For one reason or another, many of them haven't been able to sock away much money in the form of cash savings or other readily liquid assets. If you're income rich and cash poor, here's a herd of cash cows mooing to be milked:

- **You:** Put yourself on a budget by eliminating life's little excesses. Rent a DVD for a couple of bucks instead of forking over the better part of $20 to gaze at a first-run flick while munching on pricey popcorn. Don't buy so many fancy designer outfits. Skip that expensive ski vacation, and check out the local museums instead. Avoid overpriced foofoo coffee, take a lunch to work, and eat dinner at home. Stifle the urge to be the first one on your block to own the latest electronic gadget. Stop smoking. Squirrel away all the money you don't waste on frivolities. You'll be astonished to see how quickly your savings grow.
- **GI financing:** Contrary to what you may think, GI financing isn't restricted to veterans. The GI we're referring to here is known as *generous in-laws*. Some parents help their children, married or not, purchase property by giving their kids cash for a down payment. Assuming that your parents have owned their home a long time, it's probably worth considerably more today than it was when they bought it way back when. If they get a loan on their house to obtain cash that they give you, their increased indebtedness doesn't affect your borrowing power.

  Under current tax law, a parent, friend, or mysterious stranger, for that matter, can give you, your spouse, and each of your kids tax-free gifts of up to $14,000 per calendar year. For example, suppose that you're happily married, have three adorable kids, and have truly generous in-laws. To help you buy your dream home, your munificent mother-in-law bestows a $70,000 gift ($14,000 per family member) upon the family. Ditto your fabulous father-in-law, for a total gift of $140,000 from your in-laws. (And if this gifting happens near the end of the year, they could each give you a gift in December and another in January, which would increase the total to a truly grand $280,000. Now aren't you sorry about all those dreadful things you said about them?)
- **Your employer:** If you're relocating at the request of your employer, find out whether your company will pay some or all of your down payment and other home purchase costs as an employee benefit. It's a deductible business expense for your employer.

- **Tax refund:** Don't fritter away next year's federal or state income tax refund on baubles like a second yacht or that spiffy new Rolls Royce. Apply it to your down payment.
- **Life insurance:** If you have a whole-life policy, check to see how much cash value you've built up. Replace the whole-life policy with more modestly priced *term* life insurance to maintain your insurance coverage (or go without life coverage if you have no one dependent upon you financially) and free up the cash value to use for a down payment.
- **Bonus:** What better way to invest that huge year-end bonus the boss promised?
- **Income tax withholding allowance:** If you're a salaried employee and you've gotten hefty tax refunds in the past, try increasing the number of dependents on your IRS W-4 form. (Complete the worksheet to see whether it makes sense.) Doing so will reduce the amount of tax that's withheld from your check (so you don't have to wait to get it back from the government). Put the extra money toward your down payment.
- **Retirement plans:** The law now allows you, if you're a first-time homebuyer, to withdraw up to $10,000 from your IRAs if you use the money to acquire your principal residence. (Married couples can each withdraw up to $10,000 from their own IRAs.) To avoid a 10-percent penalty tax for an early withdrawal (withdrawals before you reach age 59½), you must be a *first-time buyer* who hasn't owned a home for at least two years prior to the acquisition of your new primary residence. The funds must be used within 120 days of withdrawal to purchase or build your home. Many 401(k) plans also permit borrowing for a home down payment. Check with your employer's benefits office or your tax advisor.
- **Real estate:** If you own a vacation home or rental real estate that has appreciated in value, you can probably pull cash out of the property by refinancing the existing mortgage.

WARNING

Loans are a two-edged sword. Any loan that increases your overall indebtedness reduces your borrowing power accordingly. This is true whether the loan in question is an unsecured personal loan from a friend or your credit union, is secured by a mortgage on real estate, or is secured by personal property such as a car, boat, or jewelry.

- **Equity sharing:** This technique allows two or more people to buy a house that one or more of them occupies as a primary residence. For example, a nonoccupant investor pays the down payment and closing costs in return for a 25 percent interest in the property. You, as the occupant/co-owner, get a 75 percent ownership stake for making the monthly mortgage payments as well as paying the property tax, the homeowners insurance premium, and all other maintenance expenses. Any increase in value is split according to the terms of the equity-sharing agreement either after a specified period of time, such as five years, or when the property is sold.

Although unrelated people can use equity sharing, it works best between parents and their children. Given a well-crafted written agreement, equity sharing is an ideal win-win situation. Your parents get tax benefits and share in the house's appreciation while helping you buy a home. You get a home of your own with little or no cash down, you enjoy tax deductions for your specified percentage of the mortgage interest and property tax payments, and you also share in the home's appreciation. For more detailed information about drawing up a legally binding equity sharing agreement, consult a qualified real estate lawyer.

- **State or federal programs for first-time buyers:** Freddie Mac, Fannie Mae, the FHA, and many states have financial aid programs designed to assist low- or moderate-income buyers in purchasing their first home with little money down (see Chapter 4). Again, you may find that these programs define "first-time buyer" as someone who has not owned a home for just the past few years.
- **Seller (owner-carry) financing:** This technique may make it possible to purchase real estate with relatively little cash, because the seller takes some of the sale price in the form of a loan. For instance, you put 10 percent of the cash down, the owner carries back a 10 percent second mortgage, and you get an 80 percent first mortgage from a conventional lending institution (see Chapter 6 for more about seller financing used with 80-10-10 financing).

The number of owners willing to carry financing ebbs and flows like the tide. When conventional mortgage interest rates are high, many sellers offer lower-interest-rate second mortgages to help sell their houses. However, even when conventional mortgage rates are cheap, a few sellers do owner-carry financing for tax purposes (by spreading their taxable gain over multiple years) or because owner-carry financing has an attractive interest rate compared to returns they could get on other investments.

- **Private mortgage insurance (PMI):** Thanks to the availability of PMI, conventional lenders offer special loan programs for cash-poor buyers with strong incomes. If your down payment is less than 20 percent of the purchase price, you'll have to buy private mortgage insurance to protect *the lender* in case you go belly up and the lender has to foreclose. Getting PMI may increase your loan origination fee and will increase your monthly loan payment. However, without PMI, you couldn't buy with such a low down payment.
- **Stock or stock options:** Selling stock or stock options is a quick way to get your down payment. Before you do so, be sure you understand the tax consequences and make provisions to cover the state and federal capital gains taxes generated by the sale.
- **Sale of other assets:** What better time to convert your collection of rare stamps, gold coins, vintage baseball cards, agglomeration of Beanie Babies,

first-edition comic books, or whatever else is collecting dust into cold, hard, down-payment cash?

- **Lottery tickets:** Hey. Somebody always wins the lottery sooner or later. It may as well be you. Stranger things have happened. Your luck is bound to change eventually. You have our permission to squander up to a buck a week. If, however, you crave a slightly more certain way to obtain cash for a down payment, we urge you to review our previous 15 suggestions.

Excessive indebtedness

Death is nature's Draconian way of telling us to slow down. Having your mortgage application rejected because you're in hock up to your hip-huggers is the lender's gentle suggestion that you'd be wise to put your financial house in order.

Even if you're only moderately overextended, the lender has done you a tremendous favor by turning you down. If your debt-to-income ratio is too high *before* buying a house, piling on additional debt in the form of mortgage payments and homeownership expenses will probably turn your dream home into a fiscal nightmare.

Face it. Even though you're perfectly willing to shoulder the additional financial burden of homeownership, the lender is telling you that too much debt will ravage your ability to live within your means. You won't own the house; the house will own you.

TIP

Here are four ways to handle this problem:

- **Reduce long-term indebtedness.** If you're close to being able to qualify for a mortgage, paying off a chunk of installment-type debt such as a student loan or car loan will most likely bring your debt-to-income ratio within acceptable limits. Discuss this game plan with your lender. (Car loans and other long-term installment debt with ten or fewer payments remaining are typically not considered long-term debt.)

  Fannie Mae and Freddie Mac don't like total monthly payments on long-term indebtedness (including your mortgage) to exceed about 40 to 45 percent or so of your gross monthly income.

- **Expand income or restrict living expenses.** If you're living way beyond your means, you have two choices: Increase your income or, more realistically, put yourself on a stringent financial diet to reduce your blimpish budget. For help with this, read Chapter 1 (if you haven't already). It helps you identify areas where you can make budget cuts.

- **Get real.** If you have champagne tastes and an unalterable beer budget, something's gotta give. Ask your lender to define the outer limits of your realistic purchasing power. The easiest way to cut your payments for a mortgage, property taxes, homeowners insurance, and other ownership expenses is to buy a less expensive home.
- **Reach out and touch someone.** If you're lucky enough to have fiscally powerful parents or relatives to whom you can turn for financial assistance, you have a huge advantage. Consider using it. Don't let false pride about asking them for a loan or having them cosign a mortgage prevent you from owning a home. After all, in many areas of the country, property is much more expensive today than it was back in the Stone Age when your mom and dad bought their first home.

WARNING

Cosigning a mortgage is inherently risky for the co-borrowers. If you make payments late or, worse, default on your loan, you sully your cosigners' credit record every bit as much as your own. Even if you mail in your monthly loan payments long before they're due, however, the cosigners' borrowing power is reduced, because they have a contingent liability to repay your loan *if* you default. In fairness, you should discuss these financial ramifications with your co-borrowers *before* they cosign your loan papers.

Insufficient income

Even if you have plenty of cash for a down payment and no debt whatsoever, you may still experience the despair of rejection. Lenders frequently turn down loan applicants if they believe the financial burdens of homeownership will be too great. As is the case with excessive indebtedness, the lenders are trying to protect you from yourself as well as protect their own interests.

Before you throw a stink bomb in the lender's lobby, please read the section in Chapter 1 about determining how much home you can realistically afford. For example, suppose you currently aren't earning much, because the business you started last year is gushing buckets of red ink. Under the circumstances, it would probably be prudent to wait another year or two to prove conclusively to the lender — and yourself — that your business is capable of producing profits.

If (after reviewing Chapter 1) you still believe that the lender is being too paternalistic, take a look at these two suggestions that may help get your loan approved:

- **Increase your down payment.** If you're cash rich and income poor, make an even larger down payment. The more money you have in the property, the lower the lender's risk that you'll default on your mortgage.

» **Get a borrower.** Excessive indebtedness isn't the only problem a borrower can cure. This may be the perfect time to ask your parents, your rich uncle Dennis, or your buddy who just won the Publisher's Clearinghouse Sweepstakes to help you.

Credit blemishes

"You can run, but you can't hide" aptly describes the futility of trying to duck creditors. If you have pecuniary problems with the butcher, the baker, or the candlestick maker, woe be it to you if you're ever slow and sloppy when paying your bills. Creditors have a nasty way of getting even with you. They report your delinquencies and defaults to credit bureaus. These fiscal zits deface your record for years to come whenever anyone obtains a copy of your credit report.

TIP

If your credit history is a smidgen less than sparkling, one key element to getting your loan approved is immediate, detailed disclosure of any unfavorable information. Don't play games. Give the lender a complete, written explanation of all prior credit problems when you submit the loan application. Financial dings tied to one-time predicaments such as serious illness or job loss that you've satisfactorily surmounted are usually relatively easy to handle. Also, some credit card lenders, particularly ones that are part of a retail establishment (for example, department stores), may change what they report to the bureaus as a matter of "customer convenience." Macy's does not want you mad at them, so ask their credit department if it will modify what it reports for your account.

It pays to take the initiative if you have trouble obtaining a mortgage. Ask your loan officer to list all the derogatory items you must rectify to get loan approval. Instead of wasting your valuable time trying to guess what's wrong, you'll have a nice, neat (hopefully short) checklist of everything you must correct.

Here are four ways to conquer crummy credit:

» **Seek sympathetic lenders.** Lenders start with mostly the same underwriting guidelines for conventional loans. But many lenders add additional restrictions called *lender overlays* that make qualifying more stringent. For instance, at the time of this writing, FHA allows credit scores down to 580, but many lenders will not make FHA loans below 600–620. You may have to figure out if you are running up against the actual underwriting guidelines or a lender overlay. The only way to find out is to ask a few different lenders. When you interview lenders, don't be coy. Ask them whether your credit blemishes present a problem.

Depending on the magnitude of your mess, you may want to secure the services of a mortgage broker. Because they often assist people with credit problems, mortgage brokers already know which lenders will be most understanding about this kind of fiscal frailty. Mortgage brokers are typically approved with a number of lenders — and thus have more options in placing a mortgage.

- **Seek seller financing.** As we note in Chapter 5, tax advantages and high rates of return induce some sellers to offer financing for the buyers of their properties. Sellers can be more flexible when dealing with credit blemishes than conventional lenders, because they aren't hampered by so many rules and regulations. If you're financially strong today, a seller may be willing to overlook your past credit problems.
- **Seek a co-borrower.** Once again, we suggest trying to obtain the cooperation of the ever-popular co-borrower.
- **Seek savings and spruce up your credit.** If the lenders you've talked to either summarily reject your loan application or offer you outrageous loans with stratospherically high interest rates and fees, why rush to buy a home? Instead, continue renting. Concentrate on two goals — saving money for your down payment and keeping your credit record spotless. After a couple of years, lenders will be knocking at your door day and night beseeching you to honor them with your business.

Don't waste your time working with a company that says it can quickly repair your credit. You may be told that, for a fee, your legitimate credit problems will be removed from your credit report. Sound too good to be true? It is. See Chapter 3 for honest ways that you can improve your credit reputation.

Low appraisals

Did you hear the joke about the conscientious fellow who dutifully visited his friendly neighborhood dentist for a semi-annual checkup and teeth cleaning? After completing her usual meticulous, 15-minute inspection, the dentist advised our hero that his teeth passed the exam with flying colors. Then she solemnly announced that the poor guy's gums had to go. *Ta da boom!*

Believe it or not, this hilarious digression (all right, mildly hilarious) does have a point. Suppose you're a lender's dream borrower, the embodiment of perfection — plenty of cash for a down payment, no indebtedness whatsoever, incredible income, exceptional job security, and nary a spot of derogatory information anywhere in your credit history. How could you, a Champion of Creditworthiness, ever be turned down for a mortgage?

THE BEST DEFENSE IS A GREAT OFFENSE

In the American legal system, you're innocent until proven guilty. In the *Alice in Wonderland* financial realm, conversely, you're guilty until credit reporting agencies say that you're innocent.

Credit agencies and the creditors who report information to them sometimes make mistakes. Most folks don't discover these errors until they're turned down for a loan.

If that hideous fate befalls you, begin the correction process by finding the inaccuracy. For instance, if the error pertains to a charge account that's not yours, tell the credit bureau to remove the derogatory data and put it on the correct person's credit report.

Now suppose that it's your account. A creditor of yours told the credit agency that you never paid a bill when, in fact, you actually paid it in full long ago. In that case, you must go back to the source of the erroneous information and have the creditor instruct the credit bureau to correct the misinformation.

Fixing this type of error requires persistence and patience. Credit bureaus, by law, must respond to your inquiry within 30 days. If you get the brush-off from frontline customer service representatives, demand to speak to their manager. If that doesn't work, file a complaint with local government regulatory agencies.

Your best strategy is to have the blemish removed from your credit record. If the quarrelsome creditor refuses to rectify the inaccuracy, you're allowed to enter a statement of contention in your file so future creditors who obtain your credit report can read your side of the story.

Obtain a copy of your credit report to ensure that the information is accurate. If you're applying for a mortgage, ask for a copy of your credit report. After all, you're paying for it.

Once per year, you can obtain a free copy of your credit report directly from each of the credit bureaus that publish them. Equifax (800-685-1111, `www.equifax.com`), Experian (888-397-3742, `www.experian.com`), and TransUnion (800-916-8800, `www.transunion.com`) provide credit reports. So, if you want to keep a close watch on your credit reports, you can rotate, every four months, which credit bureau from which you obtain a free copy. Also know that Section 615(a) of the Fair Credit Reporting Act is a federal law that gives you the right to receive a free copy of your credit report from the credit bureau if you ask within 60 days of being turned down for a loan.

Simple. Blame the lender's appraiser, who is of the firmly held opinion that the house you're so madly infatuated with isn't worth what you so foolishly agreed to pay for it. Don't take it personally. The rejection has nothing to do with you as a fine, upstanding individual.

Low appraisals aren't restricted to transactions involving home purchases; they've sabotaged their fair share of refinances, too.

Maybe the appraiser is absolutely correct — maybe not. What you do next depends on which of the following six factors provoked the low appraisal:

- **You overpaid.** Hey, it happens. Appraisals rarely come in under the purchase price. You and your real estate agent may be suffering from a case of excessive enthusiasm regarding your dream home's fair market value. For example, just because you're willing to pay $250,000 for it doesn't mean that anyone else in the whole wide world would pay a penny over $235,000. Or the appraised value may be low because the house needs a new foundation, a new roof, and other expensive repairs that you didn't factor into your offering price. In either case, be grateful the appraiser warned you before you made a costly mistake.

  TIP

  You obviously like the house or you wouldn't have offered to buy it. If, despite the low appraisal, you still want the property, don't give up. Get your real estate agent to use the appraisal as a negotiating device to reduce the purchase price or to get an offsetting credit for the necessary corrective work. Your home inspection report can be very helpful in identifying repairs that the seller should correct at his expense. Be sure to ask that the appraiser reconsider the valuation if it was reduced due to deferred maintenance or needed repairs that have subsequently been completed properly.

  WARNING

  The seller is stuck with the property. You aren't. If the seller won't listen to reason, don't waste more of your valuable time. Instead, move on to find your true dream home. Speaking of moving on, getting another real estate agent may also be wise if you suspect that your present agent is inept or wants you to pay more than the house is worth to fatten his own commission check. A good agent's negotiating skills and knowledge of property values can save you thousands of dollars. An incompetent or unethical agent can cost you just as many thousands of dollars.

- **The home you want to buy is located in a declining market.** For several years starting in the late 2000s, lenders imposed loan restrictions on markets they consider risky because home prices in those areas were dropping. Although no longer the case in most areas of the country, a high-risk area could be as small as a specific zip code or as large as giant chunks of California and Florida. If your dream house is located in a declining market area, you'll have to put more cash down and pay higher interest rates and loan fees to offset the lender's increased risk due to actual or perceived falling property values.

Stigmatizing every single property in a zip code or, worse yet, a major metropolitan area as risky is a sledgehammer solution to the problem. Local neighborhood conditions can and do vary widely within a zip code or city. Lenders may make an exception to the dreaded declining market designation if your appraisal demonstrates conclusively that property values aren't falling within the specific geographic area where your dream house is located.

- **Prices dropped since you bought your home.** This predicament periodically clobbers folks trying to refinance a loan. Real estate is an excellent *long-term* investment. However, like the stock market, the real estate market has short-term boom-and-bust cycles. For instance, suppose you paid a record high price several years ago when you acquired your home at the pinnacle of a strong (seller's) market. In our hypothetical situation, assume that the country is now mired in a deep recession, and houses like yours are selling for far less money. If that actually happens to you, don't kill the messenger for accurately reporting current property values. (Take this as an opportunity to buy an investment property or at least ask your local tax assessor to lower your assessed value and save money on your property taxes.)

TIP

Property prices aren't fixed. They slither all over the place. A house's fair market value (FMV) is based on what buyers offer and sellers accept. *It's not a specific number — it's a price range.* To push your appraisal toward the high end of FMV, have your real estate agent give the appraiser a list of houses comparable to yours in location, condition, size, and age that sold within the past six months. Unlike good real estate agents, appraisers generally don't inspect every property on the market. If your agent toured all these houses and the appraiser didn't have time to see some of them, your agent should review the properties with the appraiser to help the appraiser understand why the highest sales are the best comparables.

- **The appraiser doesn't know property values in your area.** Suppose that, while looking for your dream home, you and your agent saw five comparable houses (near the home you want to buy) that completely justify the price you agreed to pay. If the appraisal comes in low under these circumstances, the appraiser may not know neighborhood property values.

TIP

When you suspect that the appraiser is geographically clueless, get a copy of the appraisal from the lender. Check the houses the appraiser selected to establish fair market value to see whether they're actually valid comparables for the home you want to buy. If they aren't, discuss your concerns with the lender. Find out how many appraisals the appraiser has done recently in the neighborhood. If the appraiser doesn't work in the immediate vicinity, the appraiser's opinions of value are suspect. In this situation, some lenders will have the property reappraised without charging you.

- **The appraiser did not properly value your specific property.** Maybe something unique about the property you're buying justifies the higher valuation.

Although an appraiser should take into account all the differences between the comparable properties and your dream home, the dollar value of the adjustments to the valuation are subjective. If your property has a killer view and most of the comparable properties overlook a nearby power plant, the appraiser may not have properly accounted for this superior feature of your future home.

The appraiser may not always acknowledge the size of the parcel as well as other unique features, so look at the appraisal report narrative and see whether he considered these positive benefits when reaching his final opinion of value. Yes, it's just his professional "opinion" of value and you may be able to point out inconsistencies, or some lenders may even allow you to get a second opinion in the form of another appraisal.

- **The lender is redlining.** *Redlining* is the discriminatory act of refusing to make loans in specific neighborhoods that a lender considers undesirable. Because this practice is illegal, it's the least likely explanation for a low appraisal from a reputable lender.

  Request a copy of your appraisal if you suspect redlining. After carefully reviewing the comparable sales data to establish that the appraisal is unrealistically low based on your firsthand knowledge of comps, ask the lender to explain why. If you're not satisfied with the explanation or if you get the runaround, ask for a full refund of your loan application and appraisal fees; then take your business to another lender. You may also consider filing a complaint with the appropriate agency in your state that regulates mortgage lenders.

Problem properties

Two types of residential property — cooperative apartments and fixer-uppers — are difficult to get mortgages on. The intricacies of these properties are discussed in great detail in *Home Buying For Dummies* (Wiley). This section simply highlights the financing problems associated with these types of properties.

Cooperative apartments

When you buy a house or a condominium apartment, you get a *deed* that proves you have legal title to the property. Nice and simple, isn't it?

When you buy a *cooperative apartment*, usually called a *co-op*, you get a stock certificate, which proves that you own a certain number of shares of stock in the cooperative corporation. You also get a *proprietary lease*, which entitles you to occupy the apartment you bought. The cooperative corporation that owns the building has the deed in its name. Confusing, isn't it?

In places such as New York City and San Francisco, where co-ops are common, mortgage financing on this type of property is readily available. In many other parts of this great land, however, lenders find co-ops legally daunting. They don't make co-op loans, because they refuse to accept shares of stock in a cooperative corporation as security for a mortgage. Compounding the problem, some co-ops won't permit any individual financing over and above the mortgage that the cooperative corporation has on the building as a whole.

WARNING

If only one or two lenders in your area make co-op loans, don't buy a cooperative apartment unless you're independently wealthy. You'll likely end up paying a higher mortgage interest rate due to limited competition and the lenders' concerns about the risks involved with co-op financing. Worse, what happens to you if these lenders stop making co-op mortgages and no other lenders take their place? You won't be able to sell your unit unless you find an all-cash buyer (rare birds, indeed) or you decide to carry the loan for the next buyer.

Fixer-uppers

Fixer-uppers are properties that need work to put them in pristine condition. If the house you want to buy needs only cosmetic renovations (painting, carpeting, landscaping, and the like), you probably won't have a big problem obtaining a mortgage.

However, suppose the apple of your eye is a house that needs serious structural repairs, such as a new foundation, a new roof, and the installation of new electrical and plumbing systems. We have to question the wisdom of buying such a needy property. Don't say we didn't warn you. If your dream house is a corrective-work nightmare, getting financing may be tough unless you use specific renovation loans such as the FHA 203K, Fannie Mae HomeStyles, or Freddie Mac Renovation Program. These loan programs finance both the acquisition and needed repairs.

Of particular concern is the reliability of the roof. If the appraiser sees evidence of water damage, like water stains on the ceiling, he will mention it, and you will probably have to provide a roof certification after examination by a roofing company. The lender may not allow closing until the roof is repaired.

TIP

A good real estate agent should know which lenders in your area specialize in renovation loans.

IN THIS CHAPTER

» Unraveling how scores work

» Boosting your credit score for better loan terms

Chapter 3
Scoping Out Your Credit Score

When you apply for a loan, lenders try to determine your credit risk. If they decide to loan you money, what are the odds that you'll pay them back on time? To understand your credit risk, most lenders look at your credit report and credit score. Your score ultimately influences the credit that's available to you and the terms of any mortgage that lenders offer you.

Most lenders also use a number of other facts about you to make credit decisions. They usually look at the amount of debt you can reasonably handle given your income, your employment history, and your credit history. Based on their perception of this information, as well as their specific underwriting policies and secondary market guidelines and limitations, lenders may approve your loan although your score may be a bit low, or decline your loan application despite your score being quite high. But your chances for getting approved at the best possible loan terms improve when you have a good score and the lender determines that you're a lower credit risk. This chapter gives you an overview of the importance of your credit score when you apply for a mortgage.

Defining Credit Scores

Today, the credit scoring system that the majority of the top 100 largest U.S. lending institutions use for their risk assessment needs is a FICO score — developed by Fair Isaac Corporation (`www.fico.com`) in 1989. FICO scores range from a low of 300 to a maximum of 850. The three major credit reporting agencies — Equifax, Experian, and TransUnion — provide these scores to lenders.

TIP

Understanding your credit score can help you manage your credit health. By knowing how lenders evaluate your credit risk, you can take action to lower your credit risk — and thus raise your score — over time. A better score may mean better loan options for you.

Although FICO scores are by far the most commonly used credit risk scores in the United States, a few lenders may use other scores to evaluate your credit risk. These include

- **Application risk scores:** Many lenders use scoring systems that include the FICO score but also consider information from your loan application.
- **Customer risk scores:** A lender may use these scores to make credit decisions about its current customers. Also called *behavior scores,* these scores generally consider the FICO score along with information about how you've paid that lender in the past.
- **Credit bureau scores:** The three major credit bureaus — Equifax, Experian, and TransUnion — each have developed their own scoring systems. These scores may evaluate your credit report differently from FICO scores, and in some cases a higher score may mean more risk, not less risk, as with FICO scores.

Even though these other measures are important and may come into play when a lender determines your eligibility for a mortgage, the FICO score is still the gold standard. You should understand it as well as you can so you can optimize your FICO score and be likely to get the best loan terms.

Assessing Your Credit History

Your FICO score evaluates your credit report, which is the way most U.S. businesses see your credit history. The report details your credit history as it has been reported to the credit reporting agency by lenders who have extended credit to you. Your credit report lists what types of credit you use, the length of time your accounts have been open, and whether you've paid your bills on time. It tells lenders how much credit you've used and whether you're seeking new sources of credit.

It gives lenders a broader view of your credit history than one bank's own records (unless you drew all your previous credit from that one bank).

Your credit report reveals many aspects of your borrowing activities. To give you a fair assessment, lenders should consider each piece of information on your report in relationship to the other report information. The ability to quickly, fairly, and consistently consider all this information is what makes credit scoring so useful. This section briefly highlights what information goes into your credit report and what you need to regularly check to avoid errors.

REMEMBER

Expect to pay about $20 to $35 for a lender to obtain a current copy of your standard credit report from the credit reporting agencies. A more extensive report called a Residential Mortgage Credit Report (RCMR) can cost $50 to $75. Chapter 2 tells you how to obtain a free copy of your credit reports if you want to see them before applying for a loan.

What goes into your credit report

Although each credit reporting agency formats and reports information differently, all credit reports contain basically the same kinds of information:

- **Identifying information:** Your name, current and former addresses, Social Security number, date of birth, and employment information are used to identify you. The agencies don't use these factors to calculate your score, however. Identifiers match your experience with credit to your identity and file. Updates to your identifying information (such as employer change or name change) come from information you supply to lenders.
- **Tradelines:** These are businesses or credit grantors where you have credit accounts. Lenders report each account you've established with them. They report the type of account (credit card, revolving, auto loan, mortgage, and so on), the date you opened the account, your credit limit or loan amount, the account balance, and your payment history.
- **Inquiries:** When you apply for a loan, you authorize your lender to ask for a copy of your credit report. This is how inquiries appear on your credit report. The inquiries section contains a list of everyone who accessed your credit report within the last two years. The report you see lists both *voluntary* or *hard inquiries*, spurred by your own requests for credit, and *involuntary* or *soft inquiries*, such as when lenders order your report before sending you a preapproved credit offer in the mail. (Other soft inquiries can include your creditors periodically reviewing existing accounts and insurance or employment credit checks.) Soft inquiries appear only on your own consumer-requested report; they're excluded from the credit reports lenders see and don't count against your credit score.

» **Public record and collection items:** Credit reporting agencies also collect public record information from state and county courts and information on overdue debt from collection agencies. Public record information includes bankruptcies, foreclosures, suits, wage attachments, liens, and judgments.

Along with the credit report, lenders can also buy a credit score based on the information in the report.

Check your credit report

If your credit report contains errors, the report may be incomplete or contain information about someone else. A recent Federal Trade Commission study reported that 5 percent of consumers had at least one error on one of their three major credit reports that would likely lead to being charged a higher rate of interest.

This typically happens because:

» You applied for credit under slightly different names (Robert Jones, Bob Jones, and so on), or you have several members of your family with similar names. Another common reason is that you changed your name due to a change in your marital status.

» Someone made a clerical error in reading or entering your name or address information from a handwritten application.

» Someone gave an inaccurate Social Security number, or the lender misread the number.

This type of error could also be a sign of identity theft. If, after checking into this error, you discover that your identity has been stolen, get as much of the problem resolved as you can before applying for a mortgage.

» Loan or credit card payments were inadvertently applied to the wrong account. Years ago, Robert once found that his credit was being negatively affected by a large unpaid delinquent balance at a store he had never patronized and didn't even have a location in his area.

» Information from an ex-spouse that should not be included.

If you find an error, the credit reporting agency must investigate and respond to you within 30 days. If you're in the process of applying for a loan, immediately notify your lender in writing of any incorrect information in your report. In Chapter 2, we tell you how to contact the credit reporting agencies to obtain and fix your credit report.

Understanding How Scores Work

Each credit score is calculated by a mathematical equation or algorithm that evaluates many types of information from your credit report at that agency. By comparing this information to the patterns in hundreds of thousands of past credit reports, the score identifies your level of estimated future credit risk.

For a FICO score to be calculated from your credit report, the report must contain at least one account that's been open for six months or longer. In addition, the report must contain at least one account that's been updated in the past six months. This ensures that enough recent information is in your report to calculate a score.

Your score can change whenever your credit report changes. But your score probably won't change a lot from one month to the next. In a given three-month time period, only about one in four people has a 20-point change in her credit score.

TIP

Although a bankruptcy or late payment can quickly lower your score, improving your score takes time. That's why it's a good idea to check your score (especially if you have reason to be concerned about your credit history) at least six months before applying for a mortgage. That gives you time to take corrective action if needed. If you're actively working to improve your score, you should check it quarterly or even monthly to review changes.

The higher your FICO score, the lower the potential risk you pose for lenders. But no score says whether you'll be a "good" or "bad" customer. Although many lenders use FICO scores to help them make lending decisions, each lender also has its own strategy, including the level of risk it finds acceptable for a given type of loan. There is no single minimum score used by all lenders.

FICO scores can differ between bureaus

Fair Isaac makes the FICO scores as consistent as possible among the three credit reporting agencies. If your information is exactly identical at all three credit reporting agencies, your scores from all three should be within a few points of each other. But that is rarely the case.

Sometimes your FICO score may be quite different at each of the three credit reporting agencies. The way lenders and other businesses report information to the credit reporting agencies sometimes results in different information being in your credit report at two or more of the agencies. The agencies may also report the same information in different ways. Even small differences in the information at the three credit reporting agencies can affect your scores.

Because lenders may review your score and credit report from any one of the three credit reporting agencies, go ahead and check your credit report at all three to make sure each is correct (see Chapter 2 for instructions on how to do that).

What a FICO score considers

The FICO score evaluates five main categories of information. Some, as you'd expect, are more important than others. It's important to note the following:

- **A score considers all these categories of information, not just one or two.** No one piece of information or factor alone determines your score.
- **The importance of any factor depends on the overall information in your credit report.** A given factor may be more important for some people than for others who have a different credit history. In addition, as the information in your credit report changes, so does the importance of any factor in determining your score. That's why it's impossible to say exactly how important any single factor is in determining your score — even the levels of importance shown in the following subsections are for the general population, and differ for different credit profiles. Also, the FICO score algorithm is dynamic and constantly being adjusted.
- **Your FICO score looks only at information in your credit report.** When making a credit decision, lenders often also look at other things, including your income, how long you've worked at your present job, and the kind of credit you're requesting.
- **Your score considers both positive and negative information in your credit report.** Late payments lower your score, but establishing or reestablishing a good track record of making payments on time raises your score. Unfortunately, a single delinquent account or late payment will negatively affect your FICO score much more than a handful of accounts paid on time will increase your credit score.
- **Raising your score is a bit like getting in shape.** It takes time, and there is no quick fix. In fact, quick-fix efforts can backfire. The best advice is to manage credit responsibly over time. Try to never be even one day late with your mortgage payment or other tradeline payments.

  If you have a legitimate reason for the late payment, immediately contact your credit provider and discuss the situation and ask them to waive any late penalties. Many lenders will allow a one-time late payment, and some merchants will be willing to waive late charges just by you asking. Now, this won't work if you're late multiple times, but suggesting that you'll pay the full balance due if they close your credit account can be an effective negotiating tool with many credit providers.

The percentages we give you in the following sections are based on the importance of the five categories for the general population. For particular groups — for example, people who haven't been using credit for very long — the importance of these categories may be different.

The following sections offer a complete look at the information that goes into a FICO score. For a visual graphic of what contributes to your credit score, see Figure 3-1.

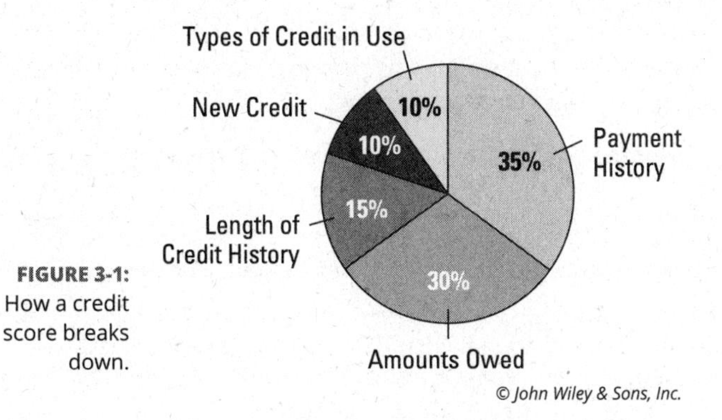

FIGURE 3-1: How a credit score breaks down.

Your loan repayment history

What's your track record for repaying creditors? One of the most important factors in a credit score is your payment history; it affects roughly 35 percent of your score. The first thing any lender wants to know is whether you've paid past credit accounts on time.

Late payments aren't an automatic "score-killer." An overall good credit picture can outweigh one or two instances of, say, late credit card payments. On the other hand, having no late payments in your credit report doesn't mean you automatically get a great score. Some 60 to 65 percent of credit reports show no late payments at all. Your payment history is just one piece of information used in calculating your credit score.

In the area of payments, your score takes the following into account:

- **Payment information on many types of accounts:** These types of accounts include credit cards such as Visa, MasterCard, American Express, PayPal Credit, and Discover, credit cards from stores or online merchants where you do business, installment loans (loans such as a mortgage on which you make regular payments), and finance company accounts.

- **Public record and collection items:** These items include reports of events such as bankruptcies, foreclosures, suits, wage attachments, liens, and judgments. They're considered quite serious, although older items and items with small amounts count less than more recent items or those with larger amounts. Bankruptcies stay on your credit report for seven to ten years, depending on the type.
- **Details on late or missed payments *(delinquencies)* and public record and collection items:** The FICO score considers how late such payments were, how much you owed, how recently they occurred, and how many you have. As a rule, a 60-day late payment isn't as damaging as a 90-day late payment. A 60-day late payment made just a month ago, however, penalizes you more than a 90-day late payment from five years ago.
- **How many accounts show no late payments:** A good track record on most of your credit accounts increases your credit score.

TIP

So how do you improve your FICO score? Consider the possibilities:

- **Pay your bills on time.** Delinquent payments and collections can have a major negative impact on your score.
- **If you've missed payments, get current and stay current.** The longer you pay your bills on time, the better your score.
- **Paying off or closing an account doesn't remove it from your credit report.** The score still considers this information, because it reflects your past credit pattern. But closing accounts that you never use can help because the number of lines of credit and the total dollar amount of available credit are factors in the credit scoring algorithms.
- **If you're having trouble making ends meet, get help.** This step doesn't improve your score immediately, but if you can begin to manage your credit and pay on time, your score gets better over time. See Chapter 2 for credit problem-solving strategies.

Amount you owe

About 30 percent of your score is based on your current debt. Having credit accounts and owing money on them doesn't mean you're a high-risk borrower who'll receive a low score. However, owing a great deal of money on many accounts can indicate that a person is overextended and is more likely to make some payments late or not at all. Part of the science of scoring is determining how much is too much for a given credit profile.

THE LOWDOWN ON HOW A FORECLOSURE CAN AFFECT YOUR FICO SCORE

A foreclosure, a *short sale* (where the lender agrees to accept less than the total amount due on a mortgage), or a *deed in lieu of foreclosure* (in which a borrower deeds his property to the lender, who then sells it and uses the proceeds of sale to repay some or all of the mortgage) lowers your credit score. If you had the misfortune to personally go through one of these negative credit events, be advised they're considered extremely serious delinquencies. They show that you failed to honor a credit obligation. Because of limitations in the way this type of delinquency is shown on credit reports, a FICO score generally doesn't distinguish among them.

The FICO score assesses negatives on your credit report by three factors:

- **Recency** (how long ago)
- **Severity** (how late)
- **Frequency** (how often)

A foreclosure is serious because you became so late in making your monthly payments (severity) that your lender terminates the loan and demands immediate repayment in full. Its impact on your credit score increases if the event was reported a short time ago (recency) or if other items on your credit report are also delinquent (frequency).

How can you improve your FICO score after a foreclosure? Typically, a foreclosure adversely affects your credit report for up to seven years. Because your payment history comprises about 35 percent of your credit score, the best way to improve your FICO score is to get current and stay current on all your other debts.

Even with an improved FICO score, however, don't expect to get a new home loan with favorable terms for five to seven years after your foreclosure. Fortunately, even homeowners with a foreclosure, short sale, or deed in lieu of foreclosure during the major economic downturn of the late 2000s are now reaching the point where such events won't be reflected negatively on their credit score. See Chapter 13 for more on foreclosures.

In the area of debts, your score takes into account the following information:

» **The amount owed on all accounts:** Note that even if you pay off your credit cards in full every month, your credit report may show a balance on those cards. The total balance on your last statement is generally the amount that will show in your credit report.

- **The amount owed on all accounts and on different types of accounts:** In addition to the overall amount you owe, the score considers the amount you owe on specific types of accounts, such as credit cards and installment loans.
- **Whether you show a balance on certain types of accounts:** In some cases, having a small balance without missing a payment shows that you've managed credit responsibly. But keep open only the credit accounts that you intend to use because having a bunch of open credit accounts with no activity can be a negative. On the other hand, closing unused credit accounts for establishments that you intend to continue to patronize that show zero balances and that are in good standing doesn't raise your score. Closing accounts you may use again in the near future only to reopen them can have an overall negative affect on your credit score. So close those accounts you know you won't be using for years, if ever, while keeping open any credit accounts that you may use in the near future.
- **How many accounts have balances:** A large number can indicate higher risk of overextension. Although many stores and online retailers want to lure you into having their specific branded or affinity credit card, it's better to consolidate all your credit to just a few of the major credit cards that are widely accepted.
- **How much of the total credit line you're using on credit cards and other *revolving credit* accounts.** Someone closer to "maxing out" on many credit cards may have trouble making payments in the future.
- **How much of installment loan accounts is still owed, compared with the original loan amounts.** For example, if you borrowed $10,000 to buy a car and you've paid back $2,000, you owe (with interest) more than 80 percent of the original loan. Paying down installment loans is a good sign that you're able and willing to manage and repay debt.

How to improve your FICO score:

- **Keep balances low on credit cards and other revolving credit.** High outstanding debt can adversely affect a score.
- **Pay off debt.** The most effective way to improve your score in this area is by paying down your revolving credit.
- **Don't close unused credit accounts that you still may use as a short-term strategy to raise your score.** Generally, this tactic doesn't work. In fact, it may lower your score. Late payments associated with old accounts won't disappear from your credit report if you close the account. Long-established accounts show you have a longer history of managing credit, which is a good thing.
- **Don't open new credit cards that you don't need, just to increase your available credit.** This approach can backfire and actually lower your score. Again, although it's tempting when your local retailer makes that great offer of

an extra 10, 20, or even 50 percent savings on today's purchases if you just open a credit account with them, don't do it — unless you're buying an extremely expensive item (although most of these deals have limits or caps) and you're able to immediately make full payment for all your monthly expenditures, plus you actually intend to use the card regularly. Otherwise, just ask for a cash discount or use one of your major credit cards that are accepted by most retailers.

Length of credit history

How established is your credit history? About 15 percent of your score is based on this area. In general, a longer credit history increases your score. However, even people who haven't been using credit long may get high scores, depending on how the rest of the credit report looks.

In this area, your score takes into account

- **How long your credit accounts have been established, in general:** The score considers both the age of your oldest account and an average age of all your accounts.
- **How long specific credit accounts have been established:** Extended responsible use of credit accounts with major credit cards and/or major retailers can have a positive effect on your credit score. This is much better than having a lot of accounts that are open for only a short period of time.
- **How long it's been since you used certain accounts:** Not using all your available credit shows self-control and responsible use of credit.

TIP

If you've been managing credit for a short time, don't open a lot of new accounts too rapidly. New accounts lower your average account age, which will have a larger (negative) effect on your score if you don't have a lot of other credit information. Also, rapid account buildup can look risky if you're a new credit user, so you don't want to accept every offer you receive in the mail for a new credit card or open a credit account with every retailer you patronized just for a one-time sign-up bonus.

New credit

Taking on a lot of new debt affects your score, too. About 10 percent of your score is based on new credit and credit applications.

WARNING

People tend to have more credit today and to shop for credit — via the Internet and other channels — more frequently than ever. Credit scores reflect this fact. However, research shows that opening several credit accounts in a short period does represent more risk — especially for people who don't have a long-established credit history.

Applying for several new credit cards or accounts also represents more risk. However, FICO scores do a good job of distinguishing between a search for *many* new credit accounts and rate shopping for *one* new account.

In the area of new credit, your score takes into account

- **How many new accounts you have:** The score looks at how many new accounts you have by type of account (for example, how many newly opened credit cards you have). It also may look at how many of your accounts are new accounts.
- **How long it's been since you opened a new account:** Again, the score looks at this info by type of account.
- **How many recent requests for credit you've made:** This is indicated by inquiries to the credit reporting agencies. Inquiries remain on your credit report for two years, although FICO scores consider inquiries only from the last 12 months. The scores have been carefully designed to count only those hard inquiries that truly impact credit risk. Inquiries for insurance or employment are soft inquiries and don't negatively affect your credit score.
- **Length of time since lenders made credit report inquiries:** The older the lender inquiries, the better. Inquiries more than a year old are ignored. In this case, being ignored is good.
- **Whether you have a good recent credit history, following past payment problems:** Reestablishing credit and making payments on time after a period of late payment behavior helps to raise a score over time, so can disputing any incorrect entries or even providing a letter of explanation.

TIP

Here are some ways to improve your FICO score:

- **Do your rate shopping for a specific loan within a focused period of time.** FICO scores distinguish between a search for a single loan and a search for many new credit lines, in part by the length of time over which inquiries occur. For more on this topic, see the section "Adding up inquiries," later in this chapter.
- **Reestablish your credit history if you've had problems.** Opening a select number of new credit accounts responsibly and paying them off on time will raise your score in the long term.
- **Request and check your own credit report and FICO score.** It's okay to do this and it doesn't affect your score because it's a "soft inquiry" — as long as you order your credit report directly from the credit reporting agency or through an organization authorized to provide credit reports to consumers, such as `www.annualcreditreport.com`.

Types of credit in use

The credit mix usually isn't a key factor in determining your score — but it's given more weight if your credit report doesn't have a lot of other information on which to base a score. About 10 percent of your score is based on this category.

In this area, your score takes into account the following factors:

- **What kinds of credit accounts you have:** Your score considers your mix of credit cards, retail accounts, installment loans, finance company accounts, and mortgage loans. Don't feel obligated to have one of each.
- **How many of each type of credit account you have:** The score looks at the total number of accounts you have. How many is too many varies on the credit type. You don't need to have one of each type. Don't open credit accounts you don't intend to use just to hype up your total. Think quality, not quantity. Apply only for credit accounts that you know you'll really need, and always use all types of credit judiciously and responsibly.

TIP

How to improve your FICO score:

- **Apply for and open new credit accounts only as needed.** Don't open accounts just to have a better credit mix or fall for the trap of thinking that more accounts is better. Years ago, common advice was that to build up your credit history, you must go out and buy something you really don't need just to establish that you can show a good payment history— our advice is to buy only what you have to buy on credit and pay it off as promised.
- **Have credit cards — but manage them responsibly.** In general, having two to three major widely accepted credit cards and installment loans (and making timely payments) raises your score.
- **Note that closing an account doesn't make it go away.** A closed account still shows up on your credit report and may be included in the score.

Adding up inquiries

A search for new credit can mean greater credit risk. This is why the FICO score counts inquiries — those requests a lender makes for your credit report or score when you apply for credit.

FICO scores consider inquiries very carefully because not all inquiries are related to credit risk. You should note three things about credit inquiries:

- **Inquiries don't affect scores very much.** For most people, one additional hard credit inquiry takes less than 5 points off their FICO score. However, inquiries can have a greater impact if you have few accounts or a short credit history. Large numbers of inquiries also mean greater risk: People with six inquiries or more on their credit reports are eight times more likely to declare bankruptcy than people with no inquiries on their reports.

- **Many kinds of inquiries aren't counted at all.** Ordering your own credit report or credit score from a credit reporting agency has no impact on your score because it's a soft inquiry. Also, the score doesn't count requests a lender makes for your credit report or score to make you a preapproved credit offer, or to review your account with them, even though you may see these inquiries on your credit report. Requests that are marked as coming from insurance companies or employers aren't counted either.
- **The score looks for *rate shopping*.** Looking for a mortgage or an auto loan may cause multiple lenders to request your credit report, even though you're looking for only one loan. To compensate for this reality, the score counts multiple inquiries in any 14-day period as just one inquiry. In addition, the score ignores *all* inquiries made in the 30 days prior to scoring. So if you find a loan within 30 days, the inquiries won't affect your score while you're rate shopping.

What FICO scores ignore

FICO scores consider a wide range of information on your credit report. However, they don't consider the following:

- Your race, color, religion, national origin, sex, and marital status

  U.S. law prohibits credit scoring from considering these facts, as well as any receipt of public assistance, or the exercise of any consumer right under the Consumer Credit Protection Act.
- Your age
- Your salary, occupation, title, employer, date employed, or employment history

Lenders may consider this information, however:

- Where you live and how long you've lived there
- Any interest rate being charged on a particular credit card or other account
- Any items reported as child/family support and divorce obligations or rental agreements
- Certain types of inquiries (requests for your credit report or score)

  The score does *not* count any requests you make, any requests from employers or insurers, and any requests lenders make without your knowledge.

- Any information not found in your credit report, including your current salary and occupation
- Any information not proven to be predictive of future credit performance

Interpreting scores

When a lender receives your FICO score, up to four *score reasons* are also delivered. These aren't reasons your score was low but rather the top reasons your score isn't higher. If the lender rejects your request for credit and your FICO score is part of the reason, these score reasons can help the lender tell you why.

TIP

These score reasons can be more useful to you than the score itself. They help you determine whether your credit report may contain errors and how you may improve your credit score. However, if you already have a high FICO score (for example, in the mid-700s or higher) some of the reasons may not be helpful because they may be marginal factors related to less important categories such as your length of credit history, new credit, and types of credit in use.

The total number of factors or score reasons that are available and used in the preparation and scoring of credit reports vary among the three major credit reporting agencies. Our recent check found that they currently use between 30 and 34 score reasons.

Getting your score

TIP

Because lenders check your score, you may want to see the same score that they see. It's easy to check your FICO score and to find out specific things that you can do to raise it. The websites for many banks, financial services sites, and credit reporting agencies offer FICO scores for a fee, as does Fair Isaac's myFICO site at `www.myFICO.com`. Information you receive includes

- Your current FICO score
- Your credit report on which your FICO score is based
- An explanation of your score, the positive and negative factors behind it, and how lenders view your credit risk
- A FICO score simulator you can use to see how specific actions, such as paying off all your card balances, would affect your score
- Specific tips on what you can do to improve your FICO score over time

In addition, you can see current information on the average interest rates for home loans for different FICO score ranges.

If you do business with one of the larger banks, you may have free access to your FICO score. Just be aware that you may not be getting the best overall deal on whatever services you're buying from those banks.

Managing your score

Follow the tips in this chapter to manage your credit score efficiently. Improving your score can help you

- Get better credit offers
- Lower your interest rates
- Speed up credit approvals

An important time to check your score is six months or more before applying for a mortgage. This gives you time to make sure your credit report information is right, correct it if it's not, improve your score if necessary, and ensure your access to the best mortgages available.

If you've been turned down for credit, the federal Equal Credit Opportunity Act gives you the right to find out why within 30 days. You're also entitled to a free copy of your credit bureau report within 60 days, which you can request from the credit reporting agencies. If your FICO score was a primary part of the lender's decision, the lender will use the score reasons to explain why you didn't qualify for the credit.

2

Locating a Loan

IN THIS PART . . .

Get familiar with mortgage basics and the jargon that you need to know.

Check out the many types of mortgages that are available when you're seeking to buy or refinance a home.

Explore alternative financing options if you're faced with a special circumstance that makes it hard for you to get a traditional mortgage.

IN THIS CHAPTER

» Understanding the basic building blocks of mortgages

» Looking at mortgage terminology

» Finding out about prepayment penalties and private mortgage insurance

Chapter 4
Fathoming the Fundamentals

Like brain surgeons, nuclear physicists, pizza makers, and all other highly skilled professionals, financial wizards have developed their own weird customs, practices, and terminology over the centuries. If you want to do business with financiers, knowing how to speak their language helps, because they rarely bother to speak yours. A steady diet of *jumbo* loan with *points* au gratin on the side and the infamous house specialty, *prepayment penalty* flambé, for dessert leaves even the hardiest borrower intellectually constipated.

Worse, some unscrupulous lenders may use your fiscal ignorance to maneuver you into getting a loan that's good for them but bad for you. Even though an assortment of loans may outwardly appear to be equally attractive, they're usually not — not by a long shot.

The good news is that lending ain't rocket science. This chapter explains what makes a loan tick and helps you speak the language of lending like a pro. (Chapter 5 takes you through the particulars of choosing the best loan for you.)

Grasping Loan Basics: Principal, Interest, Term, and Amortization

Money isn't magical. It's a commodity or consumer product like HDTVs and toasters. Lending institutions such as banks, savings and loan associations (S & Ls), and credit unions get their raw material (money) in the form of deposits from millions of people just like you. Then they bundle your cash into neat little packages called loans, which they sell to other folks who use the money to buy cars, college educations, and cottages. Lenders make their profit on the *spread* (differential) between what they pay depositors to get money and what they charge borrowers to use the money until the lender is fully repaid.

REMEMBER

All loans have the following four basic components:

- **Principal:** Even though both words are spelled and pronounced the same way, the principal we're referring to isn't that humorless old coot who ruled your high school with an iron fist. We're talking about a sum of money owed as a debt: the dollar amount of the loot you borrow to acquire whatever it is that your heart desires.
- **Interest:** No linguistic confusion here — *interest* is what lenders charge you to use their product: money. It accumulates over time on the unpaid balance of money you borrowed (the outstanding *principal*) and is expressed as a percentage called the *interest rate.* For instance, you may be paying an interest rate of 19.8 percent or more on the unpaid balance of your credit card debt. (We recommend that you pay off credit card balances as soon as possible!)

TIP

  Consumer interest for outstanding balances such as credit card debt and a car loan is *not* deductible on your federal or state income tax return. Interest paid on a home loan, conversely, can be used to reduce your state and federal income tax burdens. There's a major difference in how you borrow money. Understanding these income tax write-off rules can save you big bucks.

- **Term:** All good things come to an end sooner or later. A loan's *term* is the amount of time you're given by a lender to repay money you borrow. Generally speaking, small loans have shorter terms than large loans. For instance, your friendly neighborhood credit union may give you only four years to pay back a $20,000 car loan. That very same lender will graciously fund a loan with a 30-year term so you have plenty of time to repay the $200,000 you borrow to buy your dream home.

TIP

  Lenders allow more time to pay back large loans to make the monthly payments more affordable. For example, you'd spend $568 a month to repay a $100,000 loan with a 5.5 percent interest rate and a 30-year term. The same loan costs $818 a month with a 15-year term. Even though the 15-year loan's payment is $250 per month higher, you'd pay *far* less interest on it over the life of the loan:

$818/month × 180 months for a $100,000 loan repayment = $47,240 in interest over 15 years

versus

$568/month × 360 months for a $100,000 loan repayment = $104,480 interest over 30 years

Don't let a seemingly low monthly payment (with a longer-term loan) fool you into paying a lot more interest over the long haul.

- **Amortization:** *Amortization* is an ominous word lenders use to describe the tedious process of liquidating a debt by making periodic installment payments throughout the loan's term. Loans are *amortized* (repaid) with monthly payments consisting primarily of interest during the early years of the loan term and principal, which the lender uses to reduce the loan's balance. If your loan is *fully amortized,* it will be repaid in full by the time you've made your final loan payment. You'll gasp in astonishment and sadness when you read Appendix B and see with your own eyes how long it takes to repay half of the original loan amount.

Deciphering Mortgage Lingo

Just for the heck of it, ask the next thousand people you meet what a mortgage is. Approximately 999 of them will tell you that it's a loan used to buy a home.

Amazingly, every one of them is wrong. Common usage aside, a mortgage is *not* simply a loan. This section clarifies what a mortgage is and isn't.

So . . . what's a mortgage?

Mortgage is a word lenders use to describe a formidable pile of legal documents you have to sign to get the money you need to buy or refinance *real property.* What's real property? It's dirt — plain old terra firma and any *improvements* (homes, garages, cabanas, swimming pools, tool sheds, barns, or other buildings) permanently attached to the land.

Mortgages aren't used only to facilitate home purchases. They're used whenever people acquire any kind of real property, from vacant lots to commercial real estate such as shopping centers and the Empire State Building.

In case you're curious, anything that isn't real property is classified as *personal property.* Moveable or impermanent possessions such as stoves, refrigerators, dishwashers, washers and dryers, window treatments, flooring, chandeliers, and fireplace screens are examples of personal property items that are frequently included in the sale of real property.

Mortgages *encumber* (burden) real property by making it security for the repayment of a debt. A *first mortgage* ever so logically describes the very first loan secured by a particular piece of property. The second loan secured by the same property is called a *second mortgage,* the third loan is a *third mortgage,* and so on. You may also hear lenders refer to a first mortgage as the *senior* mortgage. Any subsequent loans are called *junior* mortgages. Money imitates life.

This type of financial claim on real property is called a *lien.* Proper liens invariably have two integral parts:

- **Promissory note:** This note is the evidence of your debt, an IOU that specifies exactly how much money you borrowed as well as the terms and conditions under which you promise to repay it.
- **Security instrument:** If you don't keep your promise, the security instrument gives your lender the right to take steps necessary to have your property sold to satisfy the outstanding balance of the debt. The legal process triggered by the security device is called *foreclosure.* We sincerely and fervently hope that the closest you ever get to foreclosure is reading about it in this book (see Chapter 14 for details).

From a lender's perspective, each junior mortgage (subsequent mortgage after the first loan on the property) is increasingly risky, because in the event of a foreclosure, mortgages are paid off in order of their numerical priority (seniority). In plain English, the second mortgage lender doesn't get one cent until the first mortgage lender has been paid in full. If a foreclosure sale doesn't generate enough money to pay off the first mortgage, that's tough luck for the second lender. Due to the added risk, lenders charge higher interest rates for junior mortgages.

How to scrutinize security instruments

The security instrument used in your transaction can vary from one state to the next depending on where the property you're financing is located. Mortgages and deeds of trust are the most common types of security instruments. Without further ado, we give you some important information about them.

Mortgages as security instruments

As a legal concept, mortgages have been around centuries longer than deeds of trust, their relatively newfangled siblings. That's why folks nearly always refer to real property loans as mortgages even if they live in one of the many states where a deed of trust is the dominant security instrument. The other states use mortgages as security instruments.

The seniority of mortgages explains why they're the prevalent security instrument in many states east of the Mississippi River, the first part of the country to be settled. Check with your real estate agent or lender to find out which kind of security instrument is used where your property is located.

Here's how mortgages operate:

- **Type of instrument:** A mortgage is a written contract that specifies how your real property will be used as security for a loan without actually delivering possession of the property to your lender.
- **Parties:** A mortgage has two parties — the mortgagor (that's you, the borrower) and the mortgagee (the lending institution). You don't get a mortgage from the lender. On the contrary, you *give* the lender a mortgage on your property. In return, the mortgage holder (lender) loans you the money you need to purchase the property.
- **Title:** *Title* refers to the rights of ownership you have in the property. A mortgage requires no transfer of title. You keep full title to your property.
- **Effect on title:** The mortgage creates a lien against your property in favor of the lending institution. If you don't repay your loan, the lender usually has to go to court to force payment of your debt by instituting a foreclosure lawsuit. If the judge approves the lender's case against you, the lender is given permission to hold a foreclosure sale and sell your property to the highest bidder.

Deeds of trust as security instruments

Mortgages and deeds of trust are both used for exactly the same purpose: They make real property security for money you borrow. However, mortgages and deeds of trust use significantly different methods to accomplish that same purpose. The following list highlights the features of a deed of trust:

- **Type of instrument:** The security given isn't a written contract. It's a special kind of deed called a *trust deed.*

- **Parties:** The trust deed involves three parties: a *trustor* (you, the borrower), a *beneficiary* (the lender), and a *trustee* (a neutral third party such as a title insurance company or lawyer who won't show any favoritism to you or the lender).
- **Title:** The trust deed conveys your property's naked legal title to the trustee, who holds it in trust until you repay your loan. Don't worry, dear reader; you retain possession of the property. Your lender holds the actual trust deed and note as evidence of the debt.
- **Effect on title:** Like a mortgage, a trust deed creates a lien against your property. Unlike a mortgage, however, the lender doesn't have to go to court to foreclose on your property. In most states, the trustee has power of sale, which can be exercised if you don't satisfy the terms and conditions of your loan. The lender simply gives the trustee written notice of your default and then asks the trustee to follow the foreclosure procedure specified by the deed of trust and state law. Most lenders prefer having their loans secured by a deed of trust. Why? Compared to a mortgage, the foreclosure process is much faster and less expensive.

For simplicity's sake in this book, we use *mortgage, deed of trust,* and the *loan* you get to buy a home as interchangeable terms. You, however, must promise us that you'll always remember the difference and who explained it to you!

Eyeing Classic Mortgage Jargon Duets

Just because you can speak mortgage fluently doesn't mean you'll be able to communicate with lenders. The following sections offer more essential loan jargon. Consider these dynamic duos: mortgage loan options such as fixed or adjustable rate, government or conventional, primary or secondary, conforming or jumbo, and long- or short-term.

Fixed or adjustable loans

FRM, ARM, or whatever — don't let the alphabet soup of mortgages available today confuse you. No matter how complicated the names sound, all loans fall into one of the following basic classifications:

- **Fixed:** This type of loan either has an interest rate or a monthly payment that never changes. A *fixed-rate mortgage (FRM)* is just what it claims to be — a mortgage that keeps the same interest rate throughout the life of the loan.

TECHNICAL STUFF

Even though you have a fixed-rate mortgage, your monthly payment may vary if you have an *impound account* (for folks who put less than 20 percent cash down when purchasing their homes). In addition to the monthly loan payment, some lenders collect additional money each month for the prorated monthly cost of property taxes and homeowners insurance. The extra money is put into an impound account by the lender, who uses it to pay the borrower's property taxes and homeowners insurance premiums when they're due. If either the property tax or the insurance premium happens to change (and they do typically increase annually), the borrower's monthly payment is adjusted accordingly.

» **Adjustable:** Either the interest rate or the monthly payment or both interest rate and monthly payment change (adjust) with this kind of loan. The following are examples of adjustable mortgages:

- An *adjustable-rate mortgage* (ARM) is a loan whose interest rate can vary during the loan's term.
- A *hybrid loan* merges an FRM and an ARM. The hybrid loan's interest rate and monthly payment are fixed for a specific period of time, such as five years, and then the mortgage converts into an ARM for the remainder of the loan term.

WARNING

Just because a mortgage's monthly payment is fixed doesn't mean the loan is a good one. For instance, some ARMs have monthly payments that don't always change, even though the loan's interest rate can change and increase. This can lead to *negative amortization*, an unpleasant situation where the loan balance increases every month, even though you faithfully make the monthly loan payments. After the subprime crisis, few lenders offer negative amortization loans. You can find an in-depth analysis of ARMs and negative amortization in Chapter 5. For now, be advised that we strongly urge you to avoid loans that have the potential for negative amortization.

Government or conventional loans

Through either insuring or guaranteeing home loans by an agency of the federal government, Uncle Sam is a major player in the residential mortgage market. Such mortgages are called, you guessed it, *government loans*. The remaining residential mortgages originated in the United States are referred to as *conventional loans*.

Here's a quick recap of government loans:

» **Federal Housing Administration (FHA):** The FHA was established in 1934 during the depths of the Great Depression to stimulate the U.S. housing market. It primarily helps low-to-moderate income folks get mortgages by issuing federal insurance against losses to lenders who make FHA loans. The FHA is not a moneylender. Borrowers must find an FHA-approved lender such as a credit union, bank, or other conventional lending institution willing to grant a mortgage that the FHA then insures. Not all commercial lenders choose to participate in FHA loan programs due to their complexities.

Depending on which county within the United States the home you want to buy is located, you may be able to get an FHA-insured loan of up to $636,150. The minimum loan amount under this program is $275,665 with a $636,150 maximum as of 2017. The loan limit varies based on the cost of housing in each area. (For current, up-to-date lending limits by area, visit the FHA Mortgage Limits web page at `https://entp.hud.gov/idapp/html/hicostlook.cfm`.)

- **Department of Veterans Affairs (VA):** Congress passed the Serviceman's Readjustment Act, commonly known as the GI Bill of Rights, in 1944. One of its provisions enables the VA to help eligible people on active duty and veterans buy primary residences. Like the FHA, the VA has no money of its own. It guarantees loans granted by conventional lending institutions that participate in VA mortgage programs. This can be an excellent program if you qualify.
- **U.S. Department of Agriculture (USDA):** The USDA oversees the Rural Housing program. This is a popular program for owner-occupied homes outside metropolitan areas. The loans offer $0 down and affordable mortgage insurance. However, there are restrictions on location, income, and assets. If you qualify, this is usually your best $0 down option, besides a VA loan.
- **Farmers Home Administration (FmHA):** Like the FHA, VA, and USDA, the FmHA isn't a direct lender. Despite its name, you *don't* have to be a farmer to get a Farmers Home Administration loan. You do, however, have to buy a home in the sticks. The FmHA insures mortgages granted by participating lenders to qualified buyers who live in rural areas.

TIP

FHA, VA, and FmHA mortgages have more attractive features — little or no cash-down payments, long loan terms, no penalties if you repay your loan early, and lower interest rates — than conventional mortgages. However, these loans aren't for everyone. Government loans are targeted for specific types of homebuyers, have maximum mortgage amounts established by Congress, and may require an inordinately long time to obtain loan approval and funding. In a desirable urban or hot market where homes generate multiple offers, buyers using government loans often lose out to people using conventional mortgages that can be funded quicker.

Primary or secondary mortgage market

Lenders make loans directly to folks like you in what's called the *primary mortgage market.* Few lending institutions keep mortgages they originate in vaults surrounded by heavily armed guards. Lenders sell most of their mortgages to pension funds, insurance companies, and other private investors as well as certain government agencies in the *secondary mortgage market.* Why do mortgage lenders sell mortgages they originate? They want to make a profit and to obtain more funds to lend.

Uncle Sam is an extremely important force in the secondary mortgage market through two federally chartered government organizations — the *Federal National Mortgage Association* (*FNMA*, or *Fannie Mae*) and the *Federal Home Loan Mortgage Corporation* (*FHLMC*, endearingly known as *Freddie Mac*). One of the primary missions of Fannie Mae and Freddie Mac is to stimulate residential housing construction and home purchases by pumping money into the secondary mortgage market.

Fannie Mae and Freddie Mac boost home purchases and construction by purchasing loans from conventional lenders and reselling them to private investors. These government programs are far and away the two largest investors in U.S. mortgages.

These programs aren't meant to subsidize rich folks. To that end, Congress establishes upper limits on mortgages Fannie Mae and Freddie Mac are authorized to purchase. Table 4-1 shows the 2017 maximum mortgage amounts for one- to four-unit properties. ***Note:*** These are the general loan limits for most areas, but if you're buying a property in a so-called "high-cost" area, the maximum mortgage amounts are 50 percent higher than those in Table 4-1.

TABLE 4-1

2017 Fannie Mae and Freddie Mac Maximum Mortgage Amounts for One- to Four-Unit Properties

# of Units	Continental U.S.	Alaska, Hawaii, Guam & U.S. Virgin Islands
1	$424,100	$636,150
2	$543,000	$814,500
3	$656,350	$984,525
4	$815,650	$1,223,475

Congress periodically readjusts these maximum mortgage amounts to reflect changes in the prevailing average price of property. Any good lender can fill you in on Fannie Mae's and Freddie Mac's current loan limits.

Conforming or jumbo loans

This delicious tidbit of information can save you big bucks: Conventional mortgages that fall within Fannie Mae's and Freddie Mac's loan limits are referred to as *conforming loans.* Mortgages that exceed the maximum permissible loan amounts are called *jumbo loans* or *nonconforming loans.*

When Congress passed the Economic Stimulus Act of 2008 (The Act), it also created a brand-new type of mortgage neatly notched between a conforming loan and a jumbo loan. We now have three tiers of mortgages:

- **True conforming loans** include loan amounts up to $424,100. These loans, also called *traditional conforming loans,* have the lowest interest rates.
- **Jumbo conforming loans** encompass loan amounts from $424,100 up to a maximum of $636,150 and are designed for high-cost areas (the precise amount varies by area). Some lenders call these conforming jumbos, super conforming, or jumbo light loans. Whatever. Loans of this size generally have interest rates anywhere from half a percent to a full percent (or more) higher than the true conforming loan.
- **True jumbos** are loans that exceed $636,150. As you'd expect, the largest loans are also the most expensive. Their interest rates usually run a full percent point or more above jumbo conforming loans.

Fannie Mae and Freddie Mac both imposed tougher qualifying standards on jumbo conforming loans than they have for true conforming loans. Some examples of these tougher standards: Jumbo conforming loans are limited to single-family dwellings, require that you have at least a 700 FICO score if your loan-to-value (LTV) ratio exceeds 75 percent (for Freddie Mac) or 80 percent (for Fannie Mae), and specify that monthly payments on your combined total debt can't exceed 45 percent of your income.

Fannie's and Freddie's jumbo conforming loan programs were originally scheduled to expire December 31, 2008, but Congress keeps extending them, and these programs are still in place as of 2017. Be sure to check with your lender regarding the current status of these loans.

You pay dearly for nonconformity. The higher the loan amount, the bigger the thud if your loan goes belly up. Reducing the loan-to-value ratio is one way lenders cut their risk. To that end, conventional lenders generally insist on more than the usual 20 percent down on jumbo loans. You'll probably be required to make at least a 25 percent cash down payment. Interest rates on nonconforming fixed-rate mortgages generally run from 3⁄8 to 1⁄2 a percentage point higher than conforming FRMs. When mortgage money is tight, the interest rate spread between conforming and jumbo FRMs is higher; when mortgage money is plentiful, the spread decreases.

TIP

If you find yourself slightly over Fannie Mae's and Freddie Mac's limit for either true conforming loans or the jumbo conforming loans, don't despair. You can either buy a slightly less expensive home or increase your cash down payment *just* enough to bring your mortgage amount under their loan limits or possibly use a small second mortgage. In Chapter 2, we include a lengthy list of financial resources you may be able to tap for additional cash.

Long-term or short-term mortgages

Any loan that's amortized more than 30 years is considered to be a *long-term mortgage.* Reversing that guideline, *short-term mortgages* are loans that must be repaid in less than 30 years. Wow. Definitions that actually make sense.

These standards harken back to less complicated times before the late 1970s when people could get any kind of mortgage they wanted as long as it was a 30-year, fixed-rate loan. Back then, choices for a short-term mortgage were nearly as limited. Homebuyers could have an FRM with either a 10- or 15-year term or a *balloon loan* with, for example, a 30-year amortization schedule and a 10-year due date. They made the same monthly principal and interest payments for ten years and then got hammered with a massive *balloon payment* to pay off the entire remaining loan balance. (The reality was that homeowners simply had to refinance the remaining loan balance through a new loan either with their current lender or another lender.)

The total interest charges on short-term mortgages are less than total interest paid for equally large long-term loans at the same interest rate because you're borrowing the money for less time. Because a lender has less risk with a short-term loan, such loans usually have lower interest rates than comparable long-term mortgages. For instance, the interest rate on a conforming 15-year, fixed-rate mortgage is generally about ½ a percentage point lower than a comparable 30-year FRM.

In our prior example (see the section "Grasping Loan Basics: Principal, Interest, Term, and Amortization"), we say that you'd spend $568 a month to repay a $100,000 FRM with a 5.5 percent interest rate and a 30-year term. The same FRM with a 15-year term and 5.5 percent interest rate costs $818 a month. If that loan has a 5 percent interest rate, its payment would drop to $791 per month. The half-point interest rate cut saves you an additional $4,860 over the life of the loan ($818 – $791 = $27 per month × 180 months). Not too shabby!

Even though short-term loans have lower interest rates than their long-term cousins, qualifying for a short-term loan is more difficult due to the higher monthly loan payments. Lenders generally don't want you spending much more than 30 to 35 percent of your gross monthly income on mortgage payments. Even if you can qualify for a short-term loan, it may not be in your best interests (pun intended) to irrevocably lock yourself into the higher monthly payments. Will higher loan payments deplete the cash reserves you ought to maintain for emergencies? Can you afford higher loan payments and still accomplish all the other financial goals we cover in Chapter 1? We devote Chapter 12 to a stimulating analysis of the pros and cons of paying off a mortgage more rapidly than is required by the lender.

Introducing the Punitive Ps

Certain warnings are drilled into people until they become as reflexive as the way your leg convulsively jerks when a doctor hits your knee with that little pointy rubber hammer. Don't stuff yourself on sweets just before sitting down to a good, healthy meal. Don't forget to floss and brush your teeth. Don't drink and drive. Think before you post something on social media! Other injurious hazards are more insidious. The following sections offer words to the wise about two of them related to mortgages.

Prepayment penalties

Some lenders punish borrowers severely for repaying all or part of their conventional loan's remaining principal balance before its due date. As punishment, they impose a charge known as a *prepayment penalty.* Prepayment penalties aren't permitted on FHA, VA, USDA, and FmHA mortgages (see the earlier section, "Government or convention loans," for more information on these kinds of mortgages).

How much money are we talking about? That depends. Maximum permissible prepayment penalties vary widely from state to state, from one lender to the next — and even from one loan to the next on mortgages offered by the same lending institution. Some lenders will waive the prepayment penalty if you get a new loan from them when you refinance your mortgage or if you're forced to pay off the loan because you sell your house.

Less sympathetic souls force you to pay upward of 3 percent on your unpaid loan balance, which equals $3,000 on every $100,000 you prepay. Even less humane lenders may insist on a penalty equal to six month's interest on your outstanding loan balance. If, for example, your mortgage's interest rate is 8 percent per annum, you'd have to pay $4,000 per $100,000 of principal you repay early.

Now that we have your attention, here's how to determine whether the lender can impose a prepayment penalty:

- **Ask:** Now that you know what to ask, don't be shy. Look your loan officer right in the eye and specifically inquire whether the loan you're considering has a prepayment penalty. If it does, we *strongly* urge you to keep looking until you find another equally wonderful mortgage without a prepayment penalty. Some lenders will be willing to negotiate and reduce or even eliminate the prepayment penalty — all you have to do is ask!
- **Read:** Even if the lender says the loan doesn't have a prepayment penalty, don't take chances. Verify that the mortgage doesn't have a prepayment penalty clause by carefully reading the federal truth-in-lending disclosure you'll receive from the lender soon after submitting your loan application. Even good lenders frequently don't know the nuances of every single loan they offer.
- **Read again:** Check, double-check, and check again. You must scrutinize one last document to be sure that your loan doesn't have a prepayment penalty — the promissory note. Read it with care. Make sure a prepayment penalty clause doesn't somehow manage to mysteriously creep into your mortgage before you sign the final loan documents.

WARNING

Some mortgages have *soft prepayment penalties*, which may be waived at the lender's discretion if you sell an owner-occupied one- to four-unit property after you've owned the property at least one year. Soft prepayment penalties are infinitely preferable to *hard prepayment penalties*, which are always enforced without exception.

You may be tempted to get a loan with a prepayment penalty, because you're absolutely certain that there's no way you'll ever pay it off early. Trust us when we say that circumstances have a way of changing when you least expect them to. Utterly unforeseen life changes force folks to sell property whether they want to or not. Divorce happens. People find their employer has transferred them to another state or worse — fired them! Folks pass away prematurely. Life happens.

TIP

You may decide, in your infinite wisdom, to get a mortgage that has a prepayment penalty. Fine. If your mom couldn't make you eat your vegetables, how can we make you follow our sage advice? At least make sure that you completely understand the terms and conditions of your mortgage contract's prepayment penalty clause regarding the following:

- **The amount you can prepay without penalty:** For instance, some lenders permit you to prepay up to 20 percent of your original loan amount or current loan balance without penalty each calendar year. Others impose a penalty from the very first dollar of any prepayment. The more you can prepay without penalty, the better.

- **When you can prepay without penalty:** You may be allowed to prepay a specific amount of money or percentage of your original loan balance quarterly without penalty. Other lenders let you prepay funds without penalty only once a year. The faster you can prepay without penalty, the better.
- **The duration of prepayment penalty:** Mortgages on owner-occupied residential property often specify that the prepayment penalty expires three to five years after loan origination. Other home mortgages have prepayment penalties over the full term of the loan. The faster the prepayment penalty vanishes, the better.
- **The severity of prepayment penalty:** Some prepayment penalties diminish in severity as the mortgage matures. You could, for example, be penalized 5 percent on any funds prepaid within one year of loan origination, 4 percent in the second year, 3 percent for the third year, and so on. Other mortgages impose the same vicious penalty as long as the prepayment clause is in effect. Declining penalties are better.

Can you tell we're not big fans of prepayment penalties?

Private mortgage insurance (PMI)

Mortgage insurance protects lenders from losses they may incur due to the dreaded double whammy of default and foreclosure. Uncle Sam provides the mortgage insurance on government loans (FHA, VA, USDA, and FmHA). Private insurance companies provide *private mortgage insurance* (PMI) on all other loans.

Who pays for this insurance? You, of course — if you want a conventional loan and can't make at least a 20 percent cash down payment on the property you're buying or refinancing. (If that doesn't apply to you, school's out. You have our permission to skip the rest of this chapter.)

"Wait a second," you say. "That seems incredibly inequitable, even for lenders. I pay for the insurance, but my lender gets the proceeds? What's in it for me?" A loan. It's the only way to get conventional financing with a low cash down payment. That's the deal. Take it or leave.

Twenty percent is a magic number to institutional lenders. They made a fascinating empirical discovery after suffering through years of expensive, unpleasant experiences with belly-flopped loans. At least a 20 percent down payment is necessary to protect their investment (the mortgage) if you cut and run on your loan. We know you're wonderful and would *never* default on your mortgage. Unfortunately, lenders don't know you nearly as well as we do.

Look at things from their perspective. Suppose that you put only 10 percent cash down. A severe recession occurs, and property values drop 15 percent. You lose your job because your business fails, and you can't make your monthly loan payments. The lender is forced to take your house away from you in a foreclosure action and sell it to satisfy your debt. Farfetched? Hardly. Read your local paper. Stranger things happen every day. Witness the jump in foreclosures in most areas in the years just before and after the 2008 financial crisis and recession.

After the poor, misunderstood lender involuntarily takes back your now vacant home, fixes it up to make it marketable, and pays the real estate commission, property transfer tax, and other customary expenses associated with the sale of your house, there won't be nearly enough money left to pay off your loan. Your lender will lose his corporate shirt. If that scenario happens too often, the lender goes belly up.

TIP

You may be able to deduct your PMI premiums on your federal tax return. For loans that commenced after 2006, borrowers with an adjusted gross income (AGI) of up to $100,000 may deduct their PMI premiums as they do mortgage interest on IRS Form 1040, Schedule A. The deduction is phased out in 10 percent increments for each $1,000 in increased income above $100,000. Above $109,000, PMI isn't tax deductible.

What you'll end up spending for PMI depends on the following factors:

- **Type of loan:** For example, ARMs generally have higher PMI premiums than FRMs. (The previous sentence would have been utterly unintelligible gibberish before you read this chapter. See how well you've mastered the lingo? We're so proud of you.) If you don't understand this sentence, check out the section "Eyeing Classic Mortgage Jargon Duets," earlier in this chapter.
- **Loan amount:** Your PMI premium is partially based on a percentage of the loan amount — the more you borrow, the more you'll pay for PMI.
- **Loan-to-value (LTV) ratio:** LTV ratio is the loan amount divided by the appraised value of the property you're buying or refinancing. The higher the LTV ratio, the greater the risk of default to the lender and, hence, the higher your PMI premium.
- **Credit Score:** Your PMI premium is also partially based on your credit score.
- **The insurance company issuing your PMI:** This is the least important factor because PMI charges usually vary relatively little from one insurance provider to the next. It can't hurt, however, to instruct your lender to shop around for the best deal.

Even though PMI charges don't usually vary much from one insurer to the next, the type of loan they insure and geographical areas of coverage can vary wildly. The late 2000s mortgage market problems made lenders more cautious. Ditto PMI insurers. MGIC (Mortgage Guaranty Insurance Corporation, the largest private mortgage insurer), Radian Group, and Genworth Financial (two other large insurers) are now much more selective about loans they'll insure. Insurers are skittish now about property in distressed markets where values are declining and loans with less than 5 percent cash down. Your lender may have to shop around to find a PMI provider who'll issue your policy.

PMI origination fees and monthly premiums change frequently. Check with your lender for specifics on PMI expenses for your loan.

PMI isn't a permanent condition. You can discontinue it by proving you have at least 20 percent *equity* in your property. Equity is the difference between your home's current market value and what you owe on it. The magic 20 percent can come from a variety of sources: an increase in property values; paying down your loan; improving the property by, for example, modernizing the kitchen or adding a second bathroom; or any combination of these factors. To remove PMI, your lender will no doubt insist that you have the property appraised (at your expense, of course) to establish its current market value. Spending a few hundred dollars for an appraisal that'll save you hundreds or more a year in PMI expenses is a wise investment. (We also thoughtfully include a section in Chapter 6 about how you may be able to use 80-10-10 financing to avoid paying PMI.)

IN THIS CHAPTER

» Understanding fixed, adjustable, hybrid, and other loan options

» Making the 15-year versus 30-year decision

» Dealing with periods of high mortgage interest rates

Chapter 5
Selecting the Best Home Purchase Loan

As you consider your mortgage options, you may quickly find yourself overwhelmed by the sheer number of choices. Should you choose a 15-year or a 30-year fixed-rate loan? What about mortgages that have variable interest rates — some adjust monthly, others every 6 or 12 months. Still others have a fixed interest rate for, say, the first one, three, five, seven, or ten years and then convert into some sort of adjustable rate. Or you can choose loans that start out as adjustable-interest-rate mortgages but allow you to elect at some future date to convert into a fixed-rate loan.

Most mortgages come with a number of bells and whistles, which means that literally tens of thousands of loan choices are available. Talk about a mortgage migraine! This chapter goes over the many options you can choose among and helps you select which ones work best for you.

Three Questions to Help You Pick the Right Mortgage

Here's a clutter-busting pain reliever. Each and every possible mortgage you may consider falls into one of two major camps: fixed-rate mortgage or adjustable-rate mortgage (if these terms are foreign to you, be sure to read Chapter 4). Later in this chapter, we delve into the details of fixed- versus adjustable-rate mortgages.

First, however, we want to help you separate the forest from the trees. Following are three questions you need to ask yourself as you weigh which type of mortgage is best for you.

How long do you plan to keep your mortgage?

From a financial perspective, this is the most important question. Many home-buyers don't expect to stay in their current homes for a long time. If that's your expectation, consider an adjustable-rate mortgage (ARM). Why? Because an ARM starts at a lower interest rate than a fixed-rate loan, so you will save interest dollars in the first few years of holding your ARM.

A mortgage lender takes more risk when lending money at a fixed rate of interest for a longer period of time. The longer the loan term, the more time lenders could experience that interest rates increase and their cost of securing funds from deposits and other sources rise. Thus, compared with an ARM, where the lender is committing to the initial interest rate for a relatively short period of time, lenders charge a premium interest rate for a fixed-rate loan.

TECHNICAL STUFF

The interest rates used to determine most ARMs are short-term interest rates, whereas long-term interest rates dictate the terms of fixed-rate mortgages. During most time periods, longer-term interest rates are higher than shorter-term rates, because of the greater risk the lender accepts in committing to a longer-term rate.

The downside to an ARM, however, is that if interest rates rise, you may find yourself paying more interest in future years than you would be paying had you taken out a fixed-rate loan from the get-go. If you're reasonably certain that you'll hold onto your home for five years or less, however, you may come out ahead with an adjustable-rate mortgage.

If you expect to hold onto your home and mortgage for more than five to seven years, a fixed-rate loan may make more sense, especially if you're not in a financial position to withstand the fluctuating monthly payments that come with an ARM. If you're expecting to stay five to ten years, consider the hybrid loans we discuss in the "Fixed-rate periods on ARMs" sidebar, later in this chapter.

How much financial risk can you accept?

Many homebuyers, particularly first-timers, take an adjustable-rate mortgage (ARM) because doing so allows them to stretch and buy a more expensive home. We Americans aren't well known for our delayed gratification discipline! Also, real estate agents and mortgage brokers (also known as salespeople), who derive commissions either from the cost of the home you buy or the size of the mortgage you take on, may encourage you to stretch. So, if you haven't already done so, please be sure to read Chapter 1 to understand how much you can really afford to borrow given your other financial needs, commitments, and goals.

If you're considering an ARM, you absolutely, positively must understand what rising interest rates — and, therefore, a rising monthly mortgage payment — can do to your personal finances. Consider taking an ARM only if you can answer yes to all the following questions:

- Is your monthly budget such that you can afford higher mortgage payments and still accomplish other important personal financial goals, such as saving for retirement, your children's future educational costs, vacations, and the like?
- Do you have an emergency reserve or "rainy day" fund, equal to at least three to six months of living expenses, which you can tap into to make the potentially higher monthly mortgage payments?
- Can you afford the highest payment allowed on the adjustable-rate mortgage? The mortgage lender can tell you the highest possible monthly payment, which is the payment you'd owe if the interest rate on your ARM went to the lifetime interest-rate cap allowed on the loan.

WARNING

Never take an ARM without understanding and being comfortable with your ability to handle the highest payment allowed. Prior to the real estate market downturn just before and after the financial crisis and severe recession of 2008, many lenders qualified borrowers for an ARM if they could pay the artificially low initial loan payments. Now lenders are far more likely to qualify you for an ARM based on your ability to afford the maximum loan payment you may have to make.

- If you're stretching to borrow near the maximum the lender allows or an amount that will test the limits of your budget, are your job and income stable? If you're a two-income household, can you keep making loan payments if one of you loses your job? If you expect to have children in the future, remember that your household expenses will rise and your disposable income may fall with the arrival of those little bundles of joy.

» Can you handle the psychological stresses of dealing with changing interest rates and mortgage payments?

If you're fiscally positioned to take on the financial risks inherent to an ARM, by all means consider one. As we discuss in the previous section, odds are you can save money in interest charges with an ARM. Relative to a fixed-rate loan, your interest rate should start lower and should stay lower if the overall level of interest rates doesn't change.

Even if interest rates do rise, as they inevitably and eventually will, they inevitably and eventually will come back down. So if you can stick with your ARM through times of high and low interest rates, you should still come out ahead.

Although ARMs do carry the risk of a fluctuating interest rate, as we discuss in the "Adjustable-Rate Mortgages (ARMs)" section, later in this chapter, almost all adjustable-rate loans limit, or *cap*, the rise in the interest rate allowed on your loan. Typical caps are 2 percent per year *(annual cap)* and 6 percent over the life of the loan *(life cap).*

TIP

Consider an adjustable-rate mortgage only if you're financially and emotionally secure enough to handle the maximum possible payments over an extended period of time. ARMs work best for borrowers who take out smaller loans than they're qualified for or who consistently save more than 10 percent of their monthly incomes. If you do choose an ARM, make sure you have a significant cash cushion that's accessible in the event that rates go up.

How much money do you need?

One factor that distinguishes the best mortgage from inferior loans is that the best mortgage is the best deal you can get. Why waste your hard-earned money on a mediocre mortgage? That's not why you bought this book. The amount of money you borrow can greatly affect your loan's interest rate. That's why it behooves you to carefully consider how much money you need.

As we point out in Chapter 4, conventional mortgages that stay within Fannie Mae and Freddie Mac loan limits established each year by Congress are called *conforming loans.* Mortgages that exceed the maximum permissible loan amounts are referred to either as *jumbo conforming loans, nonconforming loans,* or *jumbo loans.*

For example, the conforming loan limit for single-family dwellings in the continental United States was $424,100 when this book went to press. Because mortgage maximums change annually, however, be sure to check with your lender for the current Fannie Mae and Freddie Mac loan limits. If the mortgage you need far exceeds the present conforming loan limit, skip the rest of this section. If, however, your loan is within 10 percent or so of the loan limit, keep reading. Our forthcoming advice may save you major money.

Why are we making such a fuss about the loan limit? Because mortgage interest rates for conforming loans typically run anywhere from 1/4 to 1/2 percent *lower* than the interest rates for jumbo loans. Keeping the amount of money you borrow under that all-important loan limit saves you big bucks over the life of your loan.

TIP

If your mortgage slightly surpasses Fannie Mae and Freddie Mac's loan limit, we know three ways to bring it into conformity:

- **Spend less on a home.** This may seem obvious, but what the heck, we've never been accused of subtlety! The less you pay for a home, the smaller your mortgage.
- **Increase your down payment to reduce the mortgage.** We include a long list of cash cows you may be able to milk in Chapter 2.
- **Use 80-10-10 financing.** Chapter 6 has an extremely enlightening section about 80-10-10 financing techniques you may be able to use to cut your first mortgage down to size.

Now, get down to the brass tacks of understanding the major features of fixed-rate versus adjustable-rate mortgages. Keeping the previous three questions in mind (How long do you plan to keep your mortgage? How much risk can you handle? How much money do you need?), read the following sections and ponder which mortgage works best for you.

Fixed-Rate Mortgages: No Surprises

As you may have surmised from the name, fixed-rate mortgages have interest rates that are fixed (that is, the rate doesn't change) for the entire life of the loan, which is typically 15 or 30 years. With a fixed-rate mortgage, the interest rate stays the same, and the amount of your monthly mortgage payment doesn't change. Thus, you have no surprises, no uncertainty, and no anxiety over possible changes in your monthly payment as you have with an adjustable-rate mortgage.

Figure 5-1 illustrates how 30-year fixed-rate mortgage interest rates have fluctuated over the years. You can bet with 100 percent certainty that they'll continue to bounce up and down due to ever-changing economic conditions. However, we promise that once you have your very own 30-year fixed-rate loan, its interest rate won't ever change.

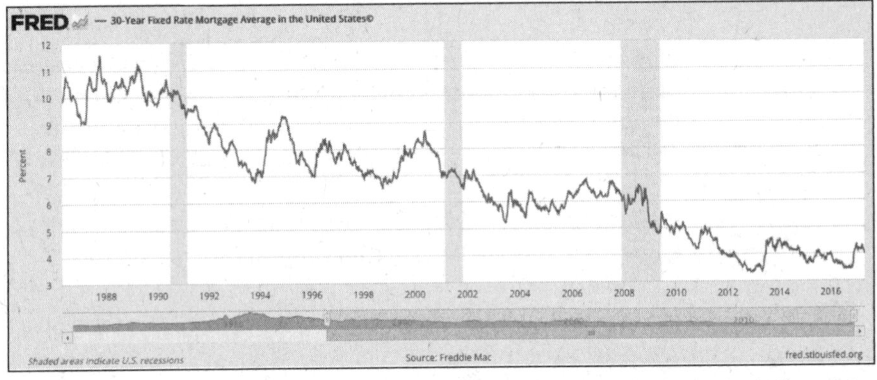

FIGURE 5-1: A long-term perspective on 30-year fixed-rate mortgage interest rates.

Because the interest rate doesn't vary with a fixed-rate mortgage, the advantage of a fixed-rate mortgage is that you always know what your monthly payment is going to be. Thus, budgeting and planning the rest of your personal finances is easier.

That's the good news. The bad news, as we allude to earlier in this chapter, is that with a fixed-rate mortgage, you pay a premium, in the form of a higher interest rate, to get a lender to commit to lending you money at a fixed rate over the full term of the mortgage. The longer the term for which a mortgage lender agrees to accept a fixed interest rate, the more risk that lender is taking.

In addition to paying a premium interest rate when you originally get a fixed-rate loan, another potential drawback to fixed-rate loans is that, if interest rates fall significantly after you have your mortgage, you face the risk of being stuck with your costly mortgage. That could happen if, for example, due to problems with your personal financial situation or a decline in the value of your property, you don't qualify to refinance, a topic we cover in Chapter 11. Even if you do qualify to refinance, doing so takes time and costs money (appraisal, loan fees, and title insurance).

Here are a couple of other possible drawbacks to be aware of with some fixed-rate mortgages:

» Fixed-rate mortgages aren't generally assumable, so if you sell during a period of high interest rates, your buyers must obtain their own financing. Finding assumable ARMs, however, is difficult.

» As with some adjustable-rate mortgages, some fixed-rate mortgages have prepayment penalties (see Chapter 4 for an explanation).

Adjustable-Rate Mortgages (ARMs)

Adjustable-rate mortgages (ARMs) have an interest rate that varies over time. On a typical ARM, the interest rate adjusts every 6 or 12 months, but it may change as frequently as monthly. Popular ARMs include *hybrid loans* where the initial interest rate is locked in for the first three, five, seven, or ten years and then adjusts after that (see the sidebar "Fixed-rate periods on hybrid-ARMs").

As we discuss later in this chapter, the interest rate on an ARM is primarily determined by what's happening to interest rates in general. Remember that interest rates are the "price" for the commodity or product known as cash money. If the price of borrowing money is increasing, then most interest rates are on the rise. In this scenario, the odds are that your ARM will also experience increasing rates, thus increasing the size of your mortgage payment. Conversely, when interest rates fall (as the price of money becomes cheaper usually due to less demand and more capital available in the market), ARM interest rates and payments eventually follow suit.

If the interest rate on your mortgage fluctuates, so will your monthly payment sooner or later. And therein lies the risk: Because a mortgage payment is probably one of your biggest monthly expenses (if not *the* biggest), an adjustable-rate mortgage that's adjusting upward can wreak havoc with your budget.

You may be attracted to an ARM or hybrid loan because it starts out at a lower interest rate than a fixed-rate loan and thus may enable you to qualify to borrow more. However, just because you can qualify to borrow more doesn't mean you can afford to borrow that much, given your other financial goals and needs. See Chapter 1 for all the details.

TIP

The right reason to consider an ARM is because you may save money on interest charges and you can afford the risk of higher payments if interest rates rise. Because you accept the risk of an increase in interest rates, mortgage lenders cut you a little slack. The initial interest rate (also known as the *teaser rate*) should be significantly less than the interest rate on a comparable fixed-rate loan. In fact, even with subsequent rate adjustments, an ARM's interest rate for the first year or two of the loan is generally lower than a fixed-rate mortgage.

Another important advantage of an ARM is that, if you purchase your home during a time of high interest rates, you can start paying your mortgage with the artificially depressed initial interest rate. If overall interest rates then decline, you can capture the benefits of lower rates without refinancing as your ARM adjusts lower.

Here's another situation when adjustable-rate loans have an advantage over their fixed-rate brethren: If, for whatever reason, you don't qualify to refinance your mortgage when interest rates decline, you can still reap the advantage of lower rates. The good news for homeowners who can't refinance and who have an ARM is that they'll receive many of the benefits of the lower rates as their ARM's interest rate and payments adjust downward with declining rates. With a fixed-rate loan, by contrast, you must refinance to realize the benefits of a decline in interest rates.

The downside to an adjustable-rate loan is that if interest rates in general rise, your loan's interest and monthly payment will likely rise, too. During most time periods, if rates rise more than 1 to 2 percent and stay elevated, the adjustable-rate loan is likely to cost you more than a fixed-rate loan.

Before you make any decision between a fixed-rate mortgage versus an adjustable-rate mortgage, please read the following sections for a crash course in understanding ARMs.

How an ARM's interest rate is determined

Most ARMs start at an artificially low interest rate. Don't select an ARM based on this rate because you'll probably be paying this low rate for no more than 6 to 12 months, and perhaps for as little as 1 month. Like other salespeople, lenders promote the most attractive features of their product and ignore the negatives. The low starting rate on an ARM is what some lenders are most likely to tell you about because profit-hungry mortgage lenders know that inexperienced, financially constrained borrowers focus on this low advertised initial rate.

The starting rate on an ARM isn't anywhere near as important as what the future interest rate is going to be on the loan. How the future interest rate on an ARM is determined is the most important issue for you to understand when evaluating an ARM — if you plan on holding onto your loan for more than a few months.

To establish what the interest rate on an ARM will be in the future, you need to know the loan's index and margin, the two of which are added together.

So ignore, for now, an ARM's starting rate and begin your evaluation of an ARM by understanding what *index* it is tied to and what *margin* it has.

What are the index and margin? We're glad you asked!

FIXED-RATE PERIODS ON HYBRID-ARMs

If you expect to keep your loan for no more than five to ten years, and if you want more stability in your monthly payments than comes with a regular ARM that locks in the initial interest rate only for a year or less, an ARM with a longer fixed-rate period may be for you. These are called hybrid-ARMs. All such loans start out as fixed-rate loans — the initial rate on the mortgage is actually fixed for three, five, seven, or even ten years — and then the loan converts into an ARM, usually adjusting every 6 to 12 months thereafter.

The longer the initial rate stays locked in, the higher the rate will be, but the initial rate of a three- to ten-year fixed-rate initial period ARM is almost always lower than the interest rate on a 30-year fixed-rate mortgage. However, because the initial rate of such loans is locked in for a longer period of time than the six-month or one-year term of regular ARMs, three- to ten-year fixed-rate ARMs have higher initial interest rates than regular ARM loans.

To evaluate these mortgages, weigh the likelihood that you'll move before the initial loan interest rate expires. For example, with a five-year ARM, if you're saving, say, 0.75 percent per year versus the 30-year fixed-rate mortgage, but you're quite sure that you'll move within five years, the five-year ARM will probably save you money. On the other hand, if you have a reasonable chance of staying put for more than five years and you don't want to face the risk of rising payments after five years, you should consider a seven- or ten-year hybrid-ARM.

You may occasionally find little difference between short-term and long-term interest rates. For example, we've seen periods when the interest-rate spread between an ARM's initial interest rate and a fixed-rate loan's interest rate was less than 1 percent. We've also seen times when the initial interest rate on a seven- or ten-year ARM was exactly the same as on a 30-year fixed-rate loan. In this type of situation, fixed-rate loans offer the best overall value.

Also, compare the rates for ARMs with varying interest-rate lock periods. You may find very little or even no difference between the five-year and seven-year fixed-rate period ARM loan. In this case, you want to take the loan with the longest fixed-rate period.

Or compare the ARM with a seven-year fixed-rate period to the ten-year fixed-rate period ARM loan, and you may decide that paying a one-quarter percent higher rate throughout the entire first ten years is acceptable to prevent a major increase after the first seven years.

Start with the index

The *index* on an ARM is a measure of general interest rate trends that the lender uses to determine changes in the mortgage's interest rate. For example, the one-year Treasury constant maturity index is a common index used for many ARMs (discussed in next section).

Suppose that the going rate on this index is approximately 2 percent. The indexes used on various ARMs theoretically indicates how much it costs the bank to take in money, for example, from people and companies investing in the bank's various accounts, which the bank can then lend to you, the mortgage borrower.

The following sections explain the most common ARM indexes. Don't worry about lenders playing games with the indexes to unfairly raise your ARM's interest rate. Lenders don't control any of the indexes we discuss. Furthermore, they're easy to verify. If you want to check the figures, you can usually find these indexes in publications such as *The Wall Street Journal* or see our recommended websites in Chapter 8 for online sources for this information.

TREASURY SECURITIES

The U.S. federal government is the largest borrower in the world. So it should come as no surprise that some ARM indexes are based on the interest rate that the government pays on some of its pile of debt. The most commonly used government interest rate indexes for ARMs are for one, three, five, and ten-year Treasuries.

The Treasury security indexes are volatile; they tend to be among the faster-moving ones around. In other words, they respond quickly to market changes in interest rates. Treasury indexes are good when interest rates are falling and lousy when rates head higher.

THE LONDON INTERBANK OFFERED RATE INDEX (LIBOR)

The *London Interbank Offered Rate Index* (LIBOR) is an average of the interest rates that major international banks charge each other to borrow U.S. dollars in the London money market. Like the U.S. Treasury indexes, LIBOR tends to move and adjust quite rapidly to changes in interest rates.

This international interest-rate index became increasingly popular as more foreign investors bought American mortgages as investments. Not surprisingly, these investors like ARMs tied to an index that they understand and are familiar with.

TIP

Be sure to ask your lender how the index tied to the ARM you're considering has changed in the last five to ten years. Figure 5-2 helps you compare the volatility of the most common indexes.

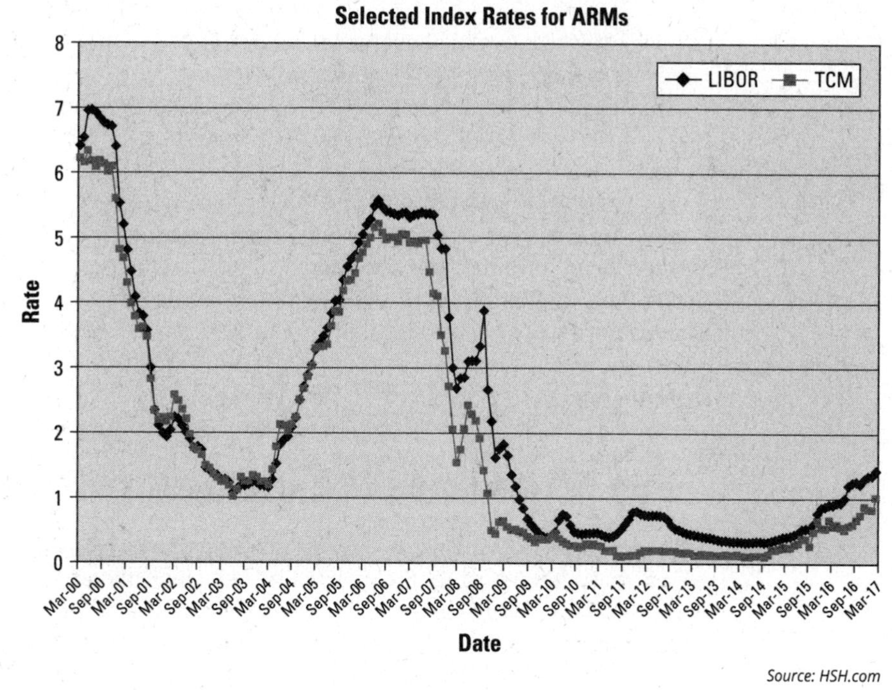

FIGURE 5-2: Selected index rates for ARMs over 30-year period.

Add the margin

The *margin*, or *spread* as it's also known, on an ARM is the lenders' profit, or markup, on the money that they lend. Most ARM loans have margins of around 2.5 percent, but the exact margin depends on the lender and the index that lender is using. When you compare several loans that are tied to the same index and are otherwise the same, the loan with the lowest margin is better (cheaper) for you.

All good things end sooner or later. After the initial interest rate period expires, an ARM's future interest rate is determined, subject to the loan's interest rate cap limitations as explained later in this section, by adding together the loan's current index value and the margin.

The following formula applies every time the ARM's interest rate is adjusted:

$$\text{Index} + \text{margin} = \text{interest rate}$$

For example, suppose that your loan is tied to the *one-year Treasury security index*, which is currently at 2.5 percent plus a margin of 2.25 percent. Thus, your loan's interest rate is

$$2.5\% + 2.25\% = 4.75\%$$

This figure is known as the *fully indexed rate.* If a loan is advertised with an initial interest rate of, say, 3.5 percent, the fully indexed rate (in this case, 4.75 percent) tells you what interest rate this ARM would rise to if the market level of interest rates, as measured by the one-year Treasury security index, stays at the same level.

Always be sure to understand the fully indexed rate on an ARM you're considering. To avoid any surprises, you also should know what the payment will be for various potentially higher interest rates during the life of your loan, including the maximum rate, so you fully understand what the maximum possible monthly payment is. Ask the lender and/or your mortgage broker to provide this payment information.

How often does the interest rate adjust?

Although some ARMs have an interest rate adjustment monthly, most adjust every 6 or 12 months, using the mortgage-rate determination formula discussed previously. In advance of each adjustment, the mortgage lender should mail you a notice, explaining how the new rate is calculated according to the agreed-upon terms of your ARM.

The less frequently your loan adjusts, the less financial risk you're accepting. In exchange for taking less risk, the mortgage lender normally expects you to pay more — such as a higher initial interest rate and/or higher ongoing margin.

What are the limits on rate adjustments?

As discussed earlier in this chapter, despite the fact that an ARM has a formula for determining future interest rates (index + margin = interest rate), a good ARM limits the magnitude of change that can occur in the actual rate you pay. These limits, also known as *rate caps,* affect each future adjustment of an ARM's rate following the expiration of the initial rate period.

Two types of rate caps exist:

- **Periodic adjustment caps:** These caps limit the maximum rate change, up or down, allowed at each adjustment. For ARMs that adjust at six-month intervals, the adjustment cap is generally plus or minus 1 percent. ARMs that adjust more than once annually generally restrict the maximum rate change allowed over the entire year as well. This annual rate cap is typically plus or minus 2 percent.

» **Lifetime caps:** Never, ever, ever take an ARM without a lifetime cap. This cap limits the highest rate allowed over the entire life of the loan. ARMs commonly have lifetime caps of 5 to 6 percent higher than the initial start rate.

WARNING

Without a lifetime cap, your possible loan payment could grow to the moon if interest rates soar again as they did in the early 1980s when rates peaked at more than 18 percent. Be sure you can handle the maximum possible payment allowed on an ARM if the interest rate rises to the lifetime cap.

TIP

You may be wondering why we stress that interest rate adjustments are capped both up and down. Who cares how much rates can go down? You will, if rates drop rapidly and your ARM responds like molasses on a subzero winter morning. As we discuss in Chapter 11, a good reason to refinance an ARM is to lower the periodic and lifetime adjustment caps accordingly if interest rates decline significantly.

Does the loan have negative amortization?

On a normal mortgage, as you make mortgage payments over time, the loan balance you owe is gradually reduced through a process called amortization (see Chapter 4). Some ARMs, however, cap the increase of your monthly payment but don't limit how much the interest rate can increase. Thus, the size of your mortgage payment may not reflect all the interest that you actually currently owe. So rather than paying the interest that's owed and paying off some of your loan principal balance every month, you may end up paying some (but not all) of the current interest that you owe.

Thus, the extra, unpaid interest that you still owe is *added* to your outstanding debt. This process of increasing the size of your loan balance is called *negative amortization.* Negative amortization is like paying only the minimum payment required on a credit card bill. You continue accumulating additional interest on the balance as long as you make only the minimum monthly payment. However, doing this with a mortgage defeats the purpose of your borrowing an amount that fits your overall financial goals (as we discuss in Chapter 1).

Some lenders try to hide the fact that an ARM they're pitching you has negative amortization. How can you avoid negative amortization loans?

» **Ask.** As you discuss specific loan programs with lenders or mortgage brokers, *be sure to tell them you don't want a loan with negative amortization.* Specifically ask them if the ARM they're suggesting has it or not.

WARNING

You must be especially wary of being pitched negative amortization loans if you're having trouble finding lenders willing to offer you a mortgage (in other words, you're considered a credit risk). Remember Robert's take on the old adage, "If it's too good to be true, *it's too good to be true.*"

» **If the loan has a monthly adjustment, ask again.** Monthly adjusting ARMs are often a warning sign of a negative amortization loan. Another red flag is an ARM with annual payment caps rather than semi-annual or annual interest rate adjustment caps.

HOW BAD IS NEGATIVE AMORTIZATION?

Negative amortization loans are also called *option ARMs* because they offer three different options for making mortgage payments. Each month you have the choice of doing one of the following:

- Making a fully amortized payment that includes principal and interest
- Making a smaller payment by paying only the loan's interest charge with no principal
- Lowering your payment even further by making a capped loan payment that doesn't cover all the loan's interest charge and results in negative amortization (an addition to your balance owed)

A disproportionately high percentage of negative amortization ARMs went into foreclosure during the late 2000s real estate market downturn. Some lenders explained this dismal fact by pointing out a disproportionately high percentage of folks who got this type of loan weren't creditworthy borrowers. That may account for part of the problem. However, it's disingenuous for lenders to express shock when people they've led into temptation succumb to the seduction of making the lowest possible monthly payment even if it results in negative amortization.

Good news. It's getting much harder to find negative amortization ARMs. Most lenders no longer offer them. If you need private mortgage insurance (PMI, which we cover in Chapter 4) because you can't make a 20 percent cash down payment, be advised that PMI companies won't insure negative amortization ARMs. If you currently have a negative amortization loan on your property, it's highly unlikely that you'll find a lender willing to give you a home equity loan (see Chapter 6 for more gory details).

UNDERSTANDING INTEREST-ONLY LOANS

As we discuss in Chapter 4, mortgages are usually *amortized* (principal repaid) with monthly payments consisting of interest plus principal used to pay off the loan. Interest-only loan payments are just that — all interest, no principal — at least in their early years.

For example, suppose that you get an interest-only (for the first five years), $250,000 fixed-rate mortgage at 6 percent interest. Your initial loan payment on this loan is $1,250 per month versus $1,500 a month on the same $250,000, traditional fixed-rate loan amortized over 30 years. The extra $250 is principal. During the next 30 years, the principal portion of each monthly $1,500 payment would get slightly larger and the interest portion slightly smaller until the loan was paid off.

Most interest-only mortgages will (after an initial time period such as three, five, seven, or ten years) begin to amortize to repay your principal over the remaining loan term. Continuing with the example we're using, after the first five years, the mortgage payment jumps from $1,250 to $1,610 to get the loan balance paid off over the remaining 25 years. Beware that some interest-only mortgages are actually balloon loans (discussed in Chapter 6), which become fully due and payable well before the typical 15- or 30-year end date of most mortgages.

During the real estate boom in the late 1990s and early 2000s, especially in high-cost housing areas, interest-only mortgages were being marketed to borrowers for their

- Minimum monthly loan payments
- Tax benefits, because 100 percent of the payment is generally tax-deductible mortgage interest

If you intend to keep your first home only a few years before moving up to your dream home, paying off the loan may be less important to you than keeping your monthly payments as low as possible. But, as we've long advised, tread carefully if you're considering an interest-only mortgage. Be sure that you understand all the conditions, especially when and by how much the payment increases when the mortgage begins amortizing. Our biggest concern with interest-only mortgages is that some people may continually use them to stretch their housing budgets. Review Chapter 1 to find out how to assess your financial condition and budget.

This may not make sense at first, but Robert contends that the only borrowers who really should consider interest-only loans are ones that actually don't need financing at all. Interest-only loans can make the most sense for wealthy borrowers who find that they're able to earn a rate of return on other investments that exceed the interest rate on the interest-only loan. For example, if an interest-only loan is 5 percent, but a business owner is consistently able to earn more than 5 percent on her investment of capital

(continued)

(continued)

back into her primary business, then an interest-only loan could make sense. In these cases, the borrowers probably don't even need financing and could make the purchase with cash but realize that their best return is leveraging funds from a lender to increase the overall return on their capital.

Fine-Tuning Your Thought Process

Now that you know darn near everything worth knowing about fixed-rate mortgages and ARMs, you're probably in a veritable frenzy of excitement about getting yourself preapproved for a loan. Not so fast, grasshopper. We have a few more words of wisdom for you.

Finding funds

Before you rush off, wouldn't it be wise to find out where the money is? Here are the big sources for home purchase mortgages:

- **Conventional loans:** As noted in Chapter 4, most U.S. residential mortgages are conventional loans originated by lending institutions such as banks, mortgage banks, credit unions, and mortgage brokers. Chapter 7 covers the merits of shopping for a loan yourself versus using a mortgage broker to assist you.
- **Government loans:** Low-income borrowers or folks with little or no cash for a down payment may be able to qualify for a variety of home loans either insured or guaranteed by an agency of the federal government. See Chapter 4 for additional information about Federal Housing Administration (FHA), Department of Veterans Affairs (VA), and USDA Rural Development (RD) loans.
- **Seller loans:** These mortgages, which are generally referred to as *owner-carry financing,* generally represent less than 5 percent of the loan market. They are, however, an extremely important loan source during periods of high mortgage interest rates and properties that may be more challenging to sell where the seller has a lot of equity. Owner-carry financing is usually structured as home purchase first mortgages, which we cover in Chapter 7, or second mortgages (we've thought of everything — see Chapter 6).

WARNING

Almost all conventional first mortgages and government loans are *fully amortized.* That means they're designed to be repaid in full by the time you make the last regularly scheduled monthly payment. Darn near all owner-carry first mortgages, conversely, come due with a generally quite large unpaid balance. This type of financing is called a *balloon loan.* As noted in Chapter 6, balloon loans can be extremely hazardous to your fiscal health if you can't repay or refinance them when they're due and payable — borrower beware!

Making the 30-year versus 15-year mortgage decision

After you decide which type of mortgage — fixed or adjustable — you desire, you have one more major choice to make. Do you prefer a 15-year or a 30-year loan term? (You may run across some odd-length mortgages — such as 20- and 40-year mortgages; however, the issues we discuss in this section remain the same as when comparing 15-year to 30-year mortgages.)

If you're stretching to buy the home of your dreams, you may not have a choice. The only loan you may qualify for is a 30-year mortgage. That isn't necessarily bad and, in fact, has advantages.

The main advantage that a 30-year mortgage has over a comparable 15-year loan is that it has lower monthly payments that free up more of your monthly income for different purposes, such as saving for other important financial goals like retirement. You may want to have more money each month so you aren't a financial prisoner in your abode. A 30-year mortgage has lower monthly payments because you have a longer time period to repay it (which translates into more payments). A fixed-rate, 30-year mortgage with an interest rate of 7 percent, for example, has payments that are approximately 25 percent lower than those on a comparable 15-year mortgage.

What if you can afford the higher payments that a 15-year mortgage requires? Should you take it? Not necessarily. What if, instead of making large payments on the 15-year mortgage, you make smaller payments on a 30-year mortgage and put that extra money to productive use?

If you do make productive use of that extra money, then the 30-year mortgage may be for you. A terrific potential use for that extra dough is to contribute it to a tax-deductible retirement account. Contributions that you add to employer-based 401(k) and 403(b) plans (and self-employed SEP-IRAs) not only give you an immediate reduction in taxes but also enable your money to compound, tax-deferred, over the years ahead. Another vehicle for tax-deductible contributions is the Health Savings Account (HSA) for those with higher deductible health plans. Everyone with employment income may also contribute to an Individual Retirement Account (IRA). Your IRA contributions may not be immediately tax deductible if your (or your spouse's) employer offers a retirement account or pension plan, but they will grow tax-free.

If you've exhausted your options for contributing to retirement accounts and an HSA, and if you find it challenging to save money anyway, the 15-year mortgage may offer you a good forced-savings program. If you elect to take a 30-year mortgage, you retain the flexibility to pay it off faster if you so choose. (Just be sure to avoid those mortgages that have a prepayment penalty.) Constraining yourself with the 15-year mortgage's higher monthly payments does carry a risk. If you stumble during tough financial times, you may not be able to meet the required mortgage payments.

Getting a Loan When Rates Are High

Over the years and decades, we've seen interest rates for conforming 30-year fixed-rate loans soar to more than 18 percent in the early 1980s and sink to a low of just over 3 percent in 2012. We can guarantee you with 100 percent certainty that mortgage rates will change. They always do. If we could only figure out a way to forecast how much and when, we'd be rich!

Earlier in this chapter, we point out three places to find a first mortgage with an interest rate *significantly* lower than what you'd pay for a new, 30-year fixed-rate loan. Just to refresh your memory, here's a recap:

- **ARMs:** Lenders charge a premium for fixed-rate loans. If you'll share the lenders' risk of possible future interest rate increases by getting an adjustable-rate mortgage, lenders will reward your adventurous spirit with a lower initial interest rate on your loan. The more often your loan adjusts, the lower your ARM's initial interest rate. ARMs that adjust every six months, for example, generally have a lower start rate than ARMs that adjust annually and so on.
- **Loan assumptions:** It's extremely unlikely that you'll find a fixed-rate mortgage you can assume. On the other hand, some ARMs are assumable for creditworthy borrowers. Nuff said.
- **Seller financing:** Some long-term homeowners no longer have mortgages on their property. These fortunate folks may offer attractive financing to qualified buyers either to get a higher purchase price or to structure their transaction as an installment sale for preferable tax treatment by the IRS. (An installment sale provides that the buyer pays the purchase price, usually plus interest, in regular payments or installments over multiple tax years to spread out and reduce the tax consequences from the sale.)

Like it or not, you may have the monetary misfortune of buying your home during a period when mortgage rates are on the high side of the cycle. If that happens, don't despair. You can refinance your loan when rates drop. Chapter 11 is chock-full of money-saving refinancing ideas.

IN THIS CHAPTER

- » Tapping home equity
- » Getting too much of a good thing: 100 percent loans
- » Financing cooperative apartments
- » Considering balloon loans

Chapter 6 Surveying Special Situation Loans

This book would've been much shorter a couple of generations ago. Many of the loans we so diligently describe in *Mortgage Management For Dummies* hadn't been invented when Richard Nixon was president.

That's no typo. *Invented* is precisely what we meant to say. Loans are indeed invented by lenders. Adjustable-rate mortgages, which occupy a significant chunk of Chapter 5, and reverse mortgages, the sole topic of Chapter 13, are two types of mortgages that didn't exist in the early 1970s.

We devote this chapter to a marvelous medley of mortgages designed to satisfy special financial requirements. If you don't see the mortgage product you desire, tell your friendly financier. That's how new loans are invented!

By the way, we use mucho loan lingo in this chapter. If you haven't read Chapter 4 yet, now's an ideal time to peruse it. Nudge. Nudge. We have many charms. Subtlety isn't one of them.

Understanding Home Equity Loans

Equity is the difference between what your house is worth in today's real estate market and how much you currently owe on it. For example, if your home's present appraised value is $225,000 and your outstanding mortgage balance is $75,000, you have $150,000 of home equity. Lucky you.

There's only one tiny problem with all that equity in your home — its utter lack of liquidity. Having equity in your house isn't like having money in your checking account or a mutual fund you can sell any day the financial markets are open. To get your hands on your home's equity, you must figure out a way to extract it from the property.

For instance, suppose you seek copious quantities of cash. If that's your dilemma, we have two suggestions. You can free up all your equity by selling your house or tap some or most of it by refinancing your mortgage.

If selling is your pleasure, rush to the nearest quality bookstore for your very own copy of the latest edition of Eric and Ray Brown's book *House Selling For Dummies* (Wiley). On the other hand, if you'd rather pull big bucks out of your home without selling it, you have the right book but the wrong chapter. We thoughtfully devote Chapter 11 to the arcane art of refinancing. This section tells you how to nibble into your equity by turning your home into an ATM.

Using home equity loans

Home equity loans may be excellent financial tools for homeowners who want to use a relatively small amount of their equity or who don't need all their money at once. For example, you may need $20,000 of that $150,000 equity to remodel your kitchen. Or perhaps your twins are heading to college next fall, and you've generously decided to pay their tuition. Folks often tap their home's equity to buy a new car or pay off unexpected medical bills.

These loans are frequently called *home equity lines of credit* or, given the mortgage industry's love of acronyms, HELOCs. *Home equity line of credit* is an appropriate term, because this type of loan is essentially a line of credit secured by a second mortgage on a property.

As long as you don't exceed the maximum loan amount previously agreed to by you and the lender, you can borrow precisely as much money as you need exactly when you need it. Take all the cash in one fell swoop or dole it out as you desire. You pay interest only on the outstanding loan balance, not your total line of credit.

WARNING

Watch out! Many home equity loans contain clauses giving lenders the unilateral right to cancel or suspend a line of credit. Suppose, for example, your lender thinks your home has declined in value due to a soft local real estate market. The lender can yank your line of credit. Woe be it to you if you just started to remodel your kitchen or were counting on using the equity to pay the twins' college tuition for next fall.

TIP

The best defense is a good offense. Instead of living in fear that your lender is going to pull the HELOC partway through your project, a prudent person like you can get the money out while the getting is good. Withdraw all funds you estimate needing *before* starting your project or *before* the tuition is due. Put the money into a fully liquid interest-bearing account (such as a money market mutual fund) to partially offset your interest charges. (The gap between the interest you pay for the HELOC and interest you earn on the funds is called the opportunity cost of money.)

Equity loans are also aptly referred to as *debt consolidation loans.* If you're burdened by consumer debt from unpaid credit card balances, installment loans, and personal loans — and you're a homeowner with sufficient equity in your property — you can use a HELOC to consolidate all your high interest rate loans into one relatively lower interest and lower monthly payment loan.

Operating instructions

There isn't a standard, one-size-fits-all format for HELOCs. On the contrary, they can be extremely flexible financial instruments.

Depending on which lender you select, you may be able to customize your personal HELOC. For instance, you could get a fixed-rate loan unless, of course, you'd rather have an adjustable-rate mortgage. Other possible options are to take your money in one lump sum, use an ATM card to make withdrawals whenever you need cash, or write checks on your credit line — it's up to you. You can opt to repay the funds you borrow in a fully amortized loan program or make interest-only payments until your loan is due. What's your pleasure?

REMEMBER

However, one common thread does run through these infinitely variable HELOCs: Every one of them is firmly secured by a lien on your home.

Because home equity loans are second mortgages, they have higher interest rates than first mortgages. That extra charge is justified because, from a lender's perspective, second mortgages are inherently riskier than firsts. Even so, interest rates on HELOCs are generally significantly lower than interest rates charged on credit cards. A home equity loan at 6 percent interest, for example, sure beats paying 18 percent interest — or more — on credit card debt.

LENDERS CAN PLAY HARDBALL ON HOME EQUITY LOANS

In the heady days of the 1990s and early 2000s when housing prices seemed like they only went up, some folks thought their homes were ATMs. Home equity loans boomed as borrowers and lenders just couldn't get enough of them. Homeowners enjoyed tapping their increasing wealth for new living room furniture, snazzy televisions, home improvements, and paying off high-cost consumer debt. Banks loved making home equity loans because they were so profitable.

When property values began to fall around 2007, lenders justifiably became concerned about getting their money back. As we note in Chapter 4, in the highly unlikely case that a prudent borrower such as yourself falls behind in your mortgage payments, your lender has the legal right to sell your house and use the proceeds of the sale to repay your loan. Mortgages are always paid off in the same order they were put on the property. The *first* mortgage used to buy your home would, therefore, be repaid before a HELOC secured by a *second* mortgage.

For example, say you paid $200,000 for your home in 1998. You put $40,000 (20 percent) cash down and got a $160,000 first mortgage. In 2005, your house appraised for $240,000. You took out a $20,000 home equity loan to remodel your kitchen. You got a great interest rate on your HELOC because the combined loan-to-value ratio for your first and second mortgage was only 75 percent of your home's fair market value ($180,000 divided by $240,000).

Suppose, unfortunately, property values fell in recent years in your town. Today your house is worth $160,000, almost $20,000 less than the current combined total of your first and second mortgage. If you default on your loan, the holder of your first mortgage could foreclose and pay off the first loan with money from the sale. Your HELOC lender would get nothing. This is called a *short sale* because the proceeds fall short of enough money to pay off both loans.

In situations like this, HELOC lenders aren't going down without a fight. They have a surprising amount of power to make life more miserable for you and the holder of the first mortgage. Your lender can, for instance, refuse to let you refinance your first mortgage unless you pay off some of your home equity loan. Your lender can also hire a collection agency to go after your other assets. Last, but not least, your bad loan remains a blemish on your credit record, which makes it more difficult for you to borrow in the future (a topic we cover in Chapter 3).

As a rule, you'll get the lowest interest rate if the total amount of your first mortgage plus the HELOC doesn't exceed 75 percent of your home's fair market value (FMV). For example, suppose that your home is worth $200,000 and you have an existing first mortgage of $130,000 on it. To obtain the most favorable financial terms in this case, you'd limit the HELOC to $20,000 ($200,000 × 75% = $150,000 less your $130,000 first mortgage).

The higher your credit score, the more you may be able to borrow. Some lenders will allow you to tap up to 90 percent of your home's FMV for the first mortgage plus HELOC. We cover how to improve your credit score in Chapter 3.

You can lose your home if you don't repay a HELOC. Unlike department store charge accounts, credit card debt, student loans, and other unsecured liabilities, home equity loans permit lenders to foreclose on property when borrowers default. And if the total of your first mortgage plus the equity loan exceeds 80 percent of your home's FMV, you'll pay higher loan origination fees and a higher mortgage interest rate on your HELOC. Be sure to review Chapter 1 so you understand how much mortgage debt you can truly afford given your overall financial situation and goals.

Considering tax consequences

All people are created equal. All debt isn't. For example, the interest charged for student loans, credit card debt, and car loans is classified as *consumer interest*. This distinction is noteworthy because consumer interest isn't tax deductible.

Mortgage interest, on the other hand, generally *is* tax deductible. One of a home equity loan's most appealing features is that the interest you pay on a HELOC *may* be deductible for both federal and state income tax purposes. Whether the interest actually is deductible depends on three IRS tests:

- **The $100,000 test:** There's a $100,000 limit on tax deductibility of home equity indebtedness. You won't go to jail or lose all your hair if your HELOC exceeds $100,000. The amount could be $10 million, and your kindly old Uncle Sam wouldn't care. Any interest charged on the portion of your equity loan in excess of $100,000, however, will be classified as consumer interest, which isn't tax deductible.
- **Capital improvements test:** Home equity loan interest is only supposed to be deductible to the extent that the proceeds from such loans are used for capital improvements to your home.

- **The market value test:** The IRS says that deductible home equity indebtedness can't exceed the fair market value of your home. For now, be advised that interest charged for any amount you borrow in excess of your home's current value is *not* tax deductible.

The amount of debt taken out on the home when it was acquired and the dreaded alternative minimum tax (AMT) may also limit the amount of home equity interest you can deduct. Chapter 9 covers the complexities of mortgage interest deductibility in awesome detail. However, these details have a way of changing. Because Congress takes devilish delight in continually revising U.S. income tax rules and regulations, it may be prudent to review the nuances of your specific situation with a tax advisor *before* you sign the dotted line for that HELOC.

Eyeing 100 Percent Home Equity Loans

As we note in Chapter 2, lenders have a disarmingly simple technique to estimate the probable risk of a mortgage. They divide the loan amount by a property's appraised value to get a *loan-to-value* (LTV) *ratio.* Referring back to our previous example, your home's LTV ratio is 60 percent if the appraised value is $150,000 and you have an existing $90,000 mortgage on it ($90,000 divided by $150,000).

The lower the LTV ratio, the lower a lender's risk of being unable to collect enough money from a foreclosure sale to repay the loan if a borrower defaults — and vice versa. Lenders compensate for riskier loans by increasing interest rates and loan fees when a conventional mortgage's LTV ratio exceeds 80 percent. High-risk borrowers must also pay for private mortgage insurance to protect lenders from losses. High LTV ratio loans aren't cheap.

Back when 30-year fixed rate loans were the only option in the mid-1970s, 95 percent loan-to-value financing was the steel-reinforced concrete ceiling for conventional mortgages. During the crazy lending days in the 1990s and early 2000s, some loans were being done up to 125 percent or more of the home's value based on the now proven false theory that home values only go up. Now, even after the very difficult lessons learned in the late 2000s, some financial institutions will lend creditworthy borrowers up to 100 percent of their home's value.

Consider the toxic consequences of 100 percent HELOCs:

- **High monthly payments:** Given the extraordinarily high level of risk associated with this loan, it has correspondingly high interest rates. For example, if the prevailing market rate on a prime 80 percent LTV ratio 30-year fixed-rate first mortgage is 6 percent, don't be surprised if your accommodating neighborhood lender wants 9 to 12 percent interest for a 100 percent HELOC.
- **Limited tax deduction:** You can't write off any of the interest charges on any portion of the HELOC loan that exceeds $100,000 *or* 100 percent of your home's appraised value at the time the loan was taken out.
- **You may not be able to sell:** Factoring in the significant transaction costs involved in selling a house, you can't pay off a 100 percent HELOC loan by selling your house if the home is worth about the same as when you took out the 100 percent HELOC. You'll have to find another source of cash to cover the debt if unforeseen circumstances force you to sell. If you can't raid your savings account or write a check to cover the difference, then you're stuck in your home whether you like it or not. If all your piggy banks are empty, you'll have to file bankruptcy and suffer the long-term damage to your credit. Your choices range from awful to dreadful.
- **They encourage additional consumer debt:** People typically take out 100 percent loans to relieve themselves from the burden of high payments on their credit card debt. Another common sales pitch is that you can deduct the interest expense on a HELOC loan, but not consumer debt. However, what the salespeople hawking these 100 percent loans don't tell you is that over time many of these borrowers ultimately run up their credit card and other consumer debts again, which places them even deeper in the credit abyss.

You can probably get a better deal on some lower interest rate credit cards than on a 100 percent loan — and without placing your home at risk of foreclosure. Because credit card rates vary from bank to bank, do some comparison shopping. There are several online sites (like Bankrate.com, CreditCards.com, ConsumerReports.org, and Kiplinger.com) that routinely provide comparison shopping information on the current lowest credit card rates.

Getting a 100 percent loan may be prudent if you use the proceeds to pay off other debt with an even more outrageous interest rate, such as an unsecured loan to pay for a medical emergency. On the other hand, if you *need* a 100 percent loan to pay for a dream vacation in Hawaii or buy a spiffy new car (when you have a perfectly good one sitting in your garage), you're exhibiting ominous signs of a severe credit management predicament. Be sure to read the sidebar "Pay attention: Warning signs of credit trouble."

PAY ATTENTION: WARNING SIGNS OF CREDIT TROUBLE

Getting a high interest rate HELOC loan to consolidate credit card debt won't necessarily solve your fiscal problems. If the only step you take to lower your monthly payments is to stretch out the length of time you take to repay the debt, you'll end up paying even more in total interest charges. Worse yet, you'll convert unsecured credit card debt into mortgage debt secured by your house. That puts your home in jeopardy of foreclosure if you don't make the scheduled monthly loan payments.

You're already in serious credit trouble if you experience six or more of the following behaviors:

- Paying only the minimum amount due on your credit cards
- Charging more each month than you make in payments
- Using credit and cash advances for items such as groceries, gas, and insurance that you used to pay for with cash
- Having a total credit balance that rarely decreases
- Being at or near your credit limit and applying for new cards or accounts
- Needing a consolidation loan to pay existing debt
- Not knowing the total amount you owe
- Experiencing feelings of anxiety and stress whenever you use your credit cards
- Draining your savings to pay debts
- Making bill payments late

Getting into debt over your head usually doesn't happen overnight. It's an insidious process. Answer the following questions to see if you're headed for a serious problem:

- Are your debts making your home life unhappy?
- Does the pressure of your debts distract you from work, fun, and even sleep?
- Are your debts affecting your reputation?
- Do your debts cause you to think less of yourself?
- Have you ever given false information to obtain credit?
- Have you ever made unrealistic promises to your creditors?
- Do you ever fear that your employer, family, or friends will discover the extent of your indebtedness?

- When faced with a difficult financial situation, does the prospect of borrowing give you an inordinate feeling of relief?
- Has the pressure of your debts ever caused you to consider getting intoxicated?
- Have you ever borrowed money without considering the rate of interest?
- Do you expect a negative response when subject to a credit investigation?
- Have you ever developed a strict regimen for paying your debts, only to break it?
- Do you justify your debts by telling yourself that you're superior to "other" people, and when you get your "break," you'll be out of debt?

If some of these danger signs describe your current predicament, get serious about dealing with your debt and spending challenges. One way to start is by getting the most recent edition of Eric's *Personal Finance For Dummies* (published by Wiley).

Taking a Closer Look at Co-Op Loans

Cooperative apartments, usually called *co-ops,* can be difficult to finance. Wait. Why sugarcoat the situation? On our patented mortgage-origination-degree-of-difficulty scale, where 1 equals a slam dunk and 10 will never happen in your lifetime no matter how much you beguile, beg, and beseech lenders, getting a co-op loan is 9.8 nearly anywhere in the United States.

That fact no doubt seems odd when you consider that condominium financing is generally affordable and plentiful. Condos and co-ops are, after all, the two most common types of attached residential dwelling units. You can't tell which is which simply by looking at a building's exterior. Why, then, is financing co-ops so tough when getting condominium loans is relatively easy?

We thought you'd never ask.

Identifying the legal structure of co-op loans

The first reason obtaining co-op financing is more difficult than financing a condo is that even though a condominium development and a cooperative apartment building may look identical physically, they have different legal structures:

» **Common interest developments or condominiums:** When you buy a common interest development (usually in the form of a condominium or townhome or planned unit development), you get a deed to your individual unit; you own real property, plus typically a prorated share of the common areas of the community. You may even get a parking space or two actually deeded to you as well. Lenders like that. They're inordinately fond of real property because they can use it as security for repayment of mortgage debt.

- **Cooperatives:** When you buy a co-op, you don't get a deed to your unit. Instead, you're issued a fancy stock certificate proving to the world that you own a specified number of shares in the cooperative corporation. In addition, you get a *proprietary lease* that entitles you to occupy the unit you bought. You do not, however, own any real property a lender can use to secure your mortgage. This deviation from normal residential real estate practices disturbs almost all lenders.

TECHNICAL STUFF

About now you're probably wondering whether cooperative apartments are some kind of ultraexpensive shell game. If you don't own the real property, who does? The cooperative corporation owns the building in which your cooperative unit is located; it holds the property's deed in its name. But because you own shares in the cooperative corporation that owns the building, that makes you a co-owner of the building as well as a tenant in the building you partly own. Does the word *discombobulated* describe how you feel about now?

Dealing with deal-killing directors

The internal management structure is another reason that buying and selling co-ops is more difficult than buying and selling a condo. Stock cooperatives are corporations governed by a board of directors elected by individual housing unit owners. Like the homeowners association in a common interest development, a co-op's board of directors is responsible for overseeing day-to-day operations, including the setting of the fees and assessments and reserves, which are critical to prudent financial planning. Some co-ops are well run, but often the assessments and reserves are kept artificially low and inadequate funds exist for expensive repairs or replacements of major building systems, such as roofing, elevators, or plumbing.

The co-op's board of directors can have a say in your desire to sell your housing unit, whereas a condo's homeowners association has essentially none as long as all the assessments are paid to date. Many cooperatives won't let individual owners sell or otherwise transfer their stock or proprietary leases without written consent from the board of directors or from a majority of other owners. That arrangement may be fine with you as a co-op owner, but it makes most lenders intensely uneasy. In their opinion, giving up your right to sell your housing unit to a creditworthy buyer is far too high a price to pay for the right to select your future neighbors.

Buying a cooperative unit isn't any easier than selling one. Would-be buyers almost always have to provide several character references plus a detailed financial statement and then submit to an intrusive interrogation by the directors. Many people find the Byzantine approval process so meddlesome that they won't consider buying a co-op. This reluctance further reduces the number of prospective purchasers for your unit.

Offers you receive from prospective purchasers must be conditioned upon subsequent approval by the board of directors. When you finally find the perfect buyers, brace yourself. These paragons may be rejected. The directors, in their infinite wisdom, may believe that your buyers have a propensity to entertain too frequently. Or perhaps they're of the opinion that your buyers can't afford to shoulder their share of the co-op's operating expenses. Whatever their rationale, valid or capricious, directors can nix your deal.

WARNING

If you haven't purchased a cooperative housing unit yet, think twice before doing so. Don't buy someone else's problem. If it's difficult to find financing when you want to buy a co-op, and equally troublesome to find prospective purchasers when you want to sell it, the real estate market is trying to tell you something. The best time to think about selling a co-op is before you buy it.

Tracking down a loan

If you're still reading, we obviously haven't dissuaded you. Trust us when we say that getting a co-op mortgage will be tough. Here's what you're up against:

- **Lack of satisfactory security:** Most lenders flatly refuse to accept shares of stock in a cooperative corporation as security for their mortgage. They want real property, which you can't provide. Remember that all the housing units in the building are, unfortunately, deeded to the co-op.
- **Lack of cooperation:** Some cooperatives won't allow financing of individual units. They'll graciously let you assume that your pro-rata share of the existing mortgage on the building as a whole, but that's all. These co-ops believe that the best proof of your creditworthiness is the ability to pay cash for your individual housing unit.

Real estate agents and cooperative building owners are excellent financial ferrets. They generally know which lenders in your area are currently making co-op loans. You may also be able to obtain financing if your employer puts in a good word for you with the lender who handles the corporate accounts. Some commercial banks offer co-op loans as an accommodation to an important business relationship.

WARNING

We strongly advise pouring cold water on your burning desire to own a cooperative unit if you discover that few lenders in your area offer co-op financing. Limited competition usually results in higher loan origination fees and interest rates. Things may get even worse. Suppose that no lenders are making co-op loans when you decide to sell. You'll either have to delay your sale until you can find an all-cash buyer or carry the loan for your buyer. Owner-carry financing, as we point out in Chapter 7, can be risky business.

Grasping Balloon Loans

Loan amortization refers to the process of repaying a debt by making periodic installment payments until the loan term is completed or you sell or refinance, whichever comes first. Speaking of firsts, be advised that first mortgages are almost always *fully amortized.* That's lender jargon to describe a loan that will be completely repaid after you make the final, regularly scheduled, monthly mortgage payment. (See Chapter 4 if you want more details on loan amortization.)

Some second mortgages are also fully amortized. However, some second mortgages come due long before they're anywhere near to being fully repaid. Any mortgage that comes due with an unpaid balance is known as a *balloon loan.* Others may be home equity interest-only loans for, say, 10 years and then fully amortize over the remaining 20 years. Thus, they will have a big jump in payment after ten years.

The final monthly installment that pays off a loan's entire remaining principal balance due is called a *balloon payment.* As you'll discover after scanning the next section, balloon payments generally resemble blimps.

Because balloons bring to mind images of birthday parties and light-hearted frivolity, it seems somewhat misleading to name these mortgages after something so benign. They're more aptly referred to as *bullet loans* by lenders who've seen balloon loans mutate into financial bullets blasting hapless borrowers who can't repay or refinance their mortgages when they come due.

We don't want to scare you away from balloon loans. They can be used to augment your cash for a down payment, reduce your interest charges, or pull equity out of your present house to buy your next home. They're useful financial resources *when used properly.* Without further ado, the following sections offer a bunch of bright balloons that you can safely consider for your edification and judicious fiscal enjoyment.

80-10-10 financing

Surprising as it may seem, some folks with hefty incomes find that it's mighty tough for them to save enough money to make a 20 percent cash down payment on their dream homes. Buyers using conventional financing who can't afford to put 20 percent cash down must purchase private mortgage insurance (PMI). As we note in Chapter 4, buying PMI increases the cost of home ownership and, ironically, makes it even more difficult to qualify for a mortgage.

Good news: You're about to discover how you may be able to circumvent those nasty PMI costs with 80-10-10 financing.

Even if you put 20 percent down, you could still end up paying a higher interest rate on your home loan if you get a jumbo first mortgage. Per our succinct section in Chapter 4, these mortgages exceed the Fannie Mae and Freddie Mac conforming loan limits. In the upcoming section, "Shrinking jumbo can slash your interest rate," we show you how to shave up to ½ percent off your first mortgage's interest rate by using 80-10-10 financing.

Using 80-10-10 financing to avoid private mortgage insurance

If you're a dues-paying member of the cash-challenged class, don't despair. Given that your income is sufficiently high, it's eminently possible to avoid getting stuck with PMI. That's why *80-10-10 financing* was invented. It's called 80-10-10 because a savings and loan association, bank, credit union, or other institutional lender provides a traditional 80 percent first mortgage, you get a 10 percent second mortgage, and make a cash down payment equal to 10 percent of the home's purchase price.

Where do you obtain the 10 percent second mortgage? The most common sources are

» **House sellers:** We provide a detailed dissertation about seller financing in Chapter 7. At this point, we'll just say that some sellers offer qualified buyers attractive secondary financing either as a sales inducement or because they want to generate income from the loan. Owner-carry second mortgages are generally less expensive than seconds made by institutional lenders such as banks and credit unions because most sellers don't charge loan origination fees — and sellers usually offer lower mortgage interest rates to boot. Seller seconds are nearly always short-term balloon loans due and payable three to five years after origination.

The institutional lender that holds the first mortgage will most likely insist upon reviewing the terms and conditions of the owner-carry second mortgage. For one thing, the lender needs to be sure you can afford to make monthly loan payments on the first mortgage plus the second without overextending yourself. The lender will also probably insist upon at least a five-year term for the second mortgage, so you'll have plenty of time to save up for the balloon payment when the second comes due. Five years will also usually allow for home appreciation to create homeowner equity that can be tapped through a HELOC loan to repay the second mortgage, or you can refinance all your debt into a single new loan. (That way, if you use your current lender, they get to charge you more points and fees!)

- **Institutional lenders:** Yes, the same friendly folks who originate your 80 percent first mortgage may also provide secondary financing. This type of loan program varies from lender to lender. Some lenders structure the second as a home equity loan; others offer a conventional second mortgage. The secondary financing may or may not be in the form of a balloon loan. If the second is fully amortized, it's usually structured as a 15-year mortgage.

TIP

Don't get hung up on terminology. Just because this type of financing is referred to as 80-10-10 doesn't mean you absolutely, categorically must put down 10 percent cash. The same principle applies if you can afford to make only a 5 percent down payment — 80-15-5 financing may be available. Because a smaller cash down payment increases the lender's risk of default, however, don't be surprised when you're asked to pay higher loan fees and a higher mortgage interest rate for 80-15-5 financing and 80-10-10 financing versus traditional financing where you make a 20 percent down payment.

Playing with the numbers

Now we're going to crunch some numbers so you can see with your own eyes 80-10-10 financing. Each of the following examples assumes the same three conditions — that the home you're buying costs $200,000, that you're making a 10 percent ($20,000) cash down payment, and that you're a creditworthy buyer:

- **PMI:** In this scenario, you didn't read this fine book and hence don't know about 80-10-10 financing. You foolishly get a $180,000 (90 percent of purchase price), 30-year fixed-rate first mortgage with an 8 percent interest rate. Your monthly loan payment is $1,322. PMI costs an additional *non-tax-deductible* $78 per month (it's possible that tax law changes enacted after this book was published may make PMI costs tax deductible, so check the current rules). You pay $1,400 per month in total loan charges.
- **Owner-carry second mortgage:** After reading this book, you diligently search until you discover a seller who'll carry a $20,000 fixed-rate second mortgage amortized on a 30-year basis. The loan, however, is due in five years. You negotiate a 7.5 percent interest rate; your payment is $140 per month. With 10 percent down and a 10 percent second, you need only a $160,000 (80 percent) 30-year fixed-rate first mortgage at 8 percent interest costing $1,175 per month. Total loan charges are $1,315 a month, $85 less per month than the PMI example — and all the interest you pay on both mortgages is tax deductible. The final advantage is that you can pay off the owner-carry second mortgage any time you want. PMI, conversely, is harder to get rid of than head lice. You're so smart.

WARNING

Not so fast, smarty. Don't forget that the second mortgage is a balloon loan. It's due and payable in five short years. You'll be dismayed to discover that 94.6 percent of your original $20,000 loan remains to be paid five years after the loan is originated. In other words, your loan balance is $18,920 $(\$20{,}000 \times 94.6\%)$ even after paying the seller $8,400 (60 monthly payments of $140) over five years. What if you can't refinance the second mortgage when it's due because you lose your job? Or what if property values drop and the appraisal comes in too low to pay off the second? Or what if interest rates skyrocket and you can't qualify for a new loan at the high mortgage rates? Now maybe you understand why they're called bullet loans.

» **Institutional lender second mortgage:** In this example, the seller of your dream home won't carry a second. Having scrutinized this book, you wisely opt for 80-10-10 financing from a bank. You get a $160,000 (80 percent) 30-year fixed-rate first mortgage at 8 percent interest costing $1,175 per month. The bank offers you a choice for your $20,000 second — either a fixed-rate mortgage (FRM) amortized over 30 years but due in 15 or a fully amortized, fixed-rate, 15-year loan. You'd pay $191 per month for the 30-year, FRM balloon loan with an 11 percent interest rate versus $225 a month for the 15-year FRM at 10.75 percent interest. What to do? What to do?

What an interesting (sorry — we couldn't resist) choice. You'd pay $1,366 per month $(\$1{,}175 + \$191)$ for an 80-10-10 that has a $16,760 balloon payment due in 15 years. Taking the fully amortized second mortgage increases your monthly payment $34 to a nice round $1,400 $(\$1{,}175 + \$225)$. On the plus side, you'd build up equity faster with that second mortgage, and there's no balloon payment to fret about. (If that kind of fiscal pressure debilitates you, either of the bank's second mortgages are preferable to the owner-carry second with its *five-year* due date.)

TIP

Truth be known, it's highly unlikely you'd keep either of the second mortgages for 15 years. Given their high interest rate, you'd wisely refinance the one you select as soon as possible (see Chapter 11) or pay it off when you sell your house and move into a magnificent mansion.

Given those assumptions, we'd advise taking the balloon second mortgage and investing the $34 a month you save in a good mutual fund. If the thought of balloon payments causes you to lose shuteye, however, you have our permission to take the fully amortized second. The choice is yours.

Shrinking jumbo can slash your interest rate

Congress sets upper limits on mortgages Fannie Mae and Freddie Mac purchase from institutional lenders for resale to private investors. These loan limits are adjusted annually to ensure that they accurately reflect changes in the U.S. national average home price. For example, the maximum single-family dwelling loan Fannie Mae and Freddie Mac could buy when this book was printed was $636,150.

That amount may have changed by now, so be sure to check with your lender to determine the present loan limit for the type of property you intend to purchase.

As we note in Chapter 4, mortgages that neatly fall within the current Fannie Mae and Freddie Mac loan limits are called *conforming loans.* Conventional mortgages over the maximum permissible loan amounts are referred to as *jumbo conforming* or *true jumbo loans.* This is a critically important financial distinction if your mortgage happens to exceed the conforming loan limit. Interest rates on jumbo conforming or true jumbo fixed-rate mortgages are normally ½ to 1½ percent higher than their conforming fixed-rate brethren.

TIP

Why pay one red cent more than you have to for your home loan? If the amount of money you need to borrow is slightly over the Fannie Mae and Freddie Mac current conforming loan limit, use the 80-10-10 financing technique to cut that costly jumbo loan down to size.

Bridge loans

It's highly unlikely that you'll remain in your first home forever. Sooner or later birth, death, marriage, divorce, job transfers, retirement, or another monumental life change will probably force you to confront the eternal seller's quandary — should you sell your present house before buying a new one or buy first and then sell?

There are, of course, risks associated with either course of action. However, we firmly believe that it's ultimately far less perilous to either sell your current house before buying a new one or to sell your house concurrently with the purchase of your next dream home. You'll also sleep a whole lot better.

Why? Because, if you're like most people, you can't afford the luxury of owning two homes simultaneously. You have to use the proceeds from the sale of your present house to acquire your next home. That's how things work in the real estate food chain.

Unfortunately, some folks create serious problems for themselves by purchasing a new home before their old one has sold — which brings us to *bridge loans,* an uncommon type of balloon loan that enables qualified borrowers to pull a portion of the equity out of their house before it sells. This financial bridge provides enough cash to complete the purchase. We're not fans of bridge loans. If you're not careful, they can be the fiscal equivalent of a dose of arsenic. Here's why:

» **Bridge loans aren't cheap.** Because a bridge loan is usually a second mortgage or HELOC (home equity line of credit), its loan origination fee and interest rate will be significantly higher than the amount you'd pay for a conventional first mortgage. A bridge loan's interest rate is directly related to the combined loan-to-value (LTV) ratio of the existing first mortgage on the house you're selling plus the bridge loan.

TIP

You'll get the best possible interest rate on the bridge loan if you keep the total amount of your old house's existing first mortgage plus bridge loan under 80 percent of the house's fair market value. From a risk assessment standpoint, lenders know that their risk of loan default increases markedly when the LTV ratio exceeds 80 percent.

- **Your cash may drain away.** You may think that your house will sell quickly. But if you're wrong, you could end up owning two houses longer than you anticipated. How many months, for instance, can you afford to pay three mortgages (first mortgage plus bridge loan on your old house and first mortgage on your new home), two property tax bills, two homeowners insurance premiums, and two sets of utility bills? How long will you be able to continue maintaining two houses, especially if they're located in two different towns? You may discover that you no longer own the houses — they own you. First, the houses will consume all your disposable income, and then they'll gobble up your savings.

WARNING

- **You could lose everything.** If property prices decline while you're trying to sell the old house, you may not be able to sell it for enough money to pay off the outstanding loans. In that case, the holder of the bridge loan may be able to foreclose on your new home to make up the shortfall.

Bridge loans are fine if you're wealthy enough to afford owning two houses for an extended period of time. We grudgingly authorize the use of a bridge loan in one other situation — if the house you're selling has a ratified offer on it, if your transaction is currently in escrow, if all the conditions of your sale have been removed, and if the sale will be completed in four weeks or less. Even under these stringent conditions, a bridge loan is risky because your deal could fall through.

WARNING

Like rattlesnakes, bridge loans should be approached with extreme caution. Consider them a last resort. Stifle the unseemly urge to obtain bridge financing so you can buy your dream home before selling your present house. A bridge loan could turn that dream into a nightmare.

Construction loans

Watch your step, please. Be careful. We're about to enter a hardhat zone. This last balloon loan is covered with a fine coat of dust — construction dust.

Like the other loans we cover in this chapter, construction financing is extremely diverse. No one standard loan instrument exists that all lenders use to finance construction projects. On the contrary, the terms and conditions of construction financing vary widely from lender to lender and project to project.

That variability isn't at all surprising when you consider the full spectrum of project types and sites. Do you need a small loan to do a little cosmetic painting and landscaping around your house; or are you about to embark upon a major rehab of an inner-city, multifamily dwelling; or do you plan to construct a country retreat from the ground up? Will your project be completed in two months or two years? Are you doing the work yourself, or will you use an architect and licensed contractors?

Financing for small, do-it-yourself type projects is usually handled with home equity loans. Funding of larger projects, on the other hand, is generally paid out in installments as each previously agreed-upon stage of construction is satisfactorily completed. You pay interest on construction funds only as they're disbursed. After your project is completed, the construction financing is customarily converted into a permanent, long-term mortgage.

TIP

Construction financing is specialized. Many lenders aren't interested in financing rehabs of major fixer-uppers or making new construction loans. Real estate agents who handle this kind of property generally know which local financial institutions offer construction loans for your specific type of project. Architects and contractors are also good bird dogs for local banks or other lenders who provide construction loans.

Renovation/remodel loans

Fannie Mae and the FHA have specialized loans that will fund both the purchase of a home and the renovation and repair costs. Fannie Mae calls its loan the HomeStyles Renovation Loan, and the FHA calls its program the 203(k) Home Improvement Loan. If a home is too beat up to qualify for traditional financing and you can't afford to pay cash for the home, then these loans may be for you.

Be aware, however, that these loans are a lot of work and are slow to close. Consequently, some listing agents aren't fond of accepting offers with renovation financing. But if there isn't a cash buyer on the horizon, the listing agent will work with you and your renovation loan. Additionally, renovation loans include a lot of nuances (for example, you're not allowed to personally perform the work; you have to use a licensed contractor), so you need to find a loan officer who is highly proficient with renovation loans. Saying all of that, these can be awesome loans — but you may not feel that way until after you're finished with the renovation!

3

Landing a Lender

IN THIS PART . . .

Walk through the process of finding the best lender for your home purchase.

Check out helpful websites that can guide you in making important mortgage decisions.

Discover what it costs to take out a mortgage and compare loans from different lenders.

Know what paperwork you'll be required to fill out and what documents you must provide to the lender.

» Narrowing the universe of lenders

» Working with mortgage brokers

» Evaluating and soliciting seller financing options

Chapter 7 Finding Your Best Lender

Hopefully, you're enjoying a fair weather day or the company of family or friends as you read our book. Now, close your eyes and think about shopping for something fun and exciting. Maybe a new summer outfit, a car, a vacation, a hot tub, or a new set of golf clubs. Surely, you didn't think of shopping for a mortgage!

However, unless you enjoy throwing away thousands of dollars, you need to shop around for the best deal on a mortgage. Whether you do the footwork yourself or hire someone competent and ethical to help you doesn't matter. But you must make sure this comparison shopping gets done.

For example, suppose you're in the market for a $150,000, 30-year fixed-rate mortgage. If, through persistent and wise shopping, you discover a mortgage with a 5.5 percent interest rate when the prevailing market rate is 6 percent, that insignificant little half-of-1-percent difference in your loan's interest rate saves you an impressive $8,640 over the 30 years you have the loan.

Obviously, the more you borrow, the more you stand to save by shopping. (But don't make the mistake of thinking that if you're borrowing relatively little because that's all you can afford, there's less value in saving a little interest. If you can afford to borrow only comparatively little, you're in no position to be throwing money away!)

So, although we're the first to admit that shopping for a mortgage is among the least fun things to do when you have a day off, get motivated to do it! Shopping smart means saving big bucks that you can put toward the more interesting and enjoyable activities in your life. This chapter can get you motivated.

Going with a Mortgage Broker or Direct Lender?

Yes, thousands of mortgage lenders are out there. However, not anywhere near that many mortgage lenders are *good* lenders or the best lenders for you. Although we encourage you to find the lowest-cost lenders, we must first issue a caution: If someone offers you a deal that's much better than any other lender's, be skeptical. Such a lender may be baiting you with a loan that doesn't currently exist, one that has hidden charges or other onerous terms, or one for which you can't qualify.

Also, if you think back to other services or products you've bought, you know the wisdom of considering the features and services you receive in addition to cost. Even if you find a low-cost loan from a lender with a reputation for great service, if the loan doesn't meet your needs and personal situation, it's not the best loan for you.

One of the first decisions you face in the loan-shopping process is deciding whether to shop on your own or to hire a mortgage broker to do the mortgage shopping for you. The following sections help you make that decision.

Considerations when using brokers

Mortgage brokers are intermediaries, independent of banks or other financial institutions that have money to lend. Mortgage brokers don't have money to lend nor can they say yay or nay to your loan application. They do, however, *originate*, that is, process loan applications.

Mortgage brokers will tell you that they can get you the best loan deal by shopping among many lenders. They may further argue that another benefit of using their services is that they can explain the multitude of loan choices, help you select a loan, and help you wade through the morass of paperwork required to get a loan. Some of the time, these assertions are accurate; but you need to know at what cost and how well these services are provided.

If your credit history and ability to qualify for a mortgage are marginal, a good mortgage broker can help polish your application and steer you to the few lenders that may offer you a loan. Brokers can also help if lenders don't want to make loans on unusual properties that you're interested in buying. For example, many lenders don't like dealing with shared-ownership housing options such as mixed-use properties (residential/commercial), co-ops, and tenancies-in-common (see Chapter 6).

How brokers are paid

So how much do you pay a mortgage broker to get you a loan that meets your needs? Mortgage brokers typically receive a slice of the amount that you borrow — usually about 1 percent, although it may be as low as 0.5 percent on big loans and as much as 2 percent on small loans. (You may actually make an out-of-pocket payment directly to the broker.)

Thus, if you're going to use a mortgage broker, you must keep in mind that conflicts of interest are inherent, because such brokers are paid a commission just like stockbrokers and salespeople at car dealerships. For example, the more you borrow, the more the mortgage broker makes. Furthermore, some lenders pay higher commissions on certain loans (their more profitable ones, not surprisingly) to encourage mortgage brokers to push them. The actual lender may also pay the broker an additional fee if you pay a higher interest rate.

TIP

If you use a broker, make sure that all commissions, fees, and lender rebates are disclosed to you in writing before you commit to go forward with a specific loan.

Do brokers add to your costs?

Although mortgage brokers earn their living from commissions, that doesn't necessarily mean that using a mortgage broker always adds to your costs of obtaining a loan. The interest rate and points for most mortgages obtained through a broker may well be the same as you'd pay if you had gotten the same loan from the same lender directly. Lenders reason that they can afford to share their normal fees with an outside mortgage broker who isn't employed by the bank, because if you had gotten the loan directly from the bank, you would have had to work with and take up the time of one of the bank's own mortgage employees.

WARNING

Some lenders, including those with the lowest rates, don't market through mortgage brokers. And sometimes a loan obtained through a mortgage broker can end up costing you more than if you had gotten it directly from the lender; for example, if the mortgage broker is taking a big commission or extra fees for himself.

TIP

If you're on the fence about using a mortgage broker, take this simple test: If you're the type of person who dreads shopping and waits until the last minute to buy a gift, a good mortgage broker can probably help you and save you money. A competent mortgage broker can be of greatest value to people who don't bother shopping around for a good deal or folks who may be shunned, due to credit blemishes, by most lenders.

Even if you plan to shop on your own, talking to a mortgage broker may be worthwhile. At the very least, you can compare the mortgages you find with the deals the brokers say they can get for you. Be aware, though, that some brokers tell you only what you want to hear — that they can beat your best find. Later, you may discover that the broker isn't able to deliver when the time comes. If you find a good deal on your own and want to check with a mortgage broker to see what he or she has to offer, you may be wise not to tell the broker the terms of the best deal you've found. If you do, more than a few brokers always come up with a mortgage that they *say* can beat it.

Coauthor Robert firmly believes that you will get your best terms only if each potential lender or mortgage broker knows that she has to give you the best combination of interest rate and points, without you telling her what loan terms her competitors offered you. If you tell the lender or mortgage broker what your best deal is, not surprisingly many will just barely beat that offer. Remember that one potential loan can outshine another in other ways — for example, maybe one lender is willing to give you a loan rate lock for 60 days at no cost. As discussed in Chapter 9, interest rate locks can be valuable because they avoid the all too common problem of your interest rate rising during your loan escrow.

Developing a list of brokers and lenders

Whether you choose to work with a mortgage broker or go to lenders directly, develop a short list of the best candidates for comparison purposes. The following sections offer our time-tested methods for making that short list as strong as possible, thus maximizing your chances of ending up with the cream of the crop.

Collecting referrals

You can find plenty of mortgage lenders and brokers in most communities. Although having a large number of choices means competition, you may have a hard time deciding where to turn.

Of the various major institutional players in the mortgage marketplace — banks, savings and loan associations, credit unions, and mortgage bankers — only mortgage bankers focus exclusively on mortgages, and the best mortgage bankers offer quite competitive rates. Smaller banks, credit unions, and savings and loans can have good deals as well. The bigger banks and online lenders, whose names you're likely to recognize from the millions they spend on advertising, may not offer the best rates, but don't eliminate them without at least a phone call or online quote.

Real estate agents and others in the real estate trade, as well as other borrowers you know, can serve as useful references for steering you toward the top-notch mortgage lenders and away from the losers. If you do a good job selecting a real estate agent (a process described in detail in Ray Brown and coauthor Eric's best-selling books *Home Buying For Dummies* and *House Selling For Dummies*, published by Wiley), your agent should help. Also consult people you know who can recommend the best people in real estate and related fields — this list could include tax advisors, attorneys, financial advisors, property managers, property inspectors, contractors, real estate investors, title insurance companies, escrow companies, and so on.

WARNING

Never blindly accept someone's lender recommendation as gospel. Some people in the real estate trade — or any other trade for that matter — may simply refer you to others who've sent them business and may not offer the best mortgage loans. For example, Mike the mortgage lender may always refer people needing tax advice to his buddy Tom the tax advisor. So when one of Tom's clients is looking for a mortgage lender, Tom returns the favor, even though he hasn't the slightest clue about the mortgage rates and types of loans his buddy Mike offers.

WARNING

Likewise, be aware that some real estate agents may refer you to lenders that don't have the best mortgage rates and programs in town. These real estate agents may not be up-to-date with who has the best loans, may not be into shopping around, or may have become comfortable doing business with certain lenders. Some real estate sales firms may have a mortgage company owned by the same parent company. Be cautious if you're directed to its in-house lender. You get the idea.

In addition to asking people in real estate–related fields for mortgage lender or broker referrals, also ask your friends and colleagues who don't work in real estate and related fields. You may get some excellent ideas for whom to contact, especially if your friends have recently shopped for a mortgage loan in your area.

Just as we caution you about forging ahead with mortgage lenders recommended by real estate folks, we also urge some skepticism about referrals from your aunt Martha and coworker Charlie. When it comes to mortgages, Martha and Charlie may be complete nitwits. They may not know the difference between an adjustable-rate mortgage and an aardvark!

TIP

Whenever somebody recommends a specific mortgage lender or mortgage broker, always ask why. The answers often prove enlightening. A world of difference stands between someone saying that she chose a given lender because it's the same bank where she has her checking account and she did no shopping around versus someone who chose a lender from among ten she considered because that lender provided lower rates and better service.

Finding lender lists

Another method for adding names to your menu of prospective lenders is to peruse the various lists of lenders you may find in print or by using your computer:

- **Bankrate and HSH Associates:** These companies provide lists of lenders' rate quotes for most areas. Visit their websites, `www.bankrate.com` and `www.hsh.com` (which we discuss in Chapter 8). Note that both of these sites receive compensation from lenders on their websites.
- **The Internet:** Numerous websites hawk mortgage loans these days. Although you may find a good deal, you may also end up in the hands of a not-so-hot lender or worse. Please be sure to read Chapter 8, in which we discuss how to use (and not be abused by) mortgage Internet sites.
- **Newspaper real estate sections:** Most larger newspaper real estate sections carry tables of selected lenders' mortgage loans (look in the weekend or Sunday edition). Don't assume, however, that such tables contain the best mortgage loans available. Many of these tables are sent to newspapers for free by publicity-seeking firms that distribute information to mortgage brokers. With that in mind, go ahead and peruse these tables for lenders offering the most competitive rates.

Interviewing and working with mortgage brokers

In this section, we explain how you can find your way to good mortgage brokers. Be sure to get answers to the following questions when choosing a mortgage broker to work with (also, see the next section is "Figuring out how to interview lenders."):

- **How many lenders does the broker do business with, and how does the broker stay up-to-date with new lenders and loans that may be better?** Some mortgage brokers, either out of habit or laziness, or for higher commissions, send all their business to just a few lenders instead of shopping around to get you the best deals. Ask brokers which lenders have approved them to represent them. Some mortgage brokers represent only one or two inconsequential lenders — not the kind of broad representation you need to find the best mortgage.
- **How knowledgeable is the broker about the loan programs, and does the broker have the patience to explain all of a loan's important features?** The more lenders a mortgage broker represents, the less likely the broker is to know the nuances of every loan. Ask how long the broker has been in business. Be especially wary of a salesperson who aggressively

pushes certain loan programs and glosses over or ignores the important points we discuss in this book for evaluating particular mortgages.

WARNING

Head for cover if a prospective mortgage broker pushes you toward *balloon loans* (see Chapter 6) and *negative amortization loans* (see Chapter 5), which thankfully have been going away in recent years. Balloon loans, which become fully due and payable a few years after you get them, are dangerous, because you may not be able to get new financing and could be forced to sell your property. Negative amortization occurs when your outstanding loan balance increases every month, even though you keep making your regular monthly mortgage payments — double ouch!

- **What's the mortgage broker's commission?** As we mention in the last section, mortgage brokers typically get a commission in the range of 0.5 to 2 percent of the amount borrowed. The commission a mortgage broker receives from the lender isn't set in stone and is negotiable, especially on larger loans. On a $75,000 loan, a 1 percent commission comes to $750. The same commission percentage on a $300,000 loan (four times bigger) amounts to a $3,000 cut for the broker. A four-times-larger loan doesn't take four times as much of the mortgage broker's time. You have every right to ask the mortgage broker what her take is. Ask for this information in writing. Remember, it's your money. You should negotiate with mortgage brokers, especially on larger loan amounts. Remember that some brokers have been known to push programs with super-high interest rates and points, which provide fatter commissions for the broker. This problem occurs most frequently with borrowers who have questionable credit or other qualification problems.

Figuring out how to interview lenders

In Chapter 9, we provide some handy-dandy worksheets that allow you to compare various lenders' mortgage programs. Our goal in this section is to help you narrow the list of candidates you're considering. As you're screening lenders you may work with, you can also begin finding out about loan programs, interest rates, and other loan terms. We strongly recommend that you read Chapter 9 before you start calling lenders or mortgage brokers.

Whether you're shopping for a mortgage broker or a lender, the following questions should come in handy:

- **What types of loans does the mortgage lender or broker specialize in?** The right lender for you is one that understands and has lots of experience with the type of real estate property that you want to finance. For example, if you're buying a co-op in a big city, a lender that focuses on lending to single-family home and condo owners in the surrounding suburbs likely won't have the best programs and be able to deliver the mortgage you need on time. This is a concern whether you're talking with a mortgage lender or mortgage broker but comes up more often with brokers. In the quest to find the loan with the lowest possible interest rate, an inexperienced mortgage broker may end up trying to place your loan with a lender that doesn't offer mortgages for the type of property you want to buy.

- **How does the lender's loan approval process work?** Specifically, who's involved in the approval, and where are these people located? The best lenders approve loans locally and don't send your loan application to a mammoth, out-of-state, corporate headquarters where some faceless committee (or computer program) decides on the fate of your loan application. Good lenders should roll up their sleeves to help you get loan approval, warn you in advance of possible problems, and suggest solutions that will help you get the best loan and terms possible. Robert has found that mortgage brokers with many years of experience are often your best option. For example, if you find a mortgage broker who was in the mortgage business in the early 2000s and was able to survive continuously through the economic challenges of the late 2000s through until today, consider using that broker.
- **How competitive are the lender's rates?** You won't be able to answer this question well until you talk with various lenders and comparison shop. As we say earlier in this chapter, just because lenders boast about low rates doesn't mean that they can deliver on their promises or that their lower rates will make up for shoddy service. If you narrow your selections down to a couple of lenders or brokers, don't hesitate to ask the lender that you like best to match the rate of the lowest-priced lender you find. Loan rates and charges are negotiable. You have nothing to lose by asking.

Be sure to ask the lender for a *written* estimate of all loan costs and fees *prior* to signing your loan application. Getting such estimates from all lenders you're considering enables you to cut through the inevitable sales pitch you hear from lenders about how competitive their rates are. See Chapter 9 for more information on comparing various lenders' mortgage offerings.

- **Does the lender speak your language and candidly answer your questions?** Good, ethical mortgage lenders and brokers can clearly explain their loan programs without using jargon or verbal obfuscation. They'll candidly disclose all fees and answer all reasonable questions. A major red flag is if you ask a question and don't get a follow-up response, which either indicates that you're dealing with someone evasive or who lacks follow-up. Good lenders meet deadlines, which is especially critical if your loan is for a home purchase. Missed deadlines can sabotage your purchase. If you're refinancing to lower your loan rate, delays cost you money and could cause you to miss out on capturing low rates if rates rise during a lender's delays.

In addition to questioning lenders and mortgage brokers you're considering working with, after you narrow down your search to the two or three strongest candidates, ask for customer references. Use the same questions in the preceding list to select the winner.

Seller Financing: The Trials and Tribulations

In addition to borrowing through traditional mortgage lenders and brokers, you may find some house sellers offering to lend you money if you agree to buy their home. Why? Because the sellers may believe that the loan will help sell their house faster and at a higher price and provide a better return on their investment dollars.

And therein lies the reason you should be highly cautious about seller financing. Generally speaking, sellers offering houses for sale with financing tend to be selling problematic houses with major flaws. It's also possible that the property may be priced well above its fair market value. Alternatively, however, the sellers may be offering financing because the local real estate market is sluggish or because they can't think of better ways to invest the proceeds of sale. Or they may be facing a large income tax bill because they have a very low tax (cost) basis in the property and want to sell by using an installment sale to spread their gain over several tax years. These latter reasons can work to your advantage.

Considering/soliciting seller financing

Some house sellers who aren't offering to provide financing may consider it; you won't know until you ask.

We advocate considering seller financing under the following conditions:

- **The property doesn't have fatal flaws.** As explained in Eric and Ray Brown's *Home Buying For Dummies* book, avoid buying a house with incurable defects. Always have an independent, qualified, credentialed professional conduct a thorough inspection before you sign the Purchase and Sale Agreement and heed their advice.
- **You can buy the property at its fair market value or less.** Seller financing is often offered on properties that aren't selling. Property that's gathering cobwebs is generally overpriced. Saving 1 percent on a seller-financed loan

won't mean much if you grossly overpay for the house. Here, if the professional independent appraisal can't support the agreed-upon purchase price, then you know you're not getting a deal.

- **The cost of the seller-financed loan is as low as or lower than you can get through a traditional mortgage lender.** Why borrow from the seller if it doesn't save you money? Of course, if you have credit problems that make borrowing from traditional lenders prohibitively costly or impossible, you have another good reason to borrow from a seller.

Overcoming borrower problems

You may be tempted to consider borrowing from a seller because of problems with your credit or financial situation. Smart house sellers will pull a copy of your credit report. If they discover blemishes, they won't grant you a loan or will charge you a much higher interest rate. Be sure the warts on your report are correct. Credit reporting agencies and creditors who report information to the agencies have been known to make mistakes.

TIP

Because you followed our advice in Chapter 3 and obtained copies of your current credit report from all three major credit reporting agencies, be sure to provide a written and detailed explanation of any credit report problems at the time you apply to the sellers for a loan if you know that they're going to pull a credit report. Another way to address a seller's concerns is to get a cosigner, such as a relative, for the loan.

If your income is low, you can try to accumulate a larger down payment to placate the lender or get a relative with sufficient income to cosign the loan. You may also be able to get a cash gift toward your down payment from a friend, employer, or family member, but the lender will require a "gift letter" indicating that the money isn't a loan and no repayment or other future services is expected or implied. You can also consider an FHA loan or, if you're a veteran, a VA loan. In Chapter 2, we provide comprehensive coverage of ways to overcome these problems.

Negotiating loan terms

Call several local lenders to find out the rate they're charging for the size and type of loan that you're contemplating (for example, 15- or 30-year fixed-rate mortgage; first or second mortgage; or owner-occupied or investment/rental property). Be sure to ask about all the fees — application, processing, appraisal, credit report, points, title policy, recording, and so on.

If you're in good financial health and can easily qualify to borrow from a traditional lender, you should expect better terms through seller financing than the traditional mortgage lenders are offering you. How much better depends in large part on how good at negotiating you are! Aim for a 1 percent reduction in the ongoing interest rate as well as on the upfront fees. For example, if traditional lenders are charging 6 percent plus 1.5 points (percent) upfront, aim to pay no more than 5 percent with 0.5 points.

Deciding whether to provide seller financing

When the time comes for you to sell your house, offering seller financing may broaden the pool of potential buyers for your property. Traditional mortgage lenders are subject to many rules and regulations that force them to deny some mortgage applications. However, making loans to borrowers rejected by banks can be risky business.

TIP

To even consider making a loan against the house you are selling, *all* the following conditions should apply to your situation:

- **Without the cash you're lending to the buyer, you should still be financially able to purchase the next home or property you desire.** Most house sellers need the proceeds from the sale of their current property to be able to buy their next one.
- **You're willing to do the necessary work to assess the creditworthiness of a borrower.** A smart mortgage lender would do the same before risking his money on a loan, so why wouldn't you?
- **If the borrower defaults, you're in a financial position where you can afford to lose much or even all of this money.** If the borrower does stop making monthly payments to you, you may have to initiate the costly process of foreclosure. You'll get the home back, but it may not be in the same pristine condition as it was when you sold it.
- **You desire income-oriented investments and are in a low tax bracket.** The interest income on a mortgage loan is taxable, so if you're in a higher tax bracket and you want interest income, you're probably better off investing in tax-free municipal bonds.

Only if all these conditions apply should you consider extending a financing offer to a prospective buyer of your house. If you're going to do that, you should then do what every smart mortgage lender would do: Thoroughly review a prospective borrower's creditworthiness. In Chapters 2 and 3, we explain how lenders do that.

» Checking out mortgage sites

Chapter 8
Searching for Mortgage Information Online

Computers, tablets, and smartphones are amazing tools. Used wisely, they may save you time and money. However, like other tools (such as a hammer), used incorrectly (remember the last time you whacked your finger with a hammer?) or for the wrong purpose (tapping a glass window comes to mind), today's technology can cause more harm than good.

Some people have mistaken assumptions about using their computers and tablet or phone apps to help them make important financial decisions. Some believe and hope that fancy technology can solve their financial problems or provide unique insights and vast profits. Often, such erroneous musings originate from propaganda put forth through "fake news" or social media about how all your problems can easily be solved if you just have the right app, spend more time on particular websites, and so on.

As computers, technology, and apps continue to proliferate, we take seriously our task of explaining how, where, and when to use the Internet to help you make important mortgage decisions. In this chapter, we highlight key concepts and issues for you to understand as well as list a few of our favorite websites.

Obeying Our Safe Surfing Tips

Before we get to specific sites that are worthy of your time, in this section we provide an overview of how we suggest using (and not being abused by) your mortgage-related web surfing or cure-all app. Specific sites, and especially apps, will come and go, but these safe surfing tips should assist you with assessing any site or app that you may stumble upon.

Shop to find out about rates and programs

The best reason that we can think of to access the Internet when you're looking for a mortgage is to discover more about the going rate for the various types of loans you're considering. Despite all the cautions we raise in this chapter, shopping for a mortgage online has some attractions:

- **No direct sales pressure:** Because you don't speak or meet with a mortgage officer (who typically works on commission) when you peruse mortgage rates online, you can do so without much pressure. That said, some sites and apps are willing to give out specific loan information only *after* you reveal a fair amount of information about yourself, including how to get in touch with you. However, on one site where you must register (with all your contact information and more) to list your loan desires, take a look at how the site pitches itself to prospective mortgage lenders: "FREE, hot leads! Every lead is HOT, HOT, HOT because the borrower has paid us a fee to post their loan request."

WARNING

Although the advantages of online shopping are many, being savvy and discrete with who and how you contact prospective lenders is worthy of a cautionary reminder. You may think you're the one shopping, but on many sites and apps, you are the one being "sold" to aggressive marketers of loan products that may not be what you need. Worse yet, many of these unscrupulous hucksters don't even have the loan products and terms they tease on their website and their real goal is to lure you in and then turn around and sell your information to others. You'll soon find yourself inundated with unwanted emails, texts, and even phone calls.

- **Shop when you like:** Because most people work weekdays when lenders and mortgage brokers are available, squeezing in calls to lenders is often difficult. Thus, another advantage of mortgage Internet shopping is that you can do it any time of any day when it's convenient for you. Just be careful that you don't provide personal information to anyone unless you're sure you want him to contact you.

Quality control is often insufficient

Particularly at sites where lenders simply pay an advertising fee to be part of the program, you should know that quality control may be nonexistent or not up to your standards. "We make your loan request available to every online lender in the world," boasts one online mortgage listing service. We don't know too many borrowers willing to work with just any old mortgage company! Some sites don't check to see whether a participating lender provides a high level of service or meets promises and commitments made to previous customers.

Again, if you're going to go loan shopping on the Internet, examine each site to see how it claims to review listed lenders. One site we're familiar with claims to demand strict ethics from the companies it lists — no lowballing or bait-and-switch tactics — and says it has removed several dozen lenders from its list for such violations. That makes us think that the site should do a better job of screening lenders upfront!

Beware simplistic affordability calculators

Be highly skeptical of information about the mortgage amount that you can afford. Most online mortgage calculators simplistically use overall income figures and the current loan interest rate to calculate the mortgage amount a borrower can "afford." These calculators are really spitting out the *maximum* a bank will lend you based on your income. As we discuss in Chapter 1, this figure has nothing to do with the amount you can *really* afford.

Such a simplistic calculation ignores your larger financial picture: how much (or little) you have put away for other long-term financial goals such as retirement or college educations for your children. Thus, you need to take a hard look at your budget and goals before deciding how much you can afford to spend on a home; don't let some slick Java-based calculator make this decision for you.

Don't reveal confidential information unless . . .

Suppose that you follow all our advice in this chapter, and you find your best mortgage deal online. You may find yourself solicited to apply for your mortgage online as well. However, as you gather your confidential financial documents, you may have an unsettling feeling and wonder just how safe and wise it is to be entering this type of information into an Internet site.

WARNING

We applaud your instincts and concerns! Here's what you should do to protect yourself:

- **Do your homework on the business.** In Chapter 7, we suggest a variety of questions to ask and issues to clarify before deciding to do business with any lender — online or offline.
- **Review the lender's security and confidentiality policies.** On reputable lender websites, you'll be able to find the lender's policies regarding how it handles the personal and financial information you may share with it. We recommend doing business only with sites that don't sell or share your information with any outside organization other than for the sole purpose of verifying your creditworthiness needed for loan approval. Be sure to choose secure sites that prevent computer hackers from obtaining the information you enter.

TIP

If you're simply not comfortable — for whatever reason — applying for a loan online, know that most online mortgage brokers and lenders offer users the ability to apply for their loan offline (at an office or via loan papers sent through the regular mail). They may charge a slightly higher fee for this service, but if it makes you feel more comfortable, consider it money well spent.

Be sure to shop offline

You may find your best mortgage deal online. However, you won't know it's the best unless and until you've done sufficient shopping offline as well. Why shop offline? You want to be able to see all your options and find the best one. Online mortgage options aren't necessarily the cheapest or the best. What good is a quote for a low mortgage rate that a lender doesn't deliver on or that you won't qualify for because of your specific property, location, or financial situation? ***Remember:*** Personal service and honoring commitments is highly important.

You may be able to save a small amount of money by taking a mortgage you find online. Some online mortgage brokers are willing to take a somewhat smaller slice of commission for themselves if they feel they're saving time and money processing your loan via an online application. As we discuss in Chapter 7, mortgage brokers' fees do vary and are negotiable. Some online mortgage brokers are willing to take less than the industry standard cut (1-plus percent).

But just because you've been offered a slightly better rate online, you shouldn't necessarily jump on it. Local lender or mortgage brokers may negotiate with you to make themselves competitive. However, you have to give them the opportunity to do so. Other things being equal, go back to the runner-up on price and give them a chance to meet or beat your best offer. You may be pleasantly surprised with the results.

Mortgage websites and apps are best used to research the current marketplace rather than to actually apply for and secure a mortgage. The reason: Mortgage lending is still largely a locally driven and relationship-based business that varies based on nuances of a local real estate market.

Beware of paid advertising masquerading as directories

Some sites on the Internet and apps offer "directories" of mortgage lenders. Most sites charge lenders a fee to be listed or to gain a more visible listing. And, just as with any business buying a yellow pages listing or Google ad, higher visibility ads cost more. Here's how one online directory lured lenders to advertise on its site:

> Sure, our basic listing is free, but we have thousands of mortgage companies in our directory. A free listing is something like a five-second radio advertisement at 2:00 a.m. on an early Sunday morning. To make your listing really work for you, you must upgrade your listing.

Upgrade, here, is a code word for *pay for it!* For example, a "gold listing" on this site costs $600 per year for one state and $360 for each additional state. What does that amount of money get the lender?

> A Gold Listing sorts your company name to the top of all listings. In addition, the Gold Listings receive a higher typeface font and a Gold Listing icon next to their name.

Then there is the "diamond listing," the "platinum listing," the "titanium listing," and you get the idea.

On another directory site, you can find a "directory enhancement program," which for $125 per year enabled a lender to buy a boldface listing and for $225 per line per year place descriptive text under the listing. Thus, prospective borrowers visiting these sites are looking at the mortgage equivalent of an online Yellow Pages advertising directory rather than a comprehensive or low-cost lender directory.

If you're considering using an Internet site or app to shop for a mortgage, first investigate the way the site derived the list of lenders. If the site isn't upfront about disclosing this information, be suspicious. Do some sleuthing like we did; click on the buttons at the site that solicit lenders to join the fray. Here you can find out how the site attracts lenders and you may also find the amount lenders are paying to be listed.

Perusing Our Recommended Mortgage Websites

In addition to seeking only the highest-quality sources for you, dear reader, we don't want you wasting your time on a wild goose chase for some unreliable website or app that's here today and gone tomorrow. In this section, we recommend a short list of our favorite mortgage sites. Yes, many more sites and apps are out there, but we don't want to bore you with a huge laundry list of mortgage-related sites. And, please remember as we discuss in Chapter 7, mortgages are distributed through numerous types of mortgage lenders and brokers. The Internet and the app craze are just simply another way that these players can reach prospective customers.

Useful government sites

Various government agencies provide assistance to low-income homebuyers as well as veterans. The U.S. Department of Housing and Urban Development's website (see Figure 8-1) at `www.hud.gov` provides information on the federal government's FHA loan program as well as links to listings of HUD and other government agency–listed homes for sale (foreclosed homes for which the owners had FHA loans; see `https://portal.hud.gov/hudportal/HUD?src=/topics/homes_for_sale`). On this site, you can also find links to other useful federal government housing–related websites.

Also, if you're a veteran, check out the VA's website (see Figure 8-2; `www.benefits.va.gov/homeloans`) operated by the U.S. Department of Veterans Affairs. In addition to information on VA loans, veterans and nonveterans alike are eligible to buy foreclosed properties on which there was a VA loan (see the website `http://listings.vrmco.com`).

The Federal Citizen Information Center (`www.pueblo.gsa.gov/housing.htm`) offers numerous free and low-cost pamphlets on home financing topics such as securing home equity loans, avoiding loan fraud, finding mortgages and home improvement loans to make your home more energy efficient, and qualifying for a low down payment mortgage. You also want to know the required lender disclosures so you know what the lender must tell you and what it means.

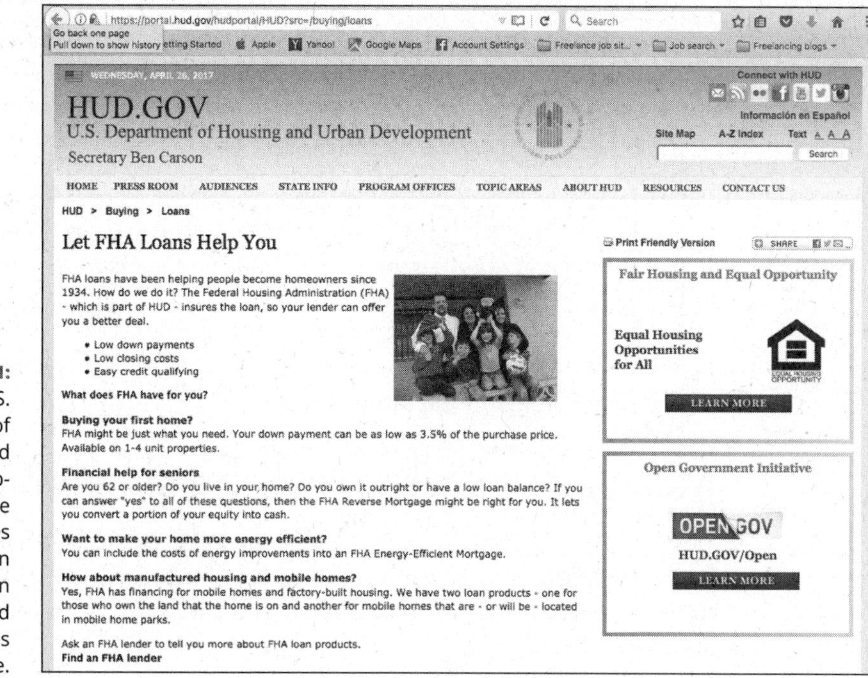

FIGURE 8-1: The U.S. Department of Housing and Urban Development website provides information on FHA loan programs and HUD homes for sale.

Source: U.S. Department of Housing and Urban Development

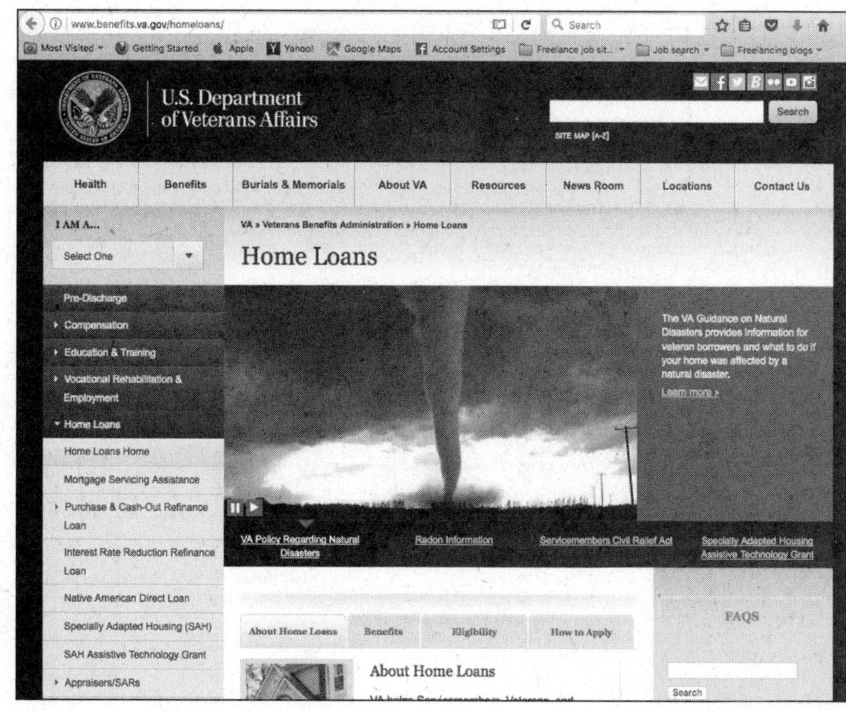

FIGURE 8-2: Visit the U.S. Department of Veterans Affairs website for information on VA loans.

Source: U.S. Department of Veterans Affairs

Fannie Mae (www.fanniemae.com) has many resources for mortgage borrowers and homebuyers. In addition to helping you find mortgage lenders for home purchases, improvements, or refinances, the site can also turn you onto helpful worksheets and counseling agencies. Freddie Mac (www.freddiemac.com) offers similar (although not as extensive) resources.

Finally, if you're trying to fix your problematic credit report, don't waste your money on so-called credit-repair firms, which often overpromise — and charge big fees for doing things that you can do yourself. In addition to following our credit-fixing advice in Chapters 2 and 3, also check out the Federal Trade Commission's website (www.ftc.gov) for helpful credit-repair and other relevant advice regarding borrowing.

Mortgage information and shopping sites

HSH Associates (www.hsh.com) is the nation's largest collector and publisher of mortgage information. If you're a data junkie, you'll enjoy perusing the HSH site, which includes up-to-date mortgage rates and graphs showing recent trends (see Figure 8-3).

Some lenders do choose to advertise online at HSH's website and you can obtain their rates through the website's ad links.

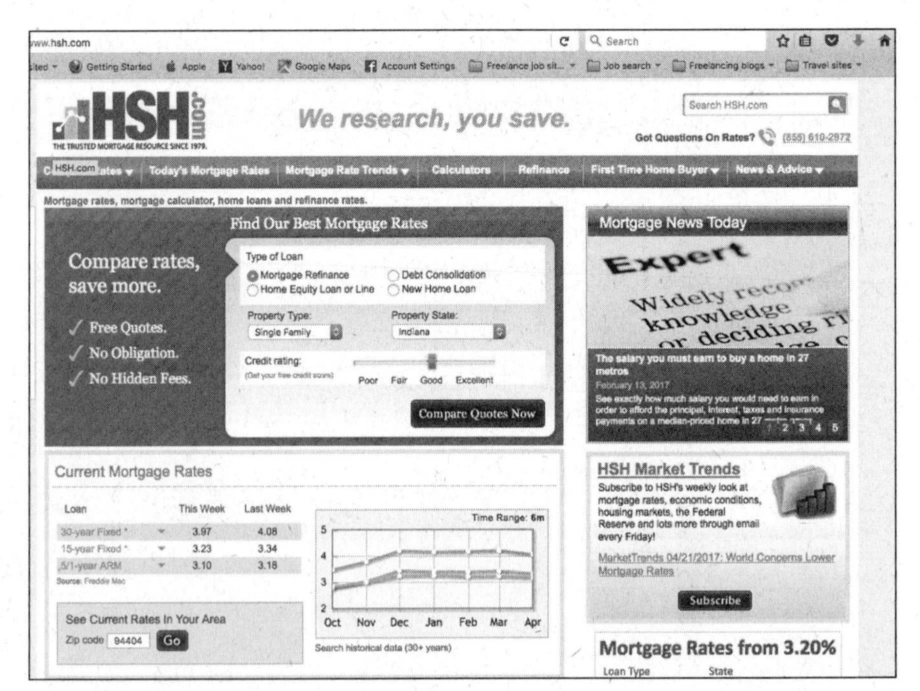

FIGURE 8-3: The website of HSH Associates, publisher of mortgage information.

Source: HSH Associates

Many online mortgage brokers and lenders provide rate quotes and assist with your loan shopping. The interactive features of some sites even allow prospective borrowers to compare the total cost of loans (including points and fees) under different scenarios (how long you keep the loan and what happens to the interest rate on adjustable-rate mortgages). Interpreting these comparisons, however, requires a solid understanding of mortgage lingo and pricing.

Two other sites that we like are `www.bankrate.com` and `www.realtor.com`. Bank Rate's site offers lots of information and perspectives on many types of consumer loans including mortgages. Realtor.com's Mortgage section is more focused on mortgages. On both sites, you can shop for specific mortgages.

» Understanding the point and interest rate tradeoff

» Recognizing loan features to avoid

» Interviewing lenders and comparing their programs

Chapter 9 Choosing Your Preferred Mortgage

In Chapter 7, we explain how to develop a short list of lenders. In this chapter, we get down to the important and often difficult business of comparing various lenders' loan programs to one another so you can choose the best. As we say throughout this book, "best" doesn't necessarily mean lowest cost, especially if the lowest cost lender you uncover has lousy service or doesn't deliver on the glowing promises in its marketing hype.

That said, clearly an important part of your selection process is pricing — namely, the amount each lender charges for a comparable loan. Mortgages require monthly payments to repay the debt. As we discuss in Chapter 1, your mortgage payment, which is comprised of *interest* (lender charges for use of the money you borrowed), and *principal* (repayment of the original amount borrowed), is likely your biggest monthly expense of homeownership and perhaps of your entire household budget. Over the life of your mortgage loan, you'll probably pay more in total interest charges than you originally paid for the home itself.

For example, suppose that you buy a home for $200,000. After making a 20 percent down payment of $40,000, you get a $160,000 loan. If you borrow that $160,000 with a 30-year fixed-rate mortgage at 7 percent, you end up paying a whopping $223,616 in interest charges over the life of your loan — more than the purchase price of the home! And those interest charges don't include various upfront fees, which we discuss later in this chapter (see the section "Other lender fees") that most mortgages carry.

However, to keep everything in perspective, rent payments for 30 years could likely total even more than the total cost of buying the home with a mortgage — and after 30 years of renting, you won't even own the home!

Taking a Look at Loan Fees

By far, the biggest expense of a mortgage is the ongoing interest charges — normally quoted as a percentage per year of the amount borrowed. You may be familiar with rates of interest if you've ever borrowed money through student loans, credit cards, or auto loans. In these cases, lenders may have charged you 9, 10, 12, or perhaps even 21 percent interest or more for the privilege of using their money. (Now you know how banks pay for their downtown corporate headquarters and the marble in their branch lobbies!) Similarly, mortgage lenders also quote you an annual interest rate on mortgage loans.

However, in addition to paying interest on your mortgage loan on an ongoing basis, most mortgages charge an upfront fee known as *basis points* or a *loan origination fee.* This section also zeros in on other lender charges such as application and processing fees as well as fees you may incur for a credit report and property appraisal.

The point and interest rate tradeoff

The interest rate on a mortgage is and should always be quoted together with the points on the loan. The points on a mortgage used to purchase a home are tax deductible in the year in which you incur them, whereas on a refinance, the points are gradually tax deductible over the life of the refinanced mortgage loan.

Mortgage lenders and brokers quote points as a percentage of the mortgage amount and require you to pay them at the time that you close on your loan. One point is equal to 1 percent of the amount that you're borrowing. For example, if lenders say a loan costs one and a half points, they mean that if you take the loan, you must pay the lender upfront 1.5 percent of the loan amount as points. On a $150,000 loan, for example, one and a half points would cost you $2,250.

Because no one enjoys paying extra costs such as these, you may rightfully be thinking that as you shop for a mortgage, you'll simply shun those loans that have high points. Don't get suckered into believing that no-point loans are a good deal. You'll find no free lunches in the real estate world. Unfortunately, if you shop for a low- or no-point mortgage, you're going to pay other ways. The relationship between the interest rate on a mortgage and that same loan's points can best be thought of as a seesaw; one end of the seesaw is the loan's interest rate, and the other end of the seesaw represents the loan's points.

So if you pay less in points, the ongoing interest rate will be higher. If a loan has zero points, it must have a higher interest rate than a comparable mortgage with competitively priced points. This fact doesn't necessarily mean that the loan is better or worse than comparable loans from other lenders. However, in our experience, lenders that aggressively push no-point loans may not be the most competitive on pricing. Lenders can price and present a prospective loan to you in many different ways, but never forget that, one way or another, lenders will make sure they cover all their costs. You need to ask a lot of questions to make sure you understand how lenders are charging you for borrowing their money so you can determine the best loan for your needs.

There are technically two types of points — *origination Points* and *discount points* — but they both are just points. Don't let a lender confuse the situation with those terms. Any points paid should get you something — namely a lower ongoing interest rate.

TIP

You may be surprised to hear us say that some people may be better off selecting a mortgage with higher points. If you pay higher points on a mortgage, the lender should lower the ongoing interest rate. This reduction may be beneficial to you if you have the cash to pay more points and want to lower the interest rate that you'll be paying month after month and year after year. If you expect to hold onto the home and mortgage for many years, the lower the interest rate, the better.

Conversely, if you want to (or need to) pay fewer points (perhaps because you're cash constrained when you take out your loan), you can elect to pay a higher ongoing interest rate. The shorter the time that you expect to hold onto the mortgage, the more this strategy of paying less now (in points) and more later (in ongoing interest) makes sense.

Take a look at a couple of specific mortgage options to understand the points/interest-rate tradeoff. For example, suppose you want to borrow $150,000. One lender quotes you 7.25 percent on a 30-year fixed-rate loan and charges one point (1 percent). Another lender quotes 7.5 percent (a difference of 0.25 percent) and doesn't charge any points. Which loan is better? The answer depends mostly on how long you plan to keep the loan.

The 7.25 percent loan costs $1,024 per month compared to $1,050 per month for the 7.5 percent mortgage. You can save $26 per month with the 7.25 percent loan, but you'd have to pay $1,500 in points to get it.

To find out which loan is better for you, divide the cost of the points by the monthly savings ($\$1{,}500 \div \$26 = 57.7$). This result gives you the number of months (in this case, 58) that it will take you to recover the cost of the points. Thus, if you expect to keep the loan for less than 58 months (almost five years), choose the no-points loan. If you plan to keep the loan more than 58 months, pay the points. If you keep the loan for the remaining 25-plus years needed to repay it, you'll save $7,850 ($26 a month for 302 months).

TIP

To make a fair comparison of mortgages from different lenders, have the lenders provide interest rate quotes in writing for loans with the same number of points. For example, ask the mortgage contenders to tell you what their fixed-rate mortgage interest rate would be at one point. Also, make sure that the loans are for the same term — for example, 30 years. This comparison of loans using identical terms will allow you to see whether certain lenders are more competitive than others. Recall that money is a commodity or product just like any other consumer product and that certain money "sellers" (lenders) will be more aggressive with their pricing of their product than others. Your job is to find the lender that offers the product (money) at the lowest price based on your specific needs.

Annual percentage rates

Truth-in-lending law requires lenders to calculate a loan's *Annual Percentage Rate (APR)* when quoting interest rates. In theory, this calculation gives prospective borrowers a way to figure out whether a 30-year fixed-rate loan at 7 percent interest and one point is a better deal than a 6.75 percent mortgage and two points.

APR is a figure that states the total annual cost of a mortgage expressed by the *actual* rate of interest paid over the full term of the loan. In addition to the loan's stated interest rate, the APR also includes prepaid finance charges, such as its loan origination fee and other add-on loan fees and costs. As a result, a mortgage's APR will always be higher than the interest rate quoted by a lender. The only exception is a no-points, no-fees mortgage, in which case the APR will equal the loan's quoted interest rate.

WARNING

APR doesn't solve all your problems with understanding mortgage rates. For one thing, folks usually don't keep their fixed-rate loans for the full 15- or 30-year term. As a result, their mortgage's actual APR will be higher than the quoted APR because its points and loan fees are spread out over fewer years. Calculating the

APR of an adjustable-rate mortgage (ARM) that may or may not adjust monthly, semiannually, or annually based on movement of an index that's impossible to determine when you get the loan is an exercise in futility.

Our advice is simple: When comparing loans from various lenders, make sure the lenders provide interest rate quotes for loans with the identical points and loan terms. The next section explains a few other common prepaid financing charges.

Other lender fees

After swallowing the fact that you're paying points on your mortgage, you may think that no other upfront fees will come your way. Unfortunately, you'll find no shortage of upfront loan-processing charges to investigate when you make mortgage comparisons. Understanding all of a lender's fees is vital; these fees come out of your pocket. If you don't understand the fees, you may end up with an unnecessarily high-cost loan or come up short of cash when the time comes to close on your loan. If you're taking out a new mortgage loan to finance a home purchase, not being able to close could put the kibosh on buying your dream home.

Be sure to ask each lender whose loans you're seriously considering for a written itemization of all upfront financing charges:

- **Lender fees:** All lenders have lender fees such as processing fees, underwriting fees, and doc prep fees. These fees can approach or exceed $1,000. These fees all get included (along with any points) into a category called Origination Charges on your upfront Loan Estimate. These fees are charged when the loan closes.
- **Application fee:** Most lenders don't charge an upfront application fee, but some do. The application fee may be refundable if the loan is denied. The easiest way to avoid a problem is to avoid lenders that charge upfront application fees (except for the appraisal, which we discuss later in this list).
- **Credit report:** Your credit report tells a lender how well you manage your finances. Expect to pay $15 to $25 or so (protest significantly higher amounts) for the lender to obtain a current copy of yours. If you know that you have blemishes such as late credit card payments on your report, address those problems before you apply for your mortgage. Otherwise, you're wasting your time and money by applying for a loan that you'll be denied. You may obtain a free copy of your credit report from any lender who recently turned you down

for a loan because of derogatory information on your credit file. The lender is legally required to give you a copy of the report. The credit report provider can provide the report as well. If you need to clean up problems on your credit report, see our detailed discourse on the subject in Chapter 2.

- **Appraisal:** Mortgage lenders require an independent assessment from an appraiser to determine whether the property that you want to buy is worth the amount you agreed to pay for it. If you're refinancing, an appraisal is required to ensure that the home is worth more than enough to justify the amount of mortgage money you seek to borrow. The cost of an appraisal varies with the size, complexity, and value of property. Expect to pay $400-plus for the appraisal of a modestly priced, average-type property. You'll probably have to pay this fee prior to the appraisal.

  Lenders generally require an appraisal because if you overpay for your property and home values decline or you end up in financial trouble, experience has shown that some borrowers are likely to walk away from the property and leave the lender holding the bag. That's how many foreclosures happened in the late 2000s' real-estate market downturn.

  Most appraisals must be paid for upfront. In this case, the appraisal fee is not refundable if the loan is denied or if the appraisal comes in low. If you paid for the appraisal, you are entitled to a copy of the appraisal. If you did not pay for the appraisal upfront, chances are you're not on the hook for the cost of the appraisal, nor do you have the right to a copy of the appraisal.

To reduce your chances of throwing away money on a mortgage for which you may not qualify, ask the lender whether your application may be turned down for some reason. For example, disclose any potential problems — of which you are aware — on your credit report.

Also, be aware as you shop for mortgages from lender to lender because just as some lenders have no-point mortgages, some lenders also have *no-fee* mortgages. If a lender is pitching a no-fee loan, odds are that the lender will charge you more in the ongoing interest rate or points on your loan. If they're hyping their no-points loan, watch out for the fees and higher interest rates. They're going to get you one way or another!

So you don't spend any more than you need to on your mortgage and so you get the mortgage that best meets your needs, the time has come to get on with the task of understanding the available mortgage options.

Avoiding Dangerous Loan Features

Just as with any product or service you may buy, some mortgages come with "features" we think you should avoid. Just as you shouldn't buy a flimsy umbrella that will break in the first wind and rainstorm or a car model with known defects, what follows are loan bells and whistles you should bypass.

Prepayment penalties

As we discuss in Chapter 4, a prepayment penalty is a mortgage provision that penalizes you for paying off the loan balance faster than is required by the loan's payment schedule. Note that some lenders won't enforce the loan's prepayment penalties when you pay off a mortgage early because you sold an owner-occupied, one- to four-unit property. Beware of mortgages with so-called *hard prepayment penalties* that must be paid without any exceptions.

Prepayment penalties can amount to as much as several percentage points of the amount of the mortgage balance that you pay off early. Although some states place limits on prepayment penalties mortgage lenders may levy on owner-occupied residential property, the charges may still be stiff. For example, on a $150,000 mortgage balance with a 4 percent prepayment penalty, you'll get socked with a $6,000 surcharge for paying your loan off. A $300,000 mortgage with a similar prepayment penalty would sock you $12,000. (Of course, you may be thinking that you should have such problems as to have such piles of extra cash sitting around in your investment accounts!)

Not as common with residential loans, but many commercial loans even have a "loan lockout" period (typically three to seven years) in which you can't prepay the loan under any circumstances. This not only prevents you from prepaying the loan but also may severely limit your ability to sell the property unless the new buyer assumes the current loan (which also requires an additional fee and the lender's approval of the new buyer). Just be sure that you understand each of these loan features and consider various future scenarios that may occur and could hamper your flexibility in selling the property or prepaying the loan.

So how do you discover whether a given mortgage loan comes with a prepayment penalty? As you're shopping for a mortgage, be sure to ask each lender whether the loan has a prepayment penalty. Also, know that many of the no-point or no-fee mortgages we discuss earlier in this chapter have prepayment penalties. In addition to asking about possible prepayment penalties as you shop for a mortgage, when you think you've settled on a loan, carefully review the federal truth-in-lending disclosure and the promissory note (actual loan agreement) to look for any mentions of prepayment penalties and under what conditions such penalties apply.

Negative amortization

As you make mortgage payments over time, the loan balance you still owe is *amortized* (gradually reduced). The reverse of this process — increasing the size of your mortgage balance — is called *negative amortization.* Negative amortization pops up more often on mortgages that lenders consider risky to make. If you're having trouble finding lenders willing to offer you a mortgage, be especially careful.

Negative amortization is what happens, for example, when you pay only the minimum payment required on a credit card bill. You continue accumulating additional interest on the balance as long as you make only the minimum monthly payment. However, as we discuss in Chapter 1, allowing negative amortization to occur with a mortgage defeats the purpose of your borrowing an amount that fits your overall financial goals.

As we discuss in Chapter 5, some adjustable-rate mortgages (ARMs) cap the increase of your monthly payment but not the increase of the interest rate. Thus, the size of your mortgage payment may not reflect the interest actually due for that payment. So, rather than paying the interest that's owed and paying off some of your loan balance every month, you may end up paying only a portion of the interest you owe; the extra interest you owe is added to, and thus increases, your outstanding debt. In two words — not good!

Some lenders (and mortgage brokers) aren't forthcoming about the fact that an ARM they're pitching you has negative amortization. So how can you avoid negative amortization loans? Start by asking lenders while you're shopping. Also, as with uncovering prepayment penalties, when you're getting serious about a loan, review the federal truth-in-lending disclosure and the promissory note the mortgage lender provides you. Be sure to do this well ahead of the loan's funding date so you have time to negotiate loan charges and fees before it's too late.

If you don't understand the legalese in the promissory note, ask for a plain-English explanation. Remember that your loan is likely the single largest purchase you make, so you want to be absolutely sure that you understand all terms and conditions. *Don't* think that you have to approve the new loan so you can learn what's in it! Take the time upfront to understand the exact terms of the proposed mortgage.

Comparing Lenders' Programs

Whether you're in the market to buy a home or you're seeking to refinance an existing mortgage, you need to get serious about securing a mortgage and initiate the shopping process. (As we discuss in Chapter 2, we believe that you'll strengthen your negotiating position with a property seller by taking the time to get preapproved for a mortgage before submitting an offer to buy a home.)

Whether you do the mortgage shopping yourself or hire a competent mortgage broker to assist (see Chapter 7 for details about how to make this important decision), compare a variety of programs to help you assess which is best for you. Lots of facts and figures will be thrown at you, and we've found that some simple worksheets can help you keep the details straight and more easily compare various loans.

Fixed-rate mortgages interview worksheet

In Chapter 5, we walk you through the critical issues to consider when deciding between a fixed-rate mortgage (FRM) versus an adjustable-rate mortgage (ARM). So if you haven't reviewed that chapter, now is a fine time to do so.

If the security and peace of mind that come with a fixed-rate mortgage appeal to you, you may also be happy to know that shopping for a fixed-rate loan is simpler than shopping for an adjustable-rate mortgage. Simpler, unfortunately, doesn't translate into easier.

Table 9-1 can help you keep the details of various lenders' programs clear and make easier comparisons. Taking good notes also ensures that you'll have documented what you were told if any discrepancies crop up in the future. Here's a brief description of the elements you need to understand to complete the worksheet in Table 9-1:

- **Contact information:** Take the time to jot down the name of the person and the phone number that you call, because you may need to call it again, especially if it's for a loan that you're likely to take. Also, some lending institutions are huge. You may end up having your call transferred several times before reaching the final destination. Be sure to ask the person you ultimately interview for her name, direct phone number, fax number, and email address.
- **Person interviewed:** Your relationship with a lender should be with a specific person, usually the loan officer. This is the person to call if you have more

questions, to check the progress on your loan, to complain if things aren't moving the way you expected, or to offer thanks when you do get what you were promised or get good service.

- **Loan processor:** The loan processor handles your loan's paperwork from the time you submit the loan application until your loan is closed. The loan processor's job includes everything from conducting the credit investigation to preparing loan documents you'll sign prior to funding the mortgage. If possible, get the loan processor's name, direct phone number, fax number, and email address.
- **Date interviewed:** If discrepancies arise, your notation of dates could prove important.
- **Program name:** Most mortgage lenders give catchy and sometimes goofy names to various loan types. This jargon helps identify loans.
- **Interest rate:** What is the annual interest rate the lender is quoting? How long will that interest rate quote be honored? Most interest rate quotes are good for only a limited time or subject to immediate change in times when interest rates are fluctuating (especially if they're rising).
- **Points:** As we discuss earlier in this chapter (see the section "The point and interest rate tradeoff"), an interest rate quote without a quote of points is meaningless. Get the quote for points as well.
- **Fees:** Although no-fee loans exist, they're the exception. Therefore, as we highlight earlier in this chapter (see the section "Other lender fees"), ask the lender to detail any and all fees: application, processing, credit report, appraisal, notary and recording fees, and others.
- **Required down payment:** For most loans, you'll be asked for a 10 or 20 percent down payment. So be sure to ask how much down payment is required for the loan terms the lending officer is quoting. Generally speaking, the smaller the required down payment percentage, the greater the risk to the lender of losing money if you default, so the higher the interest rate and/or points you'll pay.

  As we discuss in Chapter 4, try to make at least a 20 percent cash down payment to avoid paying private mortgage insurance (PMI). The 80-10-10 financing technique we describe in Chapter 6 is another way to eliminate the need for PMI. (Most lenders, rather than thinking in terms of percentage down payments, think instead in terms of loan-to-value ratios — that is, the loan amount divided by the value of the property. For example, a lender may say that it allows an 80 percent loan-to-value ratio: That's the same as saying that it requires a down payment of 20 percent of the value of the property.)
- **Loan amount allowed:** All loan programs limit the size of the loans (the amount of money you borrow) that the terms and conditions apply to. What

good is a low interest rate and point quotation if it applies only to loan amounts smaller than you're seeking? Ask what size loans the terms apply to. Loans that are "conforming," or below certain secondary mortgage market loan amount limitations, are almost always cheaper than loans that exceed these guidelines.

- **Term (number of years):** Over how many years will the loan be repaid? Typically, a loan is for 30 years, but some are repaid over 15 years. Under unusual circumstances, other lengths of time may apply. If you need assistance deciding which mortgage period makes the best sense for you, be sure to see Chapter 5.
- **Prepayment penalties:** We strongly recommend avoiding loans with prepayment penalties, if there's any chance you'll need to sell the property during the first few years of ownership. Tell lenders upfront that you don't want to consider any loans with these costs or up to what limit you'd consider. For example, a prepayment penalty for up to three years may be acceptable if you have taken a guaranteed three-year job assignment in the area but know that you'll be moving for your next opportunity. When you discuss individual loan programs, be sure to confirm that the mortgage under consideration doesn't include prepayment penalties.
- **Assumability:** This feature allows you to pass on the remaining balance of your mortgage to a creditworthy buyer of your house. Conventional fixed-rate residential loans generally aren't assumable, but some government loans (FHA, VA) may be assumable. Commercial and multifamily residential property loans, even fixed-rate, often can be negotiated to be assumable at a fee paid by the incoming buyer. For example, upon lender approval of the creditworthiness of the buyer and payment of a 1 to 2 percent fee of the then-current loan balance, the lender will allow the commercial loan to be assumed.
- **Estimated monthly payment:** How much are you going to pay each month for your mortgage? With an ARM, be sure to know the maximum monthly loan payments that could be in your future. Ask so you'll have this vital information when you review your expected monthly housing costs (see Chapter 1).
- **Owner-occupied requirements:** Lenders have also learned that their risk is lower with residential loans on homes where the borrower is the owner-occupant. If you'll be living in the property at the time the loan is made, be sure you ask for the owner-occupied loan terms. Non-owner-occupied residential one- to four-unit loans are readily available but typically are quoted higher in interest rates (one-fourth to one-half of a percentage point).
- **Other issues discussed:** Make note of any other issues of importance you discussed with the lender. Again, your notes may come in handy if any discrepancies arise down the road.

TABLE 9-1 Comparing Fixed-Rate Mortgage Programs

Lenders' Names:				
Loan officer name, phone number, fax number, and email address				
Loan processor name, phone number, fax number, and email address				
Person interviewed				
Date interviewed				
Program name				
Interest rate				
Points				
Fees				
Application & processing				
Credit report				
Appraisal				
Notary & recording				
Other				
Loan-to-value ratio allowed				
Loan amount allowed				
Term (number of years)				
Prepayment penalties				
Assumability				
Rate lock terms				
Estimated monthly payment				

A CLOSER LOOK: RATE LOCK TERMS

Most lenders will agree to hold firm on interest rates and other terms they quote to you (usually for a 30-day period). For a nominal fee or slight interest rate increase, lenders will typically commit to hold rates and other terms firm for up to 60 to 90 days without any upfront lock fees. The obvious benefit to you is that this commitment, or *rate lock* as it's often called, provides you peace of mind and one less surprise down the road if mortgage rates suddenly skyrocket before your loan is funded.

Paying a fee for a rate lock is analogous to buying insurance. When you lock the rate, you transfer the risk of something bad happening (for example, interest rates increasing) onto the lenders, who can hedge their risk by using various financial transactions. The longer you ask for the rate to be locked, the more you will pay.

So is "buying" rate lock insurance worth the cost when you secure a mortgage? Consider that on most mortgages, a 60-day rate lock — a length of time we highly recommend — will likely end up costing you about one-eighth to one-fourth additional points. On a $200,000 mortgage, that works out to $250 to $500.

Now, that amount is nothing to disregard — after all, that kind of money could treat you to some good dinners at your favorite restaurant. However, compare that cost to the extra expense of having to pay a 0.5 percent higher ongoing interest rate over the life of a 30-year $200,000 loan if you don't lock in your rate and rates jump up. If interest rates are at 7 percent and then rise to 7.5 percent, you'd end up paying approximately $24,480 more over the life of the loan.

No one we know can accurately predict where interest rates are heading over the next few months. World events can often impact interest rates (especially negatively or upward), so you certainly have no control over the interest rate market. If you don't want the stress on yourself and your budget, better to lock in your rate when you know which loan and lender you're going to choose. Also, be sure to get a lender's rate lock terms *in writing*. Verbal assurances should be viewed as worthless.

Adjustable-rate mortgages interview worksheet

In Chapter 5, we discuss the major features and differences among the various adjustable-rate mortgages (ARMs). We also compare ARMs to fixed-rate loans. If you haven't perused that chapter yet, please do so now.

Few financial products or services are as difficult to shop for as an ARM. We're not trying to scare you but simply prepare you for the reality of the sometimes-complex issues that confront ARM shoppers.

Table 9-2 is designed to make shopping for an ARM easier on you. Taking good notes of the details of ARMs you're shopping for serves two purposes. First, you'll discover more information. Second, your notes will help you hold lenders accountable for their statements and promises. Here's a brief description of the elements in Table 9-2:

- **Contact information:** Make note of the lender's name and phone number, because you may need to call in the future, especially if it's for a loan you're likely to take. Also, some lenders are large, and you may end up having your call transferred before reaching the final destination. Be sure to ask the person you interview for her name, direct line, fax number, and email address.
- **Person interviewed:** Your relationship with a lender should be with a specific person, usually the loan officer. This may not be the first person you initially speak with, but eventually you want to have a specific person to call if you have more questions, to check the progress on your loan, to complain if things aren't moving the way you expected or would like, and to thank when you do get what you were promised.
- **Loan processor:** The loan processor handles your loan's paperwork from the time you submit your loan application until your loan is closed. The loan processor's job includes everything from conducting the credit investigation to preparing loan documents you'll sign prior to funding the mortgage. If possible, get the loan processor's name, direct phone number, fax number, and email address.
- **Date interviewed:** If discrepancies arise, your notation of dates could prove important.
- **Program name:** Most mortgage lenders give catchy and sometimes goofy names to various loan types. This jargon helps identify loans.
- **Starting interest rate:** ARMs typically start at a relatively low interest rate compared with current fixed-rate loans. So, as we note in Chapter 5, don't get seduced by a low-starting, so-called *teaser* interest rate.
- **Index used for future rate determination:** As we discuss in Chapter 5, an ARM is tied to a particular index, such as the interest rate on treasury bills or certificates of deposit. Knowing and understanding the particular index a lender uses is critical, because some indexes move more rapidly than others. You also need to know the overall trends for interest rates. Are they likely to

rise or fall over the next few years? Combined with your best estimate of how long you'll own the property, or how many years till you refinance, will have a major impact on your decision about which ARM index will work best for you.

- **Margin:** The margin is the percentage that a lender adds to the index to determine your ARM's future interest rate. This is a fixed amount but determines the interest rate you'll pay. The lower the margin, the better (with all other terms the same). So be sure to ask what the margins are on the ARMs you're considering. See Chapter 5 for more details on margins.
- **Periodic interest rate adjustment cap:** Most ARMs adjust every 6 or 12 months. A good ARM, as we discuss in Chapter 5, limits or caps the amount of the increase (typically to 2 percent per year). In addition to finding out what the adjustment cap is, also inquire about the dollar amount your monthly payment could increase to avoid surprises.
- **Lifetime interest rate adjustment cap:** A good ARM also caps the maximum interest rate allowed over the life of the loan — typically 5 to 6 percent over the loan's starting rate. In addition to understanding the highest interest rate allowed on your mortgage, also ask what that means in terms of your potential maximum monthly payment.
- **Negative amortization:** As we discuss earlier in this chapter (see the section "Negative amortization"), this situation occurs when your ARM's monthly loan payment doesn't cover all the interest you owe on the loan. In other words, your loan payment doesn't even fully pay the interest that accrued over the last month on the outstanding loan balance. As a result, the loan balance gets bigger each month, which can be financially disastrous for you. We vigorously recommend avoiding loans with this toxic feature.
- **Points:** As discussed earlier in this chapter (see the section "The point and interest rate tradeoff"), an interest rate quote without a quote of points is meaningless. Get the quote for points as well.
- **Fees:** Although no-fee loans exist, they're the exception. Therefore, as we highlight earlier in this chapter (see the section "Other lender fees"), ask the lender to detail any and all fees: application, processing, credit report, appraisal, notary and recording fees, and others.
- **Required down payment:** On most loans, you'll be asked for a 10 or 20 percent down payment. So be sure to ask how much down payment is required for the loan terms the lending officer is quoting. Generally speaking, the smaller the required down-payment percentage, the higher the interest rate and/or points you'll pay. As we discuss in Chapter 4, try to make at least a 20 percent down payment.

- **Loan amount allowed:** All loan programs limit what size loans the terms and conditions apply to. What good is a competitive interest rate and point quotation if it applies only to loan amounts smaller than what you're seeking? Always ask what size loans the terms apply to.
- **Term (number of years):** Over how many years will the loan be repaid? The typical term is 30 years, but some loans are repaid over 15, 20, or 25 years; and under unusual circumstances, other lengths of time may apply. You can literally find a lender these days that will customize your loan to your specific needs. Want a 17-year loan because that's your time frame for wanting to retire? You can likely find it. If you need assistance thinking through what length mortgage makes the most sense for you, be sure to see Chapter 5.
- **Prepayment penalties:** As discussed earlier in this chapter, we implore you to avoid loans with prepayment penalties. Tell lenders upfront that you don't want to consider loans with such costs, and when discussing individual loan programs, be sure to confirm that the mortgage(s) under discussion don't include prepayment penalties.
- **Assumability:** This feature allows you to pass on the remaining balance of your mortgage to a creditworthy buyer of your house if you both desire. Most adjustable-rate loans are assumable. However, because your house will likely have appreciated in value by the time you're ready to sell, under normal financial conditions future buyers of your property will probably be able to obtain their own financing under better terms than they'd get by assuming your loan. For one, they're likely to want to borrow more money than the current balance of your loan now. Thus, we don't think that this is a feature you should go out of your way to find as you shop for an ARM. If a loan is assumable, you may care to ask how the terms of the loan may change and whether there's a limit on the number of times the loan may be assumed.
- **Rate lock terms:** You can lock in the rate on an ARM. See the sidebar "A closer look: Rate lock terms" for a discussion of rate locks.
- **Estimated monthly payment:** With an ARM, you should inquire both how much you're going to pay each month initially and after your rate adjusts fully to the index rate for your mortgage, including knowing the absolute maximum payment that could ultimately challenge your budget. You'll want this important payment information as you review your expected monthly housing costs (see Chapter 1).
- **Other issues discussed:** Make note of any other issues of importance you discussed with the lender. Again, your notes may come in handy if any discrepancies arise down the road.

TABLE 9-2 Comparing Adjustable-Rate Mortgage Programs

Lenders' Names:				
Loan officer name, phone number, fax number, and email address				
Loan processor name, phone number, fax number, and email address				
Person interviewed				
Date interviewed				
Program name				
Starting interest rate				
Index used for future rate determination				
Margin				
Periodic interest rate cap ___ % every ___ months — monthly payment may increase $ ___ every ___ months				
Lifetime interest rate cap ___ %, which would translate into a $ ___ monthly payment				
Negative amortization				
Points				
Fees				
Application & processing				
Credit report				
Appraisal				
Notary & recording				
Other				
Loan-to-value ratio allowed				
Loan amount allowed				
Term (number of years)				
Prepayment penalties				
Assumability				
Rate lock terms				
Estimated monthly payment				
Maximum monthly payment				

Applying with One or More Lenders

If you do your homework and pick a good lender with a reputation for low rates, quality service, and honesty, applying for one mortgage should be fine.

However, you may be tempted to apply with more than one mortgage lender (or broker). That way, if your first-choice lender doesn't deliver, you have a backup. Because of the additional time and money involved in applying for more than one mortgage, we recommend that you consider doing so only under the following circumstances:

- **You have credit problems.** Applying to more than one mortgage lender may make sense if you know you have credit problems that may lead to having your loan application denied. Read Chapters 1 and 2 to whip your finances and credit record into shape before you embark on the home-buying journey.
- **You're buying a physically or legally "difficult" property.** It's impossible, of course, to know in advance all the types of property idiosyncrasies that will upset a particular lender. If you're buying a home for which you need a mortgage, reduce your chances for unpleasant surprises by asking your real estate agent and property inspector whether any aspects of the property may give a lender cause for concern. This is especially true if the property is a mixed-use property (has residential plus either commercial or retail space components) or one that is no longer consistent with current zoning. Why? If the property is severely damaged or destroyed in a fire or other disaster, the lender is concerned that local officials won't allow the property to be rebuilt to the same or better condition. If you're refinancing an existing home, you should know by now whether aspects of your property make getting a mortgage challenging.

TIP

If you end up applying for loans with two different lenders, we recommend that you tell both lenders that you're applying elsewhere and why. If you don't, when the second lender pulls your credit report, the first lender's recent inquiry will show up. Don't be surprised if you have to pay for two appraisals and two sets of credit reports. Lenders generally require their own documentation.

» Filling out the Uniform Residential Loan Application

» Understanding other documents in the process

Chapter 10
Managing Mortgage Paperwork

In this chapter, we review the forms you're commonly asked to complete in the mortgage-application process. If you're working with a skilled person at the mortgage lending or brokerage company, that person can help you navigate and beat into submission most of this dreaded paperwork.

But we know you probably have some questions about what kinds of information you're required to provide versus information you don't have to provide. You also may be uncomfortable revealing less-than-flattering facts about your situation, facts you feel may jeopardize your qualifications for a mortgage. And finally, no matter how good the mortgage person you're working with is, the burden is still on you to pull together many facts, figures, and documents. So here we are, right by your side to coach you.

Pounding the Paperwork

For a mortgage lender to make a proper assessment of your current financial situation, the lender needs details. Lots of them! Thus, mortgage lenders or brokers ask you to sign a form authorizing and permitting them to make inquiries of your employer, the financial institutions that you do business with, the Internal Revenue Service, and so on.

Mortgage lenders provide you with an incredibly lengthy list of documents that they require with mortgage applications, including the following:

- Pay stubs, typically for the most recent 30 consecutive days
- Two most recent years' W-2 forms
- Two most recent years' federal income tax returns
- Signed IRS Form 4506-T Request for Transcript of Tax Return
- Year-to-date profit-and-loss statement and current balance sheet if you're self-employed
- Copies of past two months' bank, money market, and investment account statements
- Recent statements for all outstanding mortgages
- Copy of current declarations pages for homeowners insurance policies in force
- Home purchase contract (if you're financing to buy a home)
- Rental agreements for all rental properties
- Divorce decrees
- Federal corporate tax returns for the past two years
- Partnership federal tax returns for the past two years
- Partnership K-1s for the last two years
- Condo or homeowners association documentation — such as CC&Rs, (covenants, conditions, and restrictions) bylaws, articles of incorporation, budget, reserve study, current regular assessment amount owed, if any, special assessments due now or approved for the future, if any, contact name, address, and phone number
- Title report, abstract, and survey
- Property inspection report and pest control inspection report (if you're buying a home)
- Gift letter — the source of any funds being used toward your down payment must sign indicating that these funds are a "gift" and are not required to be repaid
- Receipts for deposits (if you're buying a home)

Don't despair at the length of the list. This list covers all possible situations, so some of the items won't apply to you.

Still, you may rightfully ask, "Why do lenders require so much information?"

Most of the items on this laundry list are required to prove and substantiate your current financial status to the mortgage lender and, subsequently, to other organizations that may buy your loan in the future in the secondary mortgage market. Pay stubs, tax returns, and bank- and investment-account statements help to document your income and assets. Lenders assess the risk of lending you money and determine how much they can lend you based on these items.

If you're wondering why lenders can't take your word about the personal and confidential financial facts and figures, remember that some people don't tell the truth. Lenders have no way of knowing who is honest and who isn't. The unfortunate reality is that lenders have to assume that all their loan applicants may lie given the opportunity.

Even though lenders require all this myriad documentation, some buyers still falsify information. And some mortgage brokers, in their quest to close more loans and earn more commissions, even coach buyers to lie to qualify for a loan. One example of the way people cheat: Some self-employed people create bogus tax returns with inflated incomes. Although a few people have gotten away with such deception, we don't recommend this wayward path. Also, lenders have become smarter, too, and now typically rely only on tax returns that they receive directly from the IRS or the state taxing authority.

If you can't qualify for a mortgage without resorting to trickery, getting turned down is for your own good. Lenders have criteria to ensure that you'll be able to repay the money you borrow and that you don't get in over your head.

WARNING

Falsifying loan documents is committing perjury — and fraud is *not* in your best interests, even if you won't get impeached for it. Mortgage lenders can catch you in your lies. How? Well, some mortgage lenders have you sign IRS Form 4506-T (Request for Transcript of Tax Return) — typically at the time you submit your loan application — that allows them to request *directly from the IRS* copies of the actual tax returns that you filed with the IRS.

Besides the obvious legal objections, lying on your mortgage application can lead to your having more mortgage debt than you can really afford. If you're short on a down payment, for example, alternatives are available (see Chapter 2). If the down payment isn't a problem but you lack the income to qualify for the loan, check out loans known as "No Doc" or NIVs (no income verification) or stated income loans that don't require documentation of income. Also, see Chapter 2 for other ideas on overcoming low income or credit problems.

Filling Out the Uniform Residential Loan Application

U.S. mortgage lenders and brokers use the Uniform Residential Loan Application to collect needed data about home purchases and proposed loans. Many lenders use this standardized document, known in the mortgage trade as *Form 1003*, because they sell their mortgages to investors. When mortgage loans are resold, government organizations called *Fannie Mae* and *Freddie Mac* agree (if the mortgage loans meet federal standards) to guarantee the repayment of principal and interest, which makes it easier for lenders to sell the loans and more desirable for investors to buy them.

Some mortgage lenders may expect you to complete this form on your own. Other lenders and brokers help you fill out the form or even go so far as to complete it for you.

If you let someone fill out the Uniform Residential Loan Application for you, be *sure* the information on the form is accurate and truthful. Ultimately, *you're* responsible for the accuracy and truthfulness of your application. Also be aware that, in their sales efforts, some mortgage lenders and brokers may invite you to their offices or invite themselves to your home or office to complete this form for you or with you. Although we have no problem with good service, we do want you to keep in mind that you're not beholden or obligated to any lenders or brokers. It's your money and your home purchase, so — as we discuss in Chapter 7 — be sure to shop around for a good loan officer or mortgage broker.

In the following sections, we explain the major elements on the Uniform Residential Loan Application.

1. Borrower information

This section of the loan application (see Figure 10-1) is where you begin to provide personal information about yourself as well as any co-borrower you're buying with or currently own the property with. You also detail your employment and income sources in this lengthy and important section.

To be completed by the **Lender:**
Lender Loan No./Universal Loan Identifier ______________ Agency Case No. ______________

Uniform Residential Loan Application

Verify and complete the information on this application. If you are applying for this loan with others, each additional Borrower must provide information as directed by your Lender.

Section 1: Borrower Information.
This section asks about your personal information and your income from employment and other sources, such as retirement, that you want considered to qualify for this loan.

1a. Personal Information

Name *(First, Middle, Last, Suffix)*

Alternate Names – *List any names by which you are known or any names under which credit was previously received (First, Middle, Last, Suffix)*

Social Security Number ______-____-______
(or Individual Taxpayer Identification Number)

Date of Birth *(mm/dd/yyyy)* ____/____/______

O **U.S. Citizen**
O **Permanent Resident Alien**
O **Non-Permanent Resident Alien**

O I am applying for **individual credit.**
O I am applying for **joint credit.** Total Number of Borrowers: ______
Each Borrower intends to apply for joint credit. ***Your initials:*** ______

List Name(s) of Other Borrower(s) Applying for this Loan *(First, Middle, Last, Suffix)*

Marital Status
O Married
O Separated
O Unmarried*
**Single, Divorced, Widowed, Civil Union, Domestic Partnership, Registered Reciprocal Beneficiary Relationship*

Dependents *(not listed by another Borrower)*
Number ______
Ages ______

Contact Information
Home Phone (___) ___-_____
Cell Phone (___) ___-_____
Work Phone (___) ___-_____ **Ext.** ______
Email ______

Current Address
Street ______ Unit # ______
City ______ State ______ Zip ______ Country ______
How Long at Current Address? ____ Years ____ Months O Own O Rent ($ ______ /month) O No primary housing expense

If at Current Address for LESS than 2 years, list Former Address ☐ ***Does not apply***
Street ______ Unit # ______
City ______ State ______ Zip ______ Country ______
How Long at Former Address? ____ Years ____ Months O Own O Rent ($ ______ /month) O No primary housing expense

Mailing Address – *if different from Current Address* ☐ ***Does not apply***
Street ______ Unit # ______
City ______ State ______ Zip ______ Country ______

Military Service – Did you (or your deceased spouse) ever serve, or are you currently serving, in the United States Armed Forces? O**NO** O**YES**
If YES, check all that apply:
☐ Currently serving on active duty with projected expiration date of service/tour ____/______ *(mm/yyyy)*
☐ Currently retired, discharged, or separated from service
☐ Only period of service was as a non-activated member of the Reserve or National Guard
☐ Surviving spouse

FIGURE 10-1: The first part of Section 1 summarizes your personal information.

The lender also wants to know where you've been living recently. If you've been in your most recent housing situation for at least two years, you don't need to list your prior residence. Lenders are primarily looking for stability here. Most lenders also request a letter from your landlord to verify that you've paid your rent in a timely fashion. If you've moved frequently in recent years, most lenders check with previous landlords. If your application is on the borderline, good references can tip the scales in your favor. If you've paid the amount you owed on time, you should be fine. If you haven't, you should explain yourself, either by separate letter to the lender or in the blank space on Page 4 of the application.

Your recent work history is important to a mortgage lender (Figure 10-2). Unless you're financially independent (wealthy) already, your lender knows that your employment income determines your ability to meet your monthly housing costs. As with your prior housing situation, lenders seek borrowers with stability, which can help push a marginal application through the loan-approval channels. To lenders, recent stability of the borrower in where he lives, where he works, and the source and amount of his income translates into predictability or future stability, which results in lower risk.

1b. Current Employment/Self Employment and Income ☐ *Does not apply*

Employer or Business Name ________ Phone (____)____-______
Address ________
City ________ State ____ Zip ________

Position or Title ________
Start Date ____/______ *(mm/yyyy)*
How long in this line of work? ____ Years ____ Months

Check if this statement applies:
☐ I am employed by a family member, property seller, real estate agent, or other party to the transaction.

☐ **Check if you are the Business Owner or Self-Employed** ○ I have an ownership share of less than 25%. ○ I have an ownership share of 25% or more. **Monthly Income (or Loss)** $ ________

Gross Monthly Income
Base $________/month
Overtime $________/month
Bonus $________/month
Commission $________/month
Military Entitlements $________/month
Other $________/month
TOTAL $________ **/month**

1c. IF APPLICABLE, Complete Information for Additional Employment/Self Employment and Income ☐ *Does not apply*

Employer or Business Name ________ Phone (____)____-______
Address ________
City ________ State ____ Zip ________

Position or Title ________
Start Date ____/______ *(mm/yyyy)*
How long in this line of work? ____ Years ____ Months

Check if this statement applies:
☐ I am employed by a family member, property seller, real estate agent, or other party to the transaction.

☐ **Check if you are the Business Owner or Self-Employed** ○ I have an ownership share of less than 25%. ○ I have an ownership share of 25% or more. **Monthly Income (or Loss)** $ ________

Gross Monthly Income
Base $________/month
Overtime $________/month
Bonus $________/month
Commission $________/month
Military Entitlements $________/month
Other $________/month
TOTAL $________ **/month**

1d. Previous Employment/Self-Employment and Income ONLY IF your Current Employment is LESS than 2 years. ☐ *Does not apply*

Employer or Business Name ________
Address ________
City ________ State ____ Zip ________
Position or Title ________
Start Date ____/____ *(mm/yyyy)* **End Date** ____/____ *(mm/yyyy)*

☐ **Check if you were the Business Owner or Self-Employed**

Previous Gross Monthly Income
$________

© Fannie Mae, Freddie Mac. Reprinted with permission.

FIGURE 10-2: The middle part of Section 1 details your employment.

If you've held your recent job for at least the past two years, that's the only position you need to list (unless you currently work more than one job, in which case you should list all current jobs separately). Otherwise, you must list your prior employment to cover the past two-year period.

We know that, in this ever-changing economy, some people change jobs fairly frequently and not always out of personal choice. Perhaps you've held a position for only a few months (or less) and feel it would make your loan application look more attractive to simply leave the position off your forms. Others, who have had gaps in their employment, either because they took advantage of changing jobs to engage in other activities or because it took some time to find a suitable new position, may be tempted to discreetly gloss over gaps in employment.

TIP

What do we advise? Well, our overall perspective is that a mortgage application is somewhat like a résumé. You should absolutely present your information in a positive and truthful way. It's better to show the employment gap than to have the lenders uncover it, which they can do because they often ask for the dates of your employment when verifying information with your employers.

As for leaving off a short-term or part-time job, the choice is up to you. This section of the application doesn't state that you must list every position.

Remember that lenders don't mind some job hopping. If they see frequent job changes, then the *prospects for continued employment* section of the *verification-of-employment request* that your current employer receives from the lender will be more important.

This section of the application also asks that you list the monthly income from prior jobs. You don't provide your monthly income from your current job here because it's provided in the next section of the application.

You may also wonder (and be concerned about) why the lender wants your current and previous employers' phone numbers. Shortly before your loan is ready to close, the lender may call your current employer to verify that you're still employed, but verification of employment is usually done through current pay stubs and W-2s.

It's highly unlikely that lenders will call your previous employers unless they need to verify an outstanding question about employment dates or similar information.

If you have other income sources, such as child support or alimony, list and describe them in the last portion of this section (see Figure 10-3). The more income you can list, the more likely you are to qualify for a mortgage with the most favorable terms for you. (To ensure that you "get credit" for child support or alimony payments received, you must be able to prove receipt of the funds. This requirement can get sticky because the ex-spouse may be asked to provide a canceled check. See, there's a good reason to remain on good terms with your ex.)

1e. Income from Other Sources ☐ ***Does not apply***

Include income from other sources below. Under Income Source, choose from the sources listed here:

• Alimony	• Child Support	• Interest and Dividends	• Mortgage Differential Payments	• Royalty Payments	• Unemployment Benefits
• Automobile Allowance	• Disability	• Notes Receivable	• Retirement (*e.g., Pension, IRA*)	• Separate Maintenance	• VA Compensation
• Boarder Income	• Foster Care	• Public Assistance		• Social Security	• Other
• Capital Gains	• Housing or Parsonage	• Mortgage Credit Certificate		• Trust	

NOTE: *Reveal alimony, child support, separate maintenance, or other income ONLY IF you want it considered in determining your qualification for this loan.*

Income Source – *use list above*	**Monthly Income**
	$
	$
	$
Provide TOTAL Amount Here	**$**

© Fannie Mae, Freddie Mac. Reprinted with permission.

FIGURE 10-3: The last part of Section 1 details your other (non-employment) income sources.

2. Financial information — assets and liabilities

In Section 2 (see Figure 10-4), you present your personal balance sheet, which summarizes your assets and liabilities. Your *assets* include bank checking and savings accounts, money market funds, retirement accounts, and other accounts you have.

Section 2: Financial Information — Assets and Liabilities. This section asks about things you own that are worth money and that you want considered to qualify for this loan. It then asks about your liabilities (or debts) that you pay each month, such as credit cards, alimony, or other expenses.

2a. Assets – Bank Accounts, Retirement, and Other Accounts You Have

Include all accounts below. Under Account Type, choose from the account types listed here:

- Checking
- Savings
- Money Market
- Certificate of Deposit
- Mutual Fund
- Stocks
- Stock Options
- Bonds
- Retirement (*e.g., 401k, IRA*)
- Bridge Loan Proceeds
- Individual Development Account
- Trust Account
- Cash Value of Life Insurance (*used for the transaction*)

Account Type – *use list above*	**Financial Institution**	**Account Number**	**Cash or Market Value**
			$
			$
			$
			$
			$
		Provide TOTAL Amount Here	**$**

2b. Other Assets You Have ☐ ***Does not apply***

Include all other assets below. Under Asset Type, choose from the asset types listed here:

- Earnest Money
- Proceeds from Sale of Non-Real Estate Asset
- Proceeds from Real Estate Property to be sold on or before closing
- Sweat Equity
- Employer Assistance
- Rent Credit
- Secured Borrowed Funds
- Trade Equity
- Unsecured Borrowed Funds
- Other

Asset Type – *use list above*	**Cash or Market Value**
	$
	$
	$
Provide TOTAL Amount Here	**$**

2c. Liabilities – Credit Cards, Other Debts, and Leases that You Owe ☐ ***Does not apply***

List all liabilities below (except real estate) and include deferred payments. Under Account Type, choose from the types listed here:

- Revolving (*e.g., credit cards*)
- Installment (*e.g., car, student, personal loans*)
- Open 30-Day (*balance paid monthly*)
- Lease (*not real estate*)
- Other

Account Type – *use list above*	**Company Name**	**Account Number**	**Unpaid Balance**	*To be paid off at or before closing*	**Monthly Payment**
			$	☐	$
			$	☐	$
			$	☐	$
			$	☐	$
			$	☐	$

2d. Other Liabilities and Expenses ☐ ***Does not apply***

Include all other liabilities and expenses below. Choose from the types listed here:

- Alimony
- Child Support
- Separate Maintenance
- Job Related Expenses
- Other

	Monthly Payment
	$
	$
	$

FIGURE 10-4: Section 2 asks for what you have and what you owe.

Liabilities are any loans or debts you have outstanding. The more of these financial obligations you have, the more unwilling a mortgage lender is to lend you a large amount of money.

If you have the cash available to pay off high-cost consumer loans, such as credit card and charge card balances and auto or other consumer loans, consider doing so now (note the box you can check off indicating you intend to pay off certain loans before closing). These debts generally carry high interest rates that aren't tax deductible, and they hurt your chances of qualifying for a mortgage (see Chapters 2 and 3 for an explanation of this matter). When paying off credit cards (revolving accounts), we suggest not closing them without first discussing it with your loan officer. Closing accounts can hurt your credit score in the short term.

Note (in the last part of this section) that you are to list child support and alimony payments that you make as well as out-of-pocket expenses related to your job if you aren't self-employed. These monthly expenses are like debts in the sense that they require monthly feeding.

3. Financial information — real estate

Section 3 (see Figure 10-5) continues over onto Page 4 and includes space for the details of real estate you already own. If you still own a home and are trying to sell it or have an offer on it but that transaction is pending, you should list that property in this section. This is where you also include any second home or rental income properties.

If you make a profit from such holdings, that profit can help your chances of qualifying for other mortgages. Conversely, *negative cash flow* (property expenses exceeding income) from rentals reduces the amount that a mortgage lender will lend you. Most mortgage lenders want a copy of your tax return (and possibly copies of your rental agreements with tenants) to substantiate the information you enter in this space. Investment real estate is often owned in separate legal entities for tax and reduced liability purposes, so be prepared to provide your personal tax return, including the IRS form 1065 (Schedule K-1) for each of your real estate holdings.

Net monthly rental income (which lenders now calculate) refers to the difference between your rental real estate's monthly rents and expenses (excluding depreciation). *Rental property* is any property that you've bought for the purpose of renting it out. Therefore, *net monthly rental income* is the profit or loss that you make each month on rental property (excluding depreciation). If you've recently purchased the rental property, the lender counts only 75 percent of the current rent that you're collecting. If you've held your rental property long enough to complete a tax return, most lenders use the profit or loss (excluding depreciation) reported on your tax return.

Section 3: Financial Information — Real Estate. This section asks you to list all properties you currently own and what you owe on them. ☐ ***I do not own any real estate***

3a. Property You Own **If you are refinancing, list the property you are refinancing FIRST.**

Address
Street ______ Unit # ______ City ______ State ______ Zip ______

Property Value	Status: Sold, Pending Sale, or Retained	Monthly Insurance, Taxes, Association Dues, etc. Not Included in Mortgage Payment	For Investment Property Only: Monthly Rental Income	For Investment Property Only: For LENDER to Calculate: Net Monthly Rental Income
$		$	$	$

Mortgage Loans on this Property ☐ ***Does not apply***

Creditor Name	Account Number	Monthly Mortgage Payment	Unpaid Balance	*To be paid off at or before closing*	Type: FHA, VA, Conventional, USDA-RD, Other	Credit Limit *(if applicable)*
		$	$	☐		$
		$	$	☐		$

3b. IF APPLICABLE, Complete Information for Additional Property ☐ ***Does not apply***

Address
Street ______ Unit # ______ City ______ State ______ Zip ______

Property Value	Status: Sold, Pending Sale, or Retained	Monthly Insurance, Taxes, Association Dues, etc. Not Included in Mortgage Payment	For Investment Property Only: Monthly Rental Income	For Investment Property Only: For LENDER to Calculate: Net Monthly Rental Income
$		$	$	$

Mortgage Loans on this Property ☐ ***Does not apply***

Creditor Name	Account Number	Monthly Mortgage Payment	Unpaid Balance	*To be paid off at or before closing*	Type: FHA, VA, Conventional, USDA-RD, Other	Credit Limit *(if applicable)*
		$	$	☐		$
		$	$	☐		$

FIGURE 10-5: Section 3 has you list real estate you already own.

4. Loan and property information

The information you include in the *Loan purpose* section (see Figure 10-6) indicates to the lender whether you plan to use the mortgage to buy a home, refinance an existing loan, or something else like construct a new home. Mortgage lenders and the investors who ultimately buy these types of mortgages want to know why you want to borrow money. So, in this section, you provide the address and the property value (usually the purchase price if you're buying the home).

The lender also wants to know whether the property is your primary or secondary residence or is an investment property (in this section, you also estimate expected rental income). Your answers to these questions determine which loans your property is eligible for and the terms of the loans. From a lender's perspective, construction loans (which are usually short-term loans) and investment-property loans are riskier and therefore cost you more than other loans.

Section 4: Loan and Property Information. This section asks about the loan's purpose and the property you want to purchase or refinance.

4a. Loan and Property Information

Loan Amount $ ______ **Loan Purpose** ○ Purchase ○ Refinance ○ Other ______

Property Address Street ______
Unit # ______ City ______ State ______ Zip ______
County ______ Number of Units ______ **Property Value** $ ______

Occupancy ○ Primary Residence ○ Second Home ○ Investment Property ○ FHA Secondary Residence

1. Mixed-Use Property. If you will occupy the property, will you set aside space within the property to operate your own business? *(e.g., daycare facility, medical office, beauty/barber shop)* ○ NO ○ YES

2. Manufactured Home. Is the property a manufactured home? *(e.g., a factory built dwelling built on a permanent chassis)* ○ NO ○ YES

4b. Other New Mortgage Loans on the Property You are Buying or Refinancing ☐ *Does not apply*

Creditor Name	Lien Type	Monthly Payment	Loan Amount/ Amount to be Drawn	Credit Limit *(if applicable)*
	○ First Lien ○ Subordinate Lien	$	$	$

4c. Rental Income on the Property You Want to Purchase **For Purchase Only** ☐ *Does not apply*

Complete if the property is a 2-4 Unit Primary Residence or an Investment Property	Amount
Expected Monthly Rental Income	$
For LENDER to Calculate: Expected Net Monthly Rental Income	$

4d. Gifts or Grants You Have Been Given or Will Receive for this Loan ☐ *Does not apply*

Include all gifts and grants below. Under Source, choose from the sources listed here:
• Relative • Unmarried Partner • Employer • Religious Nonprofit • Community Nonprofit • Federal Agency • State Agency • Local Agency • Other

Asset Type *(Cash Gift, Gift of Equity, Grant)*		Source – *use list above*	Cash or Market Value
	○ Deposited ○ Not Deposited		$
	○ Deposited ○ Not Deposited		$

FIGURE 10-6: Section 4 details the purpose of your loan and how you plan on using the property.

WARNING

You may be tempted (and some mortgage brokers and lender representatives have also been tempted) to lie on this part of the mortgage application to obtain more favorable loan terms. Be aware that lenders can — and sometimes do — challenge you to prove that you're going to live in the property if they suspect otherwise. Even after closing on a purchase and their loan, lenders have been known to ask for proof — such as a copy of a utility bill in your name — that you're living in the property. Some lenders have even been known to send a representative around to knock on the borrower's door to see who's living in the property. (Lender's only really require proof of owner-occupancy at the time of the loan closing and possibly a short time thereafter, but they don't care if months later the borrower relocates and uses the property as an income property.)

To ensure that the money for your down payment and closing costs isn't coming from another loan that may ultimately overburden your ability to repay the money they're lending you, mortgage lenders want to know the source of funds for your down payment and closing costs. Ideally, lenders want to see the down payment and closing costs coming from your personal savings. Tell the truth — lenders have many ways to trip you up in your lies here. For example, they ask to see the last several months of your bank or investment account statements to verify, for example, that someone else, such as a benevolent relative, didn't give you the money last week.

TIP

If you're receiving money from a relative as a gift to be used toward the down payment, have the gift giver write a short note (your broker/lender can provide a standardized gift letter) confirming that the money is indeed a present that you do *not* have to repay. Lenders are often suspicious that such payments are loans that must be repaid and that will add to your debt burden and risk of default. But in recent years, it has become so much more difficult for younger people to buy homes that it's quite common for parents and relatives to offer "no repayment required" funds to family members seeking to purchase their first condo or starter home.

5. Declarations

Figure 10-7 shows what this section looks like. Many of these questions are potential red flags to lenders or designed to see whether you're giving answers consistent with the rest of your application.

If one of your answers in this section is likely to raise a red flag, then be sure to attach an explanation that honestly provides lenders with the background and details so they understand whether any negative situations were likely unusual or one-time events. Often showing how you dealt with unexpected challenges in life head-on, without making excuses, can be a positive aspect in the overall evaluation of your loan application.

6. Acknowledgments and agreements

If you haven't been honest on this form, here's your last chance to rethink what you're doing (see Figure 10-8). Remember, these days with the advent of "big data" and electronic records for everything we do financially, there is no such thing as getting away with misleading or lying in your loan application. The best policy is full and complete disclosure and transparency. Lenders know that almost everyone has one or more issues with his credit or employment or living situations, so be upfront and offer any details that may give lenders a comfort level with what happened and why you're a good risk for the pending loan.

Section 5: Declarations. This section asks you specific questions about the property, your funding, and your past financial history.

5a. About this Property and Your Money for this Loan

A. Will you occupy the property as your primary residence? If YES, have you had an ownership interest in another property in the last three years? If YES, complete (1) and (2) below: (1) What type of property did you own: primary residence (PR), FHA secondary residence (SR), second home (SH), or investment property (IP)? (2) How did you hold title to the property: by yourself (S), jointly with your spouse (SP), or jointly with another person (O)	○NO ○YES ○NO ○YES ________ ________
B. If this is a Purchase Transaction: Do you have a family relationship or business affiliation with the seller of the property?	○NO ○YES
C. Are you borrowing any money for this real estate transaction (*e.g., money for your closing costs or down payment*) or obtaining any money from another party, such as the seller or realtor, that you have not disclosed on this loan application? If YES, what is the amount of this money?	○NO ○YES $________
D. 1. Have you or will you be applying for a mortgage loan on another property (not the property securing this loan) on or before closing this transaction that is not disclosed on this loan application? 2. Have you or will you be applying for any new credit (*e.g., installment loan, credit card, etc.*) on or before closing this loan that is not disclosed on this application?	○NO ○YES ○NO ○YES
E. Will this property be subject to a lien that could take priority over the first mortgage lien, such as a clean energy lien paid through your property taxes (*e.g., the Property Assessed Clean Energy Program*)?	○NO ○YES

5b. About Your Finances

F. Are you a co-signer or guarantor on any debt or loan that is not disclosed on this application?	○NO ○YES
G. Are there any outstanding judgments against you?	○NO ○YES
H. Are you currently delinquent or in default on a federal debt?	○NO ○YES
I. Are you a party to a lawsuit in which you potentially have any personal financial liability?	○NO ○YES
J. Have you conveyed title to any property in lieu of foreclosure in the past 7 years?	○NO ○YES
K. Within the past 7 years, have you completed a pre-foreclosure sale or short sale, whereby the property was sold to a third party and the Lender agreed to accept less than the outstanding mortgage balance due?	○NO ○YES
L. Have you had property foreclosed upon in the last 7 years?	○NO ○YES
M. Have you declared bankruptcy within the past 7 years? If YES, identify the type(s) of bankruptcy: ☐ Chapter 7 ☐ Chapter 11 ☐ Chapter 12 ☐ Chapter 13	○NO ○YES

© Fannie Mae, Freddie Mac. Reprinted with permission.

FIGURE 10-7: Declare yourself in Section 5; watch out for the red flags.

If you've had a mortgage broker (or anyone else) help you with this application, be sure to review the answers he provided for accuracy before you sign the agreement. Now is the time to ask yourself questions (and to review your responses) to ensure that you've presented your information in a positive but truthful light.

Section 6: Acknowledgments and Agreements. This section tells you about your legal obligations when you sign this application.

Acknowledgments and Agreements

I agree to, acknowledge, and represent the following statements to:

- The Lender (this includes the Lender's agents, service providers and any of their successors and assigns); AND
- Other Loan Participants (this includes any actual or potential owners of a loan resulting from this application (the "Loan"), or acquirers of any beneficial or other interest in the Loan, any mortgage insurer, guarantor, any servicers or service providers of the Loan, and any of their successors and assigns).

By signing below, I agree to, acknowledge, and represent the following statements about:

(1) The Complete Information for this Application

- The information I have provided in this application is true, accurate, and complete as of the date I signed this application.
- If the information I submitted changes or I have new information before closing of the Loan, I must change and supplement this application or any real estate sales contract, including providing any updated/supplemented real estate sales contract.
- For purchase transactions: The terms and conditions of any real estate sales contract signed by me in connection with this application are true, accurate, and complete to the best of my knowledge and belief. I have not entered into any other agreement, written or oral, in connection with this real estate transaction.
- The Lender and Other Loan Participants may rely on the information contained in the application before and after closing of the Loan.
- Any intentional or negligent misrepresentation of information may result in the imposition of:
  (a) civil liability on me, including monetary damages, if a person suffers any loss because the person relied on any misrepresentation that I have made on this application, and/or
  (b) criminal penalties on me including, but not limited to, fine or imprisonment or both under the provisions of federal law (18 U.S.C. §§ 1001 *et seq.*).

(2) The Property's Security

- The Loan I have applied for in this application will be secured by a mortgage or deed of trust which provides the Lender a security interest in the property described in this application.

(3) The Property's Appraisal, Value, and Condition

- Any appraisal or value of the property obtained by the Lender is for use by the Lender and Other Loan Participants.
- The Lender and Other Loan Participants have not made any representation or warranty, express or implied, to me about the property, its condition, or its value.

(4) Electronic Records and Signatures

- The Lender and Other Loan Participants may keep any paper record and/or electronic record of this application, whether or not the Loan is approved.
- If this application is created as (or converted into) an "electronic application", I consent to the use of "electronic records" and "electronic signatures" as the terms are defined in and governed by applicable federal and/or state electronic transactions laws.
- I intend to sign and have signed this application either using my: (a) electronic signature; or (b) a written signature and agree that if a paper version of this application is converted into an electronic application, the application will be an electronic record, and the representation of my written signature on this application will be my binding electronic signature.
- I agree that the application, if delivered or transmitted to the Lender or Other Loan Participants as an electronic record with my electronic signature, will be as effective and enforceable as a paper application signed by me in writing.

(5) Delinquency

- The Lender and Other Loan Participants may report information about my account to credit bureaus. Late payments, missed payments, or other defaults on my account may be reflected in my credit report and will likely affect my credit score.
- If I have trouble making my payments I understand that I may contact a HUD-approved housing counseling organization for advice about actions I can take to meet my mortgage obligations.

(6) Use and Sharing of Information

I understand and acknowledge that the Lender and Other Loan Participants can obtain, use, and share the loan application, a consumer credit report, and related documentation for purposes permitted by applicable laws.

Borrower Signature ______________________ Date *(mm/dd/yyyy)* ____/____/______

Borrower Signature ______________________ Date *(mm/dd/yyyy)* ____/____/______

FIGURE 10-8: Honesty counts in Section 6.

7. Demographic information

You may refuse to answer the questions in this section (see Figure 10-9) if you want to — this information isn't required.

The federal government tracks the ethnicity and gender of borrowers to see (among other things) whether lenders discriminate against certain people.

Section 7: Demographic Information. This section asks about your ethnicity, sex, and race.

Demographic Information of Borrower

The purpose of collecting this information is to help ensure that all applicants are treated fairly and that the housing needs of communities and neighborhoods are being fulfilled. For residential mortgage lending, federal law requires that we ask applicants for their demographic information (ethnicity, sex, and race) in order to monitor our compliance with equal credit opportunity, fair housing, and home mortgage disclosure laws. You are not required to provide this information, but are encouraged to do so. **The law provides that we may not discriminate** on the basis of this information, or on whether you choose to provide it. However, if you choose not to provide the information and you have made this application in person, federal regulations require us to note your ethnicity, sex, and race on the basis of visual observation or surname. The law also provides that we may not discriminate on the basis of age or marital status information you provide in this application.
Instructions: You may select one or more "Hispanic or Latino" origins and one or more designations for "Race." If you do not wish to provide some or all of this information, select the applicable check box.

Ethnicity
☐ Hispanic or Latino
☐ Mexican ☐ Puerto Rican ☐ Cuban
☐ Other Hispanic or Latino – *Enter origin:*
Examples: Argentinean, Colombian, Dominican, Nicaraguan, Salvadoran, Spaniard, etc.
☐ Not Hispanic or Latino
☐ I do not wish to provide this information

Sex
☐ Female
☐ Male
☐ I do not wish to provide this information

Race
☐ American Indian or Alaska Native – *Enter name of enrolled or principal tribe:*
☐ Asian
☐ Asian Indian ☐ Chinese ☐ Filipino
☐ Japanese ☐ Korean ☐ Vietnamese
☐ Other Asian – *Enter race:*
Examples: Hmong, Laotian, Thai, Pakistani, Cambodian, etc.
☐ Black or African American
☐ Native Hawaiian or Other Pacific Islander
☐ Native Hawaiian ☐ Guamanian or Chamorro ☐ Samoan
☐ Other Pacific Islander – *Enter race:*
Examples: Fijian, Tongan, etc.
☐ White
☐ I do not wish to provide this information

To Be Completed by Financial Institution (*for application taken in person*):

Was the ethnicity of the Borrower collected on the basis of visual observation or surname? ○ NO ○ YES
Was the sex of the Borrower collected on the basis of visual observation or surname? ○ NO ○ YES
Was the race of the Borrower collected on the basis of visual observation or surname? ○ NO ○ YES

The Demographic Information was provided through:

☐ Face-to-Face Interview (*includes Electronic Media w/ Video Component*) ☐ Telephone Interview ☐ Fax or Mail ☐ Email or Internet

FIGURE 10-9: Section 7 is used to track discrimination.

Introducing Other Typical Documents

All mortgage lenders and brokers have their own, individualized package of documents for you to complete. The following sections introduce some of the other common forms that you're likely to encounter.

Your right to receive a copy of the appraisal

It wasn't always the case, but you now have the right to receive a copy of the appraisal report if you paid for it. To make sure you know this, the government requires that mortgage lenders and brokers give you a written notice of your right to receive a copy of the appraisal report. (See Figure 10-10.)

FORM C-9—DISCLOSURE OF RIGHT TO RECEIVE A COPY OF AN APPRAISAL

APPLICATION NO:

PROPERTY ADDRESS:

You have the right to a copy of the appraisal report used in connection with your application for credit. If you wish to receive a copy, please write to us at the mailing address we have provided. We must hear from you no later than 90 days after we notify you about the action taken on your credit application or you withdraw your application.

In your letter, give us the following information:

____________________ (Applicant) (Date) ____________________ (Applicant) (Date)

____________________ (Applicant) (Date) ____________________ (Applicant) (Date)

FIGURE 10-10: This form outlines your rights to receive a copy of the appraisal.

Despite the fact that the notice tells you to make your request in writing, try making the request verbally to save yourself time. Then, if your request is ignored, go to the hassle of submitting a written request for your appraisal (within 90 days of the rendering of a decision to approve or reject your loan). Appraisals are good to have in your files — you never know when an appraisal may come in handy. At the very least, you can see what properties were used as comparables to yours to discover how good or bad the appraisal is.

Having an appraisal handy could be very helpful in the future if you ever feel that your property value has declined and your property taxes are based on a formula that relies on the current value of your home. Again, looking at those comparable properties used in the original appraisal and learning that they recently resold for a lower price than the property tax assessor claims your home is currently worth can be a great basis to appeal your property taxes.

Also, having the details of your home (lot size, square footage, amenities, and so on) handy in that appraisal can help you find other properties that may have recently sold in your area for lower prices and therefore are invaluable because the tax assessor will want you to prove that the stated value of your home should be lower for property tax calculation purposes.

Equal Credit Opportunity Act

It is a matter of federal law that a mortgage lender may not reject your loan because of nonfinancial personal characteristics such as race, gender, marital status, age, and so forth. You also don't have to disclose income (alimony) that you receive as a result of being divorced. (We think, however, that disclosing such income is in your best interests, because that income may help get your loan approved.)

If you have reason to believe that a mortgage lender is discriminating against you, contact and file a complaint with the state department of financial institutions, Department or Bureau of Real Estate, or whatever government division regulates mortgage lenders in your state. And start hunting around for a better, more ethical lender.

4
Profiting from Smart Mortgage Strategies

IN THIS PART . . .

Check out the many benefits of refinancing a mortgage.

Discover how you can pay off your mortgage faster and why you'd want to do so.

Find out how you can get your lender to send you money through a reverse mortgage.

» Restructuring your mortgage

» Understanding cash-out refinances

» Expediting your refinance

» Dealing with borrower's remorse

Chapter 11
Refinancing Your Mortgage

Many people imagine a mystical, esoteric difference between the mortgage used to purchase a home and a refinance *(refi)* loan. In 30 seconds or less, depending on how quickly you read, you'll know where their collective trains of thought went off the fiscal track.

In terms of principal, interest, loan term, amortization, security instruments, and all the other fascinating stuff we cover in Chapter 4, you can't find any difference between purchase and refi mortgages. And even though Chapter 5 ostensibly pertains to home purchase mortgages, everything we say about the advantages and disadvantages of fixed-rate loans versus adjustable-rate mortgages applies equally well to refinance loans. Last but not least, the financing expenses and fees we detail in Chapter 9 evenhandedly increase the cost of obtaining purchase mortgages and refi loans.

REMEMBER

The sole distinction between a purchase loan and a refinance mortgage is whether a change of property ownership occurs during the financial transaction. When you purchased your dream home, ownership of the house transferred from the seller to you. On the other hand, no change of ownership occurs when you subsequently opt to replace your existing mortgage with a new one. This chapter focuses on the strategic uses of a refi.

Refinancing Rationales

You're probably not going to refinance the mortgage on your house because you suddenly developed an insatiable urge to generate enormous loan fees for your friendly neighborhood lending institution. Here are three far more sensible reasons to refinance your mortgage:

- **To cut costs:** "A penny saved is a penny earned," is every bit as true today as it was in Ben Franklin's time, but why stop with a few lousy pennies? Think big. Lowering your monthly loan payment by replacing your present mortgage with a new one that offers a lower interest rate could save you tens of thousands of dollars over your new loan's term.
- **To restructure your financing:** Slashing your monthly mortgage payment isn't the only reason to refinance. In fact, you may need to refinance even if the new loan won't save you one red cent. For instance, suppose you have a short-term balloon loan (see Chapter 6) coming due soon that you *must* replace with long-term financing. Or maybe you want to trade in that volatile adjustable-rate mortgage (ARM) used to finance your home purchase for a more pedestrian (or predictable) fixed-rate loan so you can hit the sack each night without worrying yourself sick about the possibility of your loan's interest rate skyrocketing.
- **To pull cash out:** If you've owned your home a long time, you've probably built up quite a bit of equity in it, thanks to the combined effect of paying down a small percentage of your loan's outstanding balance every month through an amortizing loan and property appreciation. Instead of simply replacing the old mortgage with a new one of the same amount, some folks pull out additional cash, which they use for such purposes as starting a new business, helping pay for the kids' college expenses, or planning that dream trip to Antarctica to see male penguins dutifully play Mr. Mom. We suspect that you could probably come up with a couple of more ways to use some extra money if you really put your mind to it.

TIP

Refinancing a mortgage isn't like ordering dinner in a Chinese restaurant where you select one item from column A and one from column B. What the heck. It's your refi. You can do whatever you want. If you plan carefully, you may be able to accomplish all three objectives when you refinance.

THE BENEFITS OF SEASONED LOANS

Although this chapter explores the benefits of refinancing, at times it may actually be a more prudent strategy to not refinance because there can be advantages to keeping the existing loan and seeking additional sources of funds in a different manner.

If you've had your loan for several years, remember that with *all* loans, you pay more interest in the beginning of the loan and more principal later in the loan. Ask yourself this hypothetical question: If your loan had only one year left on it (12 payments), but it carried a 10 percent interest rate and a monthly payment of $1,000, would you start a new 30-year loan (360 payments) at 5 percent with a $65 payment? Of course not! That's why the age of your current loan matters when considering refinancing.

One smart idea is to look at the new monthly payments (principal + interest only) for the refinance based on the time period remaining on your current loan. For example, if your current loan has 12 years left on it (144 payments), then analyze the prospective refinance with payments over 12 years, too. Does refinancing the loan still make sense? Even if the refinancing does *not* make sense over time, you may still go with the refinance if you *really* need the new lower monthly payments to survive your current financial situation. You'll be helping yourself in the short term (with the lower payments), but you'll be hurting yourself long term (by adding many years to the life of your loan), but sometimes this is the only solution.

Cost-Cutting Refinances

When asked to rank the refi process in terms of pleasurable life experiences, most people list it just above having a tooth filled without anesthetic. Expect to be inundated with forms containing thousands of tiny boxes you must either check or, worse yet, answer in microscopic detail; to submit piles of substantiating documents to your lender; and to be slugged by a slew of expenses, such as loan application and origination fees, title insurance, escrow charges, and property appraisals.

As a rule, refinancing a mortgage is neither cheap nor easy. But when the pleasure of considering how much money you can save by doing a refi exceeds the anticipated pain of the process you have to go through to get the savings, the time to refinance has arrived.

Mortgage interest rates rise and fall periodically like a financial tide. Sometimes the fiscal tide gently kisses the shore. At other times, however, it's a tidal wave.

Over the past couple of generations, we've seen interest rates for conforming 30-year fixed-rate mortgages range from a high of over 18 percent in 1981 to a low of around 3.3 percent in 2012.

If you happen to buy a home during a period of relatively high interest rates, you'd be smart to seriously consider refinancing your mortgage when interest rates drop. To make your pondering productive and profitable, the following sections offer some important factors to consider.

Applying the 2 percent rule

Some well-intentioned but misguided people earnestly advise that there must be *at least* a 2 percentage point differential between your present mortgage's interest rate and the new loan's rate before refinancing makes economic sense. This tidbit of folk wisdom, straightforwardly referred to as the *2 percent rule,* is a simple guideline to help you gauge how quickly you'll get back refinancing costs by using money saved with your new, reduced loan payments.

Don't let the 2 percent rule intimidate you. It's merely a guideline — not the Ten Commandments.

In fairness, the 2 percent rule isn't utter hooey. The larger the spread between your present loan's interest rate and the new interest rate, the faster you'll recover your refinancing charges (loan application and origination fee, appraisal, title insurance, and the other items we detail in Chapter 9) by using savings produced by lower monthly payments. For instance, when the interest rate differential is 2 percentage points, you'll probably recover all the usual refi costs in less than two years.

If you don't plan to sell your house in the next few years, however, interest rate spreads smaller than 2 percent are perfectly fine to justify refinancing. A 1 percentage point differential between your present loan and the refi mortgage, for example, simply means that recovering your refinancing costs will take longer. If you plan to stay in your home for the life of the loan, then even a 0.5 percent rate cut can make economic sense. It's not a big deal to calculate your own refi payback scenario (see the following section).

TIP

If you have a large loan balance (especially a nonconforming loan or jumbo loan), with a decline in interest rates of even 50 basis points since you purchased your home, you owe it to yourself to explore the economics of a refi. A little dialing for dollars could save you big bucks. Nothing can stop you from refinancing your loan again (and again) if mortgage rates keep heading south.

Crunching the numbers

You don't need a PhD in accounting to determine whether a refi makes "cents." However, you must understand the fundamentals we cover in Chapter 4 before starting your analysis. By the same token, you should also understand how to find the best loan (Chapter 5), how to find good lenders (Chapter 7), and how to find your way through the mortgage maze (Chapter 9). If you haven't read these fascinating chapters yet, please do so now.

Starting the decision-making process is simple. Call a good lender. Find out what the monthly payment would be if you replaced your current loan with a new one. Then have the lender estimate the total cost to refinance your loan and get it in writing. Armed with these two vital bits of information, you can approximate how long it will take to repay the refi charges and start saving gobs of greenbacks.

TIP

Speaking of refinancing costs, one of the biggest bills coming your way is title insurance. Like it or not, you must get a new title insurance policy to protect your lender from title risks, such as delinquent property tax claims, that may have been recorded against your property since your previous title insurance policy was issued. Be sure to ask the title insurance company whether you qualify for a *refinance rate* on your new policy. Most firms will give you a sizable rate reduction — up to 30 percent off their normal title insurance policy premium — if your previous policy was issued within five years of the new policy's issuance date.

Refinancing's magic formula

Just for the fun of it, assume that your present loan payment is $1,500 a month. Your friendly lender offers you a new mortgage with a lower interest rate. Your new payment would be $1,250, which would reduce your loan payment by a sweet $250 a month. However, it would cost you a grand total of $4,000 to refinance the loan.

Now your lender pushing you to refinance, or that online article selling you on refinancing even if interest rates decline by less than 0.5 percent, won't tell you something that's very important — you won't actually save the full $250 just because your monthly mortgage payment is reduced by $250. That's your *pretax* savings. Because you'd have less mortgage interest to deduct after refinancing, your tax write-offs would be reduced accordingly. Here's a quick way to estimate the amount you'd save on an *after-tax* basis. Multiply the savings by your federal tax rate as we note in Table 1-1 of Chapter 1 and then subtract this lost tax savings from your pretax savings amount. If you're in the 28 percent tax bracket, for example, the pretax $250 slims down to $180 per month on an after-tax basis ($\$250 \times 28\% = \$70$ lost tax savings).

Now comes the important part. Figure the number of months to recover the refi costs. Here's the magic formula to figure out how long it will take you to break even if you refinance:

Refi cost ÷ after-tax monthly savings = months to break even.

Using the data in our example: $4,000 ÷ $180 = 22.2 months. Simple.

Whether you ultimately save money when you refinance depends on refi costs and after-tax monthly savings. In our example, refinancing wouldn't make sense if you expect to sell your house within the next 22 months. If you keep the loan five years, on the other hand, you'll recover the $4,000 you spent in refi costs plus a nifty $6,800 in savings ($180 per month × 60 months = $10,800 – $4,000 costs = 6,800 excellent reasons to refinance).

When we factored in the lost federal income tax savings by refinancing to a lower monthly payment, we ignored state income taxes. As you may know all too well from personal experience, some states also have significant income taxes. If you live in such a state, you'll want to factor those lost tax savings into your refinance calculations.

Fewer points don't always great loans make

The biggest refi expense is usually the discount points (used to buy down the interest rate) or loan origination fee (used to cover the lender's overhead expenses) or *points*. These are always paid upfront when you take out the loan. As we explain in Chapter 9, a point is equal to one percent of the loan amount. The relationship between the interest rate on a mortgage and that same loan's points can best be thought of as a seesaw; one end of the seesaw is the loan's interest rate, and the other end of the seesaw represents the loan's points. So, if you pay less in points, the ongoing interest rate will be higher.

Suppose that during your quest for the best loan, you find two lenders offering a 30-year fixed-rate mortgage at 6.5 percent interest. One lender wants two points for the loan. The other lender keenly desires your business and offers the same 6.5 percent rate for a mere one and a half points. Assuming that all other refi costs are equal, of course you'd grab the loan with lower points. We're proud of you, brilliant reader.

Unfortunately, most refinancing situations aren't so straightforward. Don't reflexively grab a loan simply because it has low points. Lenders usually offer a wide variety of mortgages. Some loans have relatively low points, others "no points," and a few even have "no points or fees." The tradeoff for these seemingly good deals is a higher interest rate over the life of the loan. There are no free lunches in the merciless world of high finance.

TAX TREATMENT OF REFI POINTS

After advising you that not a smidgen of difference exists between a home purchase loan and a refi loan, we blushingly wish to draw your attention to a difference — not in the mortgages, but in the way the Internal Revenue Service (IRS) treats the respective loan origination fees. We certainly don't want you to get in trouble with the IRS.

When you bought your home, the points you were charged to get your purchase mortgage were fully deductible in the year in which you paid them. However, when you refinance, the loan origination fee for your refi mortgage must be *amortized* (spread out) over the life of your new loan.

For instance, suppose that you paid two points to get a $300,000 mortgage several years ago when you bought your home. You deducted the full $6,000 ($\$300{,}000 \times 2\%$) loan fee on the federal tax return that you filed for the year you purchased your home. That was an impressive deduction. The federal government is glad to offer this as an incentive to promote home ownership.

Now you've decided to pay two points to refinance your original mortgage for a snazzy new, improved $300,000 loan with a lower interest rate. This time, though, you have to divide the $6,000 loan origination fee by the 30-year term of your mortgage, giving you a deduction of just $200 per year ($\$6{,}000 \div 30$ years).

The IRS isn't completely heartless. You may be able to immediately deduct part of the points on a refi if you use part of the refi mortgage proceeds to improve your primary residence. Again, the federal government likes to see you spend money improving and upgrading your home so they give you a tax benefit. Also, if you refinance again because interest rates continue to drop or you pay the refi loan off when you sell your house, it'll allow you to deduct the *unamortized* (remaining) portion of your points at that time. For example, if you sell your house three years after refinancing, you can deduct the remaining $5,400 ($\$6{,}000 - \$200$ per year $\times 3$ years) on your tax return for the year of your sale.

Here's how to determine whether you're really getting a bargain. On a $200,000 mortgage, for example, suppose that your new best pal, the lender, offered you either a 6.5 percent interest rate loan with a two-point loan fee ($\$200{,}000 \times 2\% = \$4{,}000$) or a 6.75 percent interest rate mortgage for one and a half points ($\$200{,}000 \times 1.5\% = \$3{,}000$).

Taking the one-and-a-half-point loan saves $1,000 ($\$4{,}000 - \$3{,}000$) in loan costs, but its monthly payment is $1,297 versus $1,264 for the mortgage with a two-point loan fee. So if you opt for the 6.75 percent mortgage, you'll pay $33 more per month ($24 after factoring in tax savings if you're in the 28 percent federal tax bracket) over the remaining term of the loan because of the higher interest rate. (We ignore tax savings in the following comparison because points and monthly interest are both ultimately deductible.) Good deal?

Consider a slight variation of our magic formula to find out:

> Refi cost ÷ after-tax monthly savings = months to break even.
>
> Per our second example: $1,000 ÷ $33 = 30 months.

In this example, take the loan with the 1.5 percent loan origination fee if you aren't planning to keep it at least 30 months. If you plan to hold the loan more than 30 months, however, pay the two-point fee to get the lower interest rate.

TIP

Do this calculation for all the different loans you're considering and then make your decision based on your best estimate of how long you plan to own this property. Remember that even if you relocate, if you hold the property as a rental, then you should consider that time frame in your calculation because you'll keep the loan in place for as long as you own the property, not just as long as you personally occupy it.

Restructuring Refinances

Like it or not, certain situations demand that you absolutely *must* replace an existing mortgage with new financing, even if you won't save a dime by doing so. In other circumstances, strange as it may seem, you voluntarily refinance your present mortgage to achieve nonfinancial benefits, such as peace of mind.

Restructuring when you need to

First, we cover forced restructuring. A philosopher once sagely observed that death is nature's way of telling us to slow down. By the same token, a balloon loan's imminent due date is a fiscal wake-up call that it's time to refinance your mortgage.

If you have a short-term first or second mortgage coming due, you have three choices:

» **Replace your short-term financing with a long-term loan.** Be proactive. You know darn good and well when your loan will be due and payable. Don't wait until the last minute to refinance it. Begin exploring your refi options long before you *must* pay off your present loan to make sure you get the optimum interest rate and terms on your new mortgage. Read Chapter 5 to decide whether a fixed-rate mortgage, adjustable-rate mortgage, or hybrid loan is your best long-term financing option.

WARNING

Refinancing may take longer than you expect — plan on 45 to 90 days — particularly if you're trying to do this during the holidays. And don't think the process will go perfectly. Documents have a disquieting way of getting lost. People are often slow responding to lender inquiries for verification of employment, verification of deposits, HOA dues, assessment certifications, and the like. Loan processors get sick or take vacations. The list of potential calamities is endless. Allow enough lead time to handle the last-minute problems that will inevitably rear their ugly heads. Don't let time bully you into paying late charges or expedite fees, or, worse yet, being rushed into taking a bad refi loan.

- **Get another short-term loan.** If you have a small second loan coming due, it may be more economical to either pay it off or replace it with a new second instead of refinancing your present first and second mortgages. By the same token, if you plan to sell your house within the next year or two, don't pay a premium for refi financing. Get a no-points, no-fee loan to tide you over. The higher interest rate you pay in the short run will be less than all those costs and fees.

TIP

If your loan is coming due, the first call you should make is not to a new lender but to your current lender. Rather than go through the expense and aggravation of a refi, see whether the holder of your present mortgage will extend the loan's due date long enough to accommodate your plans. Maybe your current lender likes that you've been a reliable borrower and will be willing to offer you favorable rates and other terms and/or discounted costs/fees if you refinance with them. Especially when owner-carry financing is involved, this approach may be the easiest way to solve your financial problem.

- **Sell the property.** If, for some reason, you can't qualify for a refi and the holder of your current loan won't extend the loan's due date until your prospects of finding a new loan improve, sell the property before it goes into foreclosure. Don't wait for a miracle. Take command of the situation instead of allowing yourself to become a victim. *House Selling For Dummies* (published by Wiley) is filled with proven ways to sell your property quickly for top dollar. The key to success is giving yourself enough lead time to market the house so you can control circumstances instead of having them control you.

Voluntary restructuring is a much more pleasant subject. You're refinancing your loan because you want to, not because you've run out of other options. Believe it or not, you may want to restructure your mortgage even if the refi won't save you money. We tell you why in the following sections.

Getting a fixed-rate to avoid ARM phobia

Some folks hate adjustable-rate mortgages (ARMs) with a passion. Suppose you happen to be one of them. Yet, ironically, you got an ARM when you bought your home a few years ago because interest rates were high then and you couldn't qualify for the 30-year fixed-rate loan you *really* wanted.

Times have changed. Your financial situation is much improved. You can finally afford to get rid of that treacherous ARM you despise.

Who cares if that new fixed-rate loan's interest rate is a smidge higher than your ARM's *present* interest rate? Everyone knows that the ARM's interest rate can rise. Your peace of mind is worth a few bucks a month. The important thing is that you won't spend any more sleepless nights worrying about future interest rate increases. Refinancing into a nice, secure fixed-rate mortgage is wonderful if you have ARM phobia.

TIP

Some ARMs can be converted to fixed-rate mortgages from the 13th to 60th month of the loan by paying a fee, usually 1 percent of the remaining loan balance. This method is usually cheaper and less aggravating than refinancing from scratch. If your ARM has this option, find out what the interest rate will be if it's converted to a fixed-rate loan. Sometimes the rate isn't competitive with new fixed-rate loans. For instance, if conforming fixed-rate loans are offered at 6.5 percent and your lender graciously allows you to convert your ARM to a fixed-rate loan at 8 percent, economics favor getting the 6.5 percent loan if you plan to keep it more than a few years.

Resetting ARM caps

Nearly any person can figure out why people who have fixed-rate loans refinance them when mortgage rates fall. These folks have no other way to get a lower interest rate. As the name implies, those interest rates are carved in stone.

Why, however, would anyone with an ARM refinance when rates drop? After all, an ARM's interest rate will adjust itself automatically in time. Wouldn't it be smarter, easier, and cheaper over the long haul to simply leave sleeping ARMs alone? Not always. The following sections offer two reasons to refinance an ARM.

Outwitting periodic adjustment caps

Here's a delightful problem most people never consider. Sometimes interest rates fall so rapidly that even adjustable-rate mortgages can't keep up with them. That's because, as we note in Chapter 5, good ARMs have periodic adjustment caps that limit how much the interest rate can be changed up *or down* during a periodic rate adjustment.

For example, suppose you have an ARM that permits interest rate adjustments once a year. Its periodic adjustment cap restricts the maximum rate increase or decrease to not more than 2 percent annually. You're confident that you can handle worst-case increases without going into catatonic payment shock. For some strange reason, handling payment decreases never concerned you.

Good news. You just received a letter from your lender saying that your ARM's current 7.75 percent interest rate will drop to 5.75 percent at the next adjustment. Once again, you congratulate yourself for not getting a fixed-rate mortgage like so many of your chicken-hearted friends. You feel slightly less pleased when you notice that the interest rate would have been even lower except for the loan's 2 percent periodic adjustment cap.

"Fair is fair," you mutter to calm yourself. "My ARM's cap works both ways. It also protects me from getting hammered by huge rate increases. And, if rates stay low, I'll get the extra savings next year anyway."

Then your next-door neighbor comes over for a visit. She proudly says that she decided to dump her fixed-rate loan and get an ARM exactly like yours from your lender. Truth be known, her adjustable-rate mortgage isn't *exactly* like yours. Its interest rate will be just 3.5 percent for the first year.

You think about all the money you'll leave on the table each month. Even if you get another maximum rate reduction, you'll be down to only 3.75 percent a year from now. Worse yet, interest rates may not remain low.

Conversely, by refinancing now, you won't have to worry about interest rates staying low. Even if rates skyrocket, your ARM's interest rate would be lower after the first periodic rate adjustment than it is now (3.5% + 2% maximum increase = 5.5% worst case 12 months from now versus 5.75% currently). How can you lose?

WARNING

As we discuss in Chapter 5, an ARM's initial interest rate is only one thing to consider when you select a mortgage. You must evaluate all the features (good and bad) of an ARM to make sure it's the best loan for you. ***Remember:*** Lenders offer ARMs because they're usually good for the lender.

Limiting lifetime caps

Good ARMs have another important feature: lifetime caps that set interest rate limits over the full term of the loan. Life-of-loan caps are usually 5 to 6 percent higher than an ARM's initial interest rate.

The initial interest rate on your neighbor's ARM isn't the only significant difference between her loan and yours. Both of your mortgages have 6 percent lifetime caps, but the similarity ends there. Because your ARM's initial interest rate was 5.25 percent, it can go as high as 11.25 percent (5.25% start rate + 6% life cap). Her loan peaks at a worst-case 9.5 percent (3.5% start rate + 6% life cap).

Most people never consider that, like fixed-rate loans, you can ratchet down an ARM's interest rate ceiling. Refinancing an ARM not only reduces your monthly payments, but it also slashes your upside interest rate risk.

Choosing the fast-forward mortgage

If you're willing to forgo small, immediate monthly savings to eventually get a huge pot of gold, you may consider replacing your present 30-year mortgage with a 15-year loan.

Robert has done this many times over the years. When starting out, Robert and his wife, Carol, could qualify for only a 30-year loan at basic market terms and not the best interest rates. But, through hard work, aggressive saving, and living below their means, after only a few years they found that they qualified for more favorable rates with their improved credit scores. At the same time, interest rates had declined and refinancing their loans was advantageous. And although all interest rates were lower across the board, this was especially true for 15-year loans, which are typically lower than the 30-year rates. So rather than refinance with a new 30-year loan, Robert and Carol were able to refinance into a 15-year loan with essentially the same monthly payment.

This restructuring plan could save you tens or even hundreds of thousands of dollars in interest charges over the life of your new, improved mortgage. We discuss the pros and cons of this radical course of action in Chapter 5.

Cash-Out Refinances

A cash-out refi differs from the cost-cutting and the restructuring refinances we cover in the preceding sections in one important aspect — instead of replacing your current loan with another one for the same amount of money, you pull extra cash out of the property when you refinance it. You can do this in two ways:

- **Get a new first mortgage.** If you're going to refinance your existing mortgage (because you want to cut costs or must restructure your financing), this situation could be an ideal opportunity to free up some of that equity you've accumulated. As long as getting extra cash won't jack up your new mortgage's interest rate and you have a good use for the money (such as investing in a profitable business or paying off a pile of high-interest-rate consumer debts), go for it. However, be sure you can afford to borrow all this extra money — see Chapter 1.

» **Get a home equity loan.** Don't disturb your existing loan if you're happy with your present first mortgage, if you want to tap only a small amount of your equity, if you won't need all the cash at once, or if you don't need the money for very long. See our discussion of home equity loans in Chapter 6.

Pulling cash out of your property *may* jack up your refi mortgage's interest rate. Why? Lenders have gathered statistical proof over the years that taking cash out of property for nonmortgage purposes (versus pouring the money right back into the home by adding a bathroom or modernizing the kitchen, for instance) increases the probability of a future loan default.

WARNING

Due to a huge increase in foreclosures between 2007 and 2012, lenders started putting cash-out refinances under a microscope. As noted in Chapter 2, lenders now impose *extremely* stringent loan restrictions on any market they consider risky because home prices in the area are declining. Be sure to ask your lender whether your property is located in what it considers a declining market. Chapter 2 covers the topic of problem appraisals in great detail.

As you know if you've read Chapter 2, lenders believe that the lower your property's loan-to-value (LTV) ratio, the lower the odds that you'll eventually default on your loan — and vice versa. Lenders generally charge higher interest rates and loan fees or make you pay mortgage insurance for *purchase* loans if the LTV ratio exceeds 80 percent. For cash-out refinances, on the other hand, many lenders jack up rates and fees when the LTV ratio exceeds 75 percent of appraised value.

To see the difference this policy makes: Suppose you put $30,000 cash down and got a $120,000 first mortgage with an 8 percent interest rate ten years ago when you bought your dream home for $150,000. The LTV ratio then was a nice, safe 80 percent (your $120,000 loan divided by the $150,000 appraised value).

Fast forward to today. You're ecstatic. Your home just appraised for $225,000. You intend to replace the faithful old loan you've had all these years with a new $180,000 first mortgage, which is 80 percent of the current appraised value ($\$180,000 \div \$225,000$). After paying off the $105,000 remaining principal balance of your old loan and $5,000 of refi expenses, you believe you'll get a check for $70,000 ($\$180,000 \text{ new loan} - \$105,000 \text{ loan payoff} - \$5,000 \text{ refi costs} = \$70,000$ cash out of the refi).

"Wow!" you think to yourself. "I'll have my $30,000 out of the house and another $40,000 to boot. And I'll still have $45,000 equity left in the property ($225,000 appraised value – $180,000 new loan). I can buy that red convertible I've been dreaming about, take a first-class cruise around the world, and still have cash in the bank when I get home. Life is good — and so is home ownership."

Not so fast, dear reader. Before you mentally spend all that cash, see whether your lender is one of those that increases interest rates 0.25 to 0.5 percent on 80 percent LTV cash-out refinances. If so, either reduce your refinance's LTV ratio to 75 percent or shop around to see whether you can find a lender with equally competitive rates on 80 percent LTV cash-out refinances. Some lenders won't even offer cash-out refinancing.

The cash you pull out of your property may seem like found money. It isn't. You probably worked pretty darn hard for the cash you used to buy your home. You're working just as hard to pay off your loan. As you can see when you read about reverse mortgages in Chapter 13, the equity you're accumulating in your property can be transformed into retirement income someday or used for another worthwhile purpose unless, of course, you squander it. Never borrow money needlessly. Your home isn't a piggy bank and if you're a "serial refinancer" always seeking to have the latest depreciable technology or consumer item, then you're asking for trouble and will miss out on one of your best sources of retirement funds — a home that you own "free and clear."

Expediting Your Refi

Most folks don't dawdle after they've made the decision to refinance their mortgage. As far as they're concerned, the sooner they get that new, improved financing in place and start saving money (or at least get a good night's sleep), the better.

If you want fast action, here are five ways to speed up the refinancing process:

- **Fill out your loan application completely.** Line out any items that don't apply to you so the lender knows you haven't overlooked them or forgotten to answer them. If you aren't sure how to answer a question, ask your loan officer for assistance instead of leaving the question blank. Incomplete applications have a mysterious way of ending up at the bottom of the loan processor's pile. See Chapter 10 for more tips on how to best complete your loan application.

- **Attach copies of all pertinent documents to your loan application.** Always include a copy of your latest pay stub. If you're self-employed, give the lender copies of your two most recent tax returns, with all the schedules. Make a file copy of the completed application in case the original gets misplaced.
- **The easier you make things for the appraiser, the faster your appraisal will be completed.** For example, if you have a floor plan of your home, give it to the appraiser to help determine square footage. Provide copies of invoices for any improvements you've made to the property since you bought it. Having copies of approved building permits for any additions or decks will also be important.
- **Don't "protect" yourself by submitting loan applications to several lenders.** Each loan application you file triggers its own set of title and appraisal requests. During a hot market or when interest rates stop declining and turn higher, having to wait for multiple applications to be evaluated at multiple lenders can take a long time. As we recommend in Chapter 7, you should shop around; but after you find your first choice, focus your time and energy on getting that application done and approved.

TIP

Comparable sales data help the appraiser establish your home's current fair market value. Appraisers will generally track down this information on their own. However, you could give the appraiser information (address, sale price, date of sale, and so on) about houses comparable to yours that have *sold* within the past six months. To be valid "comps," the properties must be similar to your home in size, age, condition, and must be located in the immediate vicinity of your house. Also, the real estate agent who represented you when you bought your home will probably be delighted to provide this information. Smart agents like to stay on the good side of their clients.

- **Don't be greedy.** When your loan is ready to fund, take the money and run. If you didn't take our advice to negotiate a "rate lock," then delaying the loan funding because you think mortgage rates may go down a notch or two further may turn out to be a costly mistake. Rates move in both directions. They could go higher, not lower, while you're waiting.

Robert's rule is that interest rates in a dynamic economic environment will always rise more rapidly than they'll fall. This is similar to what you see at your local gas station: You hear on the news that the price of a barrel of oil has dropped 10 percent, but even weeks later the price of a gallon of gas has barely dropped. However, if there is a terrorist attack in Nigeria or a fire at an oil refinery in Kazakhstan, the cost of filling your gas tank can immediately go up by $5 overnight. Don't give mortgage gods a malicious laugh at your expense.

Beating Borrower's Remorse

Residential real estate is riddled with remorse. Remorse eventually rears its repulsive head in almost every purchase, sale, and refi.

Sometimes, borrowers get a mild case of remorse to which the balm of logic can be applied. Other times, however, no amount of reasoning with the infected party will suffice — masochism reigns supreme until the disease runs its course.

If you're reading this chapter, you've most likely already suffered through a bout of buyer's remorse. Remember that sickening feeling you got after the sellers accepted your offer? You were absolutely certain you'd offered too much money for the house. To prove it, you continued visiting Sunday open houses and kept scrutinizing the classified ads searching for homes with lower asking prices that were bigger and better than the one you were buying.

Unbeknownst to you, the sellers were probably going through the exact same exercise in reverse. Shortly after they signed the contract, they convinced themselves they were giving their house away. To prove it, they spent weekends touring open houses and devoured real estate ads looking for houses with higher asking prices that weren't as nice as the one they were selling.

Exhaustion wears most buyers and sellers down eventually. Buyers see enough comps to reinforce the validity of their purchase price. Ditto sellers for the sale price. Logic prevails. Life returns to normal.

Borrower's remorse is equally devastating. This dreadful scourge appears in two incarnations whenever mortgage rates are in a state of flux.

Phase I borrower's remorse

Suppose you bought a home when interest rates were on the high end of a periodic cycle. The best loan you could get at the time was a 30-year fixed-rate mortgage at 6.5 percent interest. Now interest rates are falling, and you're agonizing. To lock (your new loan's interest rate) or not to lock?

For instance, people who replaced 6.5 percent loans with new ones when rates hit 5.5 percent kicked themselves as rates continued to fall. In a declining interest rate market, the situation wasn't much better for people who waited until rates hit 5.25 percent, 5 percent, or 4.75 percent to refinance.

Phase I borrower's remorse strikes whenever interest rates fall. Here's what it sounds like: "Darn it! Interest rates just dropped another ¼ point. I knew I should have waited a little longer to refinance my loan. Look how much more money I could have saved if only I had waited. Everyone said rates would go lower. Why didn't I listen? Why was I so impetuous? What a fool I am!"

Don't beat yourself up, dear reader. Instead of dwelling on how much money you could have saved if you had waited to refinance, focus on how much money you *are* saving each month *because* you refinanced. Sure, as it turns out you could have done a little better. On the other hand, rates may have gone up instead of down. Your new loan payment is an improvement on the old one, isn't it? You're better off financially than you were, aren't you? You know the magic formula to determine a refi's break-even point. If rates keep falling, you can refinance again. For the time being, however, savor your savings.

Phase II borrower's remorse

When dealing with mortgage rates, what goes down inevitably goes back up. It's the nature of the beast. Sooner or later, every cycle of interest-rate reductions hits rock bottom and starts north. When that happens, you enter Phase II of borrower's remorse. Phase II makes Phase I look like a walk in the park.

"Why did I wait so long to refinance? What a fool I am! Look how much money I could have saved by refinancing last month. Everyone said rates were going to start rising. Why didn't I listen? Why was I so greedy?"

Phase II is *far* worse than Phase I. All the folks who refinanced their loans while interest rates were falling are saving money. True, some of them are saving more than others because they got lower interest rates, but everyone who refinanced came out ahead to greater or lesser degrees. Some people who delayed refinancing because they wanted to get the absolute lowest possible interest rate ended up with nothing.

The only way to be sure that rates have hit bottom is to watch them start going back up again. Whenever that happens, the crush of people who waited to refinance added to the normal demand for new home purchase loans stresses the mortgage delivery system. Remember the old law of supply and demand? The demand for mortgages at times can far exceed the number of people valiantly trying to process them. Lenders will be buried under an avalanche of loan applications. Appraisers will have a two-month backlog of appraisal orders. Title companies can't churn out title reports as fast as new requests arrive. It's the fiscal equivalent of a nervous breakdown.

TIP

Suppose that you have a $200,000 loan at 6.5 percent interest with a monthly payment of $1,266. Suppose that you could refinance it today at 5 percent. Doing so would drop your payment to $1,074 — your payment would be lowered $192 per month. If you wait a little longer until rates drop to 4.875 percent, your payment would drop another $16 a month. But each month you have to wait, your loan payment is $1,266. You're spending an extra $192 a month in the hopes of *maybe* reducing your loan payment another $16 per month. Not smart. Rates go up every bit as easily as down. Don't be greedy — grab the savings while you can.

» Considering critical issues to paying down your mortgage early

Chapter 12
Paying Down Your Mortgage Quicker

After you go to all the time, trouble, and expense of securing a mortgage, you may have a hard time imagining that you'd ever want to pay off your loan quicker than required. However, years (and sometimes just months) after taking out a mortgage, some people discover that their circumstances have changed — sometimes dramatically for the better.

Perhaps your income has increased significantly, or you're the recipient of an inheritance, or that big promotion finally came through. Or maybe you're one of those rare folks who succeed in tightening your financial belt and spending less, thus freeing up more of your monthly income for other purposes. No matter, if you have some extra cash left over at the end of each month or extra balances sitting around in low interest accounts, this chapter can help you decide whether you should use that money to pay down your outstanding mortgage balance faster than necessary.

One Size Doesn't Fit All

If you speak with others or read articles or books about prepaying your mortgage, you'll come across those who think that prepaying your mortgage is the world's greatest money-saving device. Surprisingly, people have written entire books on the topic. You'll also find that some people consider it the most colossal mistake a mortgage holder can make. The reality, as you find out in this chapter, is often somewhere between these two extremes.

Everyone has pros and cons to weigh when he decides whether prepaying his mortgage makes sense. In some cases, the pros stand head and shoulders over the cons. For other people, the drawbacks to prepaying tower over the advantages. At the crux of the decision is the fact that you're paying interest on the borrowed mortgage money, but if you use your savings to pay down the loan balance, you won't then have that money working for you earning an investment return. More important, what happens if that rainy day comes along and you need those handy cash reserves?

Interest savings: The benefit of paying off your mortgage quicker

Mortgage prepayment advocates focus on how much interest you *won't* be charged. On a $100,000, 30-year mortgage at 7.5 percent interest, if you pay just an extra $100 of principal per month, you shorten the loan's term significantly. Prepayment cheerleaders argue that you'll save approximately $56,000 over the life of the loan.

It's true that by making larger-than-required payments each month, you avoid paying some interest to the lender. In the preceding example, in fact, you'll pay off your loan nearly ten years faster than required. But that's only part of the story. Read on for more.

Quantifying the missed opportunity to invest those extra payments

When you mail an additional $100 monthly to your lender, you miss the opportunity to invest that money into something that could provide you with a return greater than the cost of the mortgage interest. Have you heard of the stock market, for example?

Over the past two centuries, the U.S. stock market has produced an annual rate of return of about 9 percent. Thus, if instead of prepaying your mortgage, you put that $100 into some good stocks and earn 9 percent per year, you end up with more money over the long term than if you had prepaid your mortgage (assuming that your mortgage interest rate is below 9 percent).

Conversely, if instead of paying down your mortgage more rapidly, you put your extra cash in your bank savings account, you earn little interest. Because you're surely paying more interest on your mortgage, you lose money with this investment strategy, although you make bankers happy.

TIP

If you're contemplating paying down your mortgage more aggressively than required or investing your extra cash, consider what rate of return you can reasonably expect from investing your money and compare that expected return to the interest rate you're paying on your mortgage. As a first step, this simple comparison can help you begin to understand whether you're better off paying down your mortgage or investing the money elsewhere. Over the long term, growth investments, such as stocks, investment real estate, and investing in small business, have provided higher returns than the current cost of mortgage money.

Taxes matter but less than you think

Now, you may be thinking that — up until this point in this discussion — we haven't presented all the facts, and you'd be correct. One important detail we've left out of the discussion thus far is income taxes. (Don't we all wish we could ignore paying our income taxes!)

In most cases, all your mortgage interest is deductible on both your federal and state income tax returns (see the nearby sidebar "Not all mortgage interest is tax deductible" for exceptions). Thus, if you're paying, say, a 6 percent annual interest rate on your mortgage, after deducting that interest cost on your federal and state income tax returns, perhaps the mortgage is really costing you only about 4 percent on an after-tax basis. For most people, approximately one-third of the total interest cost of a mortgage is offset by their reduced income tax from writing off the mortgage interest on their federal and state income tax returns.

However, don't think that you can simply compare this relatively low after-tax mortgage cost of, say, 4 percent to the expected return on most investments. The flaw with that logic is that the return on most investments, such as stocks, is ultimately taxable. So, to be fair, if you're going to examine the after-tax cost of your mortgage, you should be comparing that with the after-tax return on your investments.

WARNING

NOT ALL MORTGAGE INTEREST IS TAX DEDUCTIBLE

If you're a high-income earner, are subject to the Federal Alternative Minimum Tax (AMT), or have low levels of itemized deductions, be warned that some of the itemized deductions from your mortgage interest may not effectively be tax deductible and may result in less tax savings than you think. For tax year 2017, for example, if your income exceeds $287,650 (for married couples filing jointly, it's $313,800), you lose some of your Schedule A itemized deductions (which includes mortgage interest and property taxes, too).

Also, be aware of the following standard deductions: $12,700 for married couples and $6,350 for singles for tax year 2017. Ignoring your mortgage interest deductions, if your itemized deductions total less than these threshold amounts, some of your mortgage interest is effectively not tax deductible. For example, if you're married and your itemized deductions, excluding mortgage interest, total to $10,000, then $2,600 of the mortgage interest you pay is essentially not tax deductible because you automatically qualify for the standard $12,600 deduction if you elect not to itemize.

Last but not least, IRS tax laws limit the amount of mortgage interest on your primary and a secondary residence that's tax deductible to no more than the interest on up to $1 million of mortgage debt. Also, the interest is allowed to be deducted only on debt equal to the amount you borrowed when you originally bought your home plus $100,000.

Alternatively, you could simplify matters for yourself and get a ballpark answer just by comparing the pretax mortgage cost to your expected pretax investment return. (Technically speaking, this comparison isn't as precise as the after-tax analysis because income tax considerations generally don't exactly equally reduce the cost of the mortgage and the investment return.)

Deciding Whether to Repay Your Mortgage Faster

In the first section in this chapter, we discuss the all-important comparison of the interest rate you're paying on your mortgage to the expected investment returns you can earn by investing your money. With extra cash that you have, you could pay down your mortgage and save interest or you could invest that money and earn investment returns.

But the decision of whether to pay down your mortgage faster isn't so simple. You need to weigh numerous other factors, such as the terms of your current mortgage, your overall financial situation (including your ability to fund retirement accounts), what type of investor you are, your refinancing options, and more. We discuss these factors in this section.

Does your mortgage have a prepayment penalty?

An important issue to clarify is to find out whether your current mortgage has a prepayment penalty (it shouldn't if you read and follow our sage advice in Chapter 4 before obtaining your mortgage). If your mortgage does have a prepayment penalty, it could negate some or all of your expected interest savings from paying down your mortgage early.

Just because a mortgage has a prepayment penalty doesn't mean that you shouldn't examine the possibility of prepaying it. In fact, when you investigate the prepayment terms on your mortgage, you may well find that you can prepay a significant amount of the outstanding loan principal balance (such as 20 percent per year) without being hit with a prepayment penalty.

How liquid are your assets?

If you're considering paying down mortgage debt, don't leave yourself *cash poor* (lack of liquidity). As a homeowner, you're probably already painfully aware of your home's tendency to need fixing up and maintenance over the years. Suppose your roof needs replacing and you don't have the cash to pay for it, or what if you lose your job and finding a suitable new one takes a few months?

You should have access to an emergency source of readily available funds, such as in a money market fund, of at least three to six months' worth of living expenses. Otherwise, when unexpected expenses come up, you'll have to go into hock on high interest (and non-tax-deductible) credit cards.

Have you funded retirement savings accounts?

If you have extra cash each month and you're debating the merits of paying down your mortgage versus investing the cash elsewhere, be sure you've fully contributed to retirement accounts. Through your employer, you may have access to a plan such as a 401(k) or 403(b). If you're self-employed, you could fund a SEP-IRA, for example. For 2017, the maximum SEP-IRA contribution is $54,000, which can provide great tax benefits and really contribute to your overall retirement assets as it grows over time. In all these plans, your contributions are effectively tax deductible, usually at both the federal and state levels.

By contrast, if you make extra payments on your mortgage, you get *no* tax relief from so doing. Thus, if you haven't fully funded tax-deductible retirement plans, do so before paying down your mortgage debt (unless, of course, you're going to leave the retirement money dozing away in a low-return investment such as a savings account or money market fund).

How aggressive an investor are you?

When you're deciding between paying down your mortgage and increasing your investments, you need to examine your risk tolerance. If you get antsy at the thought of your money going into stocks or other volatile investments, then paying down your mortgage faster may be the right investment for you.

Years ago when interest rates were high, Miriam and Bert were in their early 60s when they called Eric for some financial counseling. Over the years, they had accumulated about $50,000, which they had in a money market account. They knew that they didn't want to leave the money there, but they didn't know what to do with it.

Reviewing Miriam's and Bert's investments and discussing their investment likes and dislikes, Eric discerned that this couple was financially conservative and especially so about their impending retirement. They had their portfolio about equally split between stocks and bonds and weren't comfortable taking more risk.

Their outstanding mortgage balance of $32,000 was at 8 percent interest. Eric suggested that they use their cash to pay off their mortgage. He reasoned that if instead of paying the mortgage they invested half the money in stocks and half in bonds, their longer-term expected return would likely be no more than 8 percent — the cost of the mortgage. Why take the risk of investing, which Miriam and Bert didn't enjoy doing, in the hopes of getting an 8 percent return, when paying off the mortgage and saving the 8 percent interest was a sure thing?

By contrast, Phil was an aggressive 30-something investor when he consulted Eric. He invested his new savings into nearly all stocks, so he expected to be making a high enough return to beat the interest cost on his mortgage. Also, Phil likened paying down his mortgage to watching the grass grow — not very rewarding or exciting.

What are your refinancing options?

Don't forget the option of refinancing into a better mortgage. In some cases, you can lower your interest rate, thereby lowering your monthly payment. However, if you make larger-than-required monthly mortgage payments, you'll likely shave years off the repayment schedule.

Or you may choose to refinance to a shorter term. You can refinance a 30-year mortgage into a 15- or 20-year mortgage. Your payments will increase, but you'll cut the length of repayment by a third or half.

Consider another of Eric's clients. Mary had a fixed-rate mortgage and was leaning toward paying it down instead of investing her spare cash in mutual funds. Then she found out that her loan amount was just above the conforming loan limit (see Chapter 4). If she reduced the amount she borrowed by just $10,000, she would qualify for a lower interest rate on a conforming loan. She also saved by refinancing at rates that were lower than her original loan.

At these new and lower rates, Mary felt that she could earn a higher return investing her money, so not paying off her mortgage faster than necessary made sense to her. She was also able to fully deduct her mortgage interest to achieve that maximum benefit. Ask your lender for a written explanation *before* you prepay your loan.

REMEMBER

Refinancing your mortgage isn't as easy as trading one payment for another. You have to jump through the lender's hoops and spend some money out of pocket for the privilege of getting a better interest rate or term length. See Chapter 11 for the details on refinancing.

Considering psychological and nonfinancial issues

Many of the issues we suggest considering when you decide whether to pay down your mortgage balance faster are purely financial. However, we don't want to diminish or overlook the importance of psychological issues.

Specifically, would you derive any solace from paying your balance down or off completely? Miriam (whom we discuss in the preceding section) said, "I felt a tremendous sense of relief when we paid off our mortgage. Bert [my husband] thought doing so wasn't real exciting, but I feel better knowing that we don't owe any more money."

Another of Eric's clients, Kevin, chose to pay his mortgage off at the relatively young age of 35. "While I could have kept my mortgage going, paying it off completely freed me psychologically from feeling like I had to keep working as hard as my peers did at their careers. Now that I have a family, spending time with them is my first priority, not climbing career ladders."

Of course, if you have investment properties, you'll find that income property loans are always more expensive than your owner-occupied home. Interest rates for income property loans are typically 0.25 to 0.5 percent higher. So you may actually want to consider applying some of any "extra cash" to accelerate the payoff of your investment properties — of course, all the time keeping adequate reserves. If you own or plan to own rental property, then you know that savvy real estate investors always have a cash cushion for the unexpected vacancy or maintenance and repair bill.

TIP

See the latest edition of our book *Real Estate Investing For Dummies* (Wiley) to find out how you can build a real estate empire. Or, to keep your property in top shape and minimize surprises, see Robert's book *Property Management Kit For Dummies* (also published by Wiley) for everything you need to know as a landlord.

Developing Your Payoff Plan

Now, if you've made it this far in this chapter and you believe you want to pay off your mortgage faster than is required, this last section is for you. If you're certain that you want to pay down your mortgage balance quicker, it can be as simple as doing one of the following:

- Sending in a regular additional amount (such as $100 more) with each monthly payment
- Sending in extra money less regularly when you have extra cash (like when you receive that quarterly or annual bonus)
- Paying the mortgage in full if you have enough money to do so

You can mix and match these practices. Just remember, though, that once you send in extra money or pay off the loan in full, you can't take it back!

TIP

If it's important to you to understand how much sooner your mortgage will be paid off because of the extra payments you're making or plan to make, you can contact your loan officer (who should be able to do those calculations), contact your mortgage service company and ask it to do some calculations on your behalf, or use an online amortization calculator.

» Considering costs and payment choices

» Shopping for the best reverse mortgage

Chapter 13
Reverse Mortgages for Retirement Income

If you own a home, a reverse mortgage allows you to tap into its *equity* (the difference between the market value of your home less the mortgage debt owed on it) to supplement your retirement income — while you still live in your home. Because these mortgages are so different from what most people expect, it generally takes a while for the most basic information about them to make sense. Even experienced financial professionals are often surprised to learn how these loans really work, how different their costs and benefits can be, and what you have to look out for.

Are you full of questions about these types of mortgages perhaps for yourself or for an elderly relative? If so, this chapter gives you the lowdown on reverse mortgages and helps you figure out whether they're right for you.

Grasping the Reverse Mortgage Basics

A *reverse mortgage* is a loan against your home that you don't have to repay as long as you live there. In a regular, or so-called *forward* mortgage (the kind we discuss throughout the rest of this book), your monthly loan repayments make your debt go down over time until you've paid it all off. Meanwhile, your equity is rising as you repay your mortgage and as your property value appreciates.

With a reverse mortgage, by contrast, the lender sends you money, and your debt grows larger and larger as you keep getting cash advances (usually monthly), make no repayment, and interest is added to the *loan balance* (the amount you owe). That's why reverse mortgages are called *rising debt, falling equity* loans. As your *debt* (the amount you owe) grows larger, your *equity* (that is, your home's value minus any debt against it) generally gets smaller. However, your equity could increase if you're in a strong housing market where home values are rising nicely.

If your financial goal is to preserve the equity in your home, you may be able to conservatively structure your reverse mortgage so you limit the amount of equity you pull out of your property to the estimated increase in home values anticipated over future years. Now predicting future real estate appreciation is definitely an inexact science. But real estate values do generally rise over time, and you may find that if you're modest in the amount of money you receive from the lender, you haven't eroded your home equity as much as you thought.

Reverse mortgages are different from regular home mortgages in two important respects:

- To qualify for most loans, the lender checks your income to see how much you can afford to pay back each month. But with a reverse mortgage, you don't have to make monthly repayments. Thus, your income generally has nothing to do with getting a reverse mortgage or determining the amount of the loan.
- With a regular mortgage, you can lose your home if you fail to make your monthly repayments. With a reverse mortgage, however, you can't lose your home by failing to make monthly loan payments — because you don't have any to make!

A reverse mortgage merits your consideration if it fits your circumstances. Reverse mortgages may allow you to cost-effectively tap your home's equity and enhance your retirement income. If you have bills to pay, want to buy some new carpeting, need to paint your home, or simply feel like eating out and traveling more, a good reverse mortgage may be your salvation.

This section focuses on the ABCs of reverse mortgages and helps clarify any confusion you may have.

Considering common objections

Most older homeowners contemplating a reverse mortgage have worked hard for many years to eliminate their home's mortgage so they own their home free and clear. After what they've gone through, the thought of reversing that process and rebuilding the debt owed on their home is troubling. Furthermore, reverse mortgages are a relatively new type of loan that few people understand. And most of today's reverse mortgage borrowers are low-income, single seniors who have run out of other money for living expenses. Some people think reverse mortgages are only a last resort, but that isn't true.

Can you lose your home?

It's not too surprising that folks who don't fully understand reverse mortgages often have preconceived notions, mostly negative, about how they work. Seniors with home equity often erroneously think that taking a reverse mortgage may lead to being forced out of their homes or ending up owing more than the house is worth.

Seniors taking out a reverse mortgage won't be forced out of their home. Nor will they (or their heirs) end up owing more than their house is worth. Federal law defines reverse mortgages to be *nonrecourse loans*, which simply means that the home's value is the only asset that can be tapped to pay the reverse mortgage debt balance. In the rare case when a home's value does drop below the amount owed on the reverse mortgage, the borrower isn't on the hook for the extra debt. The lender assumes that risk.

WARNING

As detailed later in this chapter (see the section "When do you pay the money back?"), not keeping current with your property taxes and homeowners insurance can trigger your reverse mortgage going into default and requiring payoff. When a loan is called due and payable, the reverse mortgage borrower or the borrower's estate needs to repay only the lesser of either the loan balance or 95 percent of the home's appraised value at that time.

Would a home equity loan or second mortgage work better?

Some people who are intimidated by having to understand reverse mortgages wonder whether it would be simpler to get a home equity loan or a new mortgage that allows them to take some equity out of their home. The problem with this strategy is that you have to begin paying traditional mortgage loans back soon after taking them out.

For example, suppose that you own a home worth $200,000, with no mortgage debt. You decide to take out a $100,000, 15-year mortgage at 7 percent interest.

Although you'll receive $100,000, you'll have to begin making monthly payments of $899. No problem, you may think; you'll just invest your $100,000 and come out ahead. Wrong!

Most seniors gravitate toward safe bonds, which traditionally may yield in the neighborhood of 5 percent — a mere $416 of monthly income — an amount far short of your monthly mortgage payments. If you invest in stocks and earn the generous average return of 10 percent per year, which is by no means guaranteed, your returns would amount to more — $833 per month — but still not enough to cover your monthly mortgage payment. (We should also note that most income from stocks and bonds is taxable at both the federal and state level. By contrast, reverse mortgage payments you receive aren't taxable.) Advantage: reverse mortgage.

Here's another big drawback of taking out a traditional mortgage to supplement your retirement income. The longer you live in the house, the more likely you are to run out of money and begin missing loan payments, because you drain your principal to supplement inadequate investment returns and cover your monthly loan payment. If that happens, unlike with a reverse mortgage, the lending institution may foreclose on your loan, and you can lose your home.

Who can get a reverse mortgage?

Of course, reverse mortgages aren't for everyone. As we discuss later in this chapter (see the section "Deciding Whether You Want a Reverse Mortgage"), alternatives may better accomplish your goal. Also, not everyone qualifies to take out a reverse mortgage. Specifically, to be eligible for a reverse mortgage:

- You must own your home. In the early years of reverse mortgages, as a rule, all the owners had to be at least 62 years old. Now, in a couple, you may qualify for a reverse mortgage if one person is at least 62 years of age and the other person is younger than that. However, such a couple will qualify for lower reverse mortgage money due to the younger spouse because "life expectancy" is part of the calculation.
- Your home generally must be your *principal residence* — which means you must live in it more than half the year.
- For the federally insured *Home Equity Conversion Mortgage (HECM),* your home must be a single-family property, a two- to four-unit building, or a federally approved condominium or planned-unit development (PUD). Reverse mortgage programs will lend on mobile homes with foundations that meet the U.S. Department of Housing and Urban Development (HUD) guidelines but won't lend on cooperative apartments.

- If you have any debt against your home, you must either pay it off before getting a reverse mortgage or, as most borrowers do, use an immediate cash advance from the reverse mortgage to pay it off. If you don't pay off the debt beforehand or don't qualify for a large enough immediate cash advance to do so, you can't get a reverse mortgage.

One final and important point about qualifying for a reverse mortgage: Lenders are now required to perform a financial assessment analyzing the prospective borrower's financial situation, including credit history and monthly income and expenses. Lenders pay particular attention to whether borrowers have enough cash flow to pay their property tax and home insurance bills. If borrowers have little wiggle room in their monthly budget, lenders may require a "set aside" fund to ensure payment of property taxes and home insurance, and this set aside fund reduces how large a reverse mortgage the borrowers can get. The amount of this set aside fund may also vary depending on the age of the reverse mortgage borrowers.

How much money can you get and when?

The whole point of taking out a reverse mortgage on your home is to get money from the equity in your home. How much can you tap? That amount depends mostly on your home's worth, your age, and the interest and other fees a given lender charges. The more your home is worth, the older you are, and the lower the interest rate and other fees your lender charges, the more money you should realize from a reverse mortgage.

- For all but the most expensive homes, the federally insured Home Equity Conversion Mortgage (HECM) generally provides the most cash and is available in every state.
- In general, the most cash is available for the oldest borrowers living in the homes of greatest value over current debt (net equity) at a time when interest rates are low. On the other hand, the least cash generally goes to the youngest borrowers living in the homes of lowest value (or with high current debt) at a time when interest rates are high.

The total amount of cash you actually end up getting from a reverse mortgage depends on how it's paid to you plus other factors. You can choose among the following options to receive your reverse mortgage money:

- **Monthly:** Most people need monthly income to live on. Thus, a commonly selected reverse mortgage option is monthly payments. However, not all monthly payment options are created equal. Some reverse mortgage programs commit to a particular monthly payment for a preset number of years. Other programs make payments as long as you continue living in your home or for life. Not surprisingly, if you select a reverse mortgage program that pays you over a longer period of time, you generally receive less monthly — probably a good deal less — than from a program that pays you for a fixed number of years.

- **Line of credit:** Instead of receiving a monthly check, you can simply create a line of credit from which you draw money by writing a check whenever you need income. Because interest doesn't start accumulating on a loan until you actually borrow money, the advantage of a credit line is that you pay only for the money you need and use. If you have fluctuating and irregular needs for additional money, a line of credit may be for you. This is also the preferred way to access funds if your financial goal is to limit the equity you pull from your home to its increase in value. The size of the line of credit is either set at the time you close on your reverse mortgage loan or may increase over time. Generally, during the first 12 months, you can receive up to but no more than 60 percent of the maximum loan allowed.
- **Lump sum:** The third, and generally least beneficial, type of reverse mortgage is the lump-sum option. When you close on this type of reverse mortgage, you receive a check for the entire amount that you were approved to borrow. Lump-sum payouts usually make sense only when you have an immediate need for a substantial amount of cash for a specific purpose, such as making a major purchase or paying off an existing or delinquent mortgage debt to keep from losing your home to foreclosure. Ironically, but also a blessing, when your financial troubles are caused by falling behind on your mortgage payments, you can get a reverse mortgage to tap the remaining equity in your home to assist in resolving your immediate pending foreclosure.
- **Mix and match:** Perhaps you need a large chunk of money for some purchases you've been putting off, but you also want the security of a regular monthly income. You can usually put together combinations of the preceding three programs. Some reverse mortgage lenders even allow you to alter the payment structure as time goes on. Not all reverse mortgage programs offer all the combinations, so shop around even more if you're interested in mixing and matching your payment options.

When do you pay the money back?

As we discuss earlier in this chapter (see the section "Considering common objections"), some reverse mortgage borrowers worry about having to repay their loan balance. Here are the conditions under which you generally have to repay a reverse mortgage:

» When the last surviving borrower dies, sells the home, or permanently moves away. "Permanently" generally means that the borrower hasn't lived in the home for 12 consecutive months.

» Possibly, if you do any of the following:

- Fail to pay your property taxes
- Fail to keep up your homeowners insurance
- Let your home fall into disrepair

If you fail to properly maintain your home and it falls into disrepair, the lender may be able to make extra cash advances to cover these repair expenses. Just remember that reverse mortgage borrowers are still homeowners and therefore are still responsible for taxes, insurance, and upkeep.

What do you owe?

The total amount you will owe at the end of the loan (your loan balance) equals

» All the cash advances you've received (including any used to pay loan costs)

» Plus all the interest on them — up to the loan's nonrecourse limit (the value of the home)

If you get an adjustable-rate reverse mortgage, the interest rate can vary based on changes in published indexes (see Chapter 5). The greater a loan's permissible interest rate adjustment, the lower its interest rate initially. As a result, you get a larger cash advance with this type of loan than you do with loans that have higher initial interest rates.

You can never owe more than the value of the home at the time the loan is repaid. True reverse mortgages are *nonrecourse loans*, which means that in seeking repayment the lender doesn't have recourse to anything other than your home — not your income, your other assets, or your heirs' finances.

Even if you get monthly advances until you're 115 years old, even if your home declines in value between now and then, and even if the total of monthly advances becomes greater than your home's value — you can still never owe more than the value of your home. If you or your heirs sell your home to pay off the loan, the debt is limited by the net proceeds from the sale of your home.

How is the loan repaid?

How a reverse mortgage is repaid depends on the circumstances under which the loan ends:

- If you sell and move, you'd most likely pay back the loan from the money you get from selling your home. But you could pay it back from other funds if you had them.
- If the loan ends due to the death of the last surviving borrower, the loan must be repaid before the home's title can be transferred to the borrower's heirs. The heirs may repay the loan by selling the home, using other funds from the borrower's estate, using their own funds, or by taking out a new forward mortgage against the home.

As lenders have learned, not all reverse mortgage borrowers end up living in their homes for the rest of their lives. Some folks who originally planned to live in a particular house forever subsequently change their minds. Others develop health problems that force them to move. So it makes sense to plan for the possibility that you may sell and move some day. How much equity would be left if you did?

If, at the end of the loan, your loan balance is less than the value of your home (or your net sale proceeds if you sell), then you or your heirs get to keep the difference. The lender doesn't get the house. The lender gets paid the amount you owe on the reverse mortgage, and you or your heirs keep the rest of the house's proceeds of sale.

TIP

If you take the loan as a credit line account, be sure to withdraw all your remaining available credit before the loan ends. You have access to the money sooner that way, and the amount could be more than otherwise may be left. For example, a growing credit line could become greater than the leftover equity if the home's value decreases.

What's the out-of-pocket cost of getting a reverse mortgage?

The out-of-pocket cash cost to you with a reverse mortgage is usually limited to just two modest items. First is an application fee that covers a property appraisal (to see how much your home is worth). Second is a minimal credit check (to see whether you're delinquent on any federally insured loans).

Other costs, including the loan origination fee, can be financed with the loan. This means you can use reverse mortgage funds advanced to you at closing to pay the costs due at that time and later advances to pay any *ongoing costs,* such as monthly servicing fees. The advances are added to your loan balance and become part of what you owe — and pay interest on.

What are the other reverse mortgage costs?

The specific cost items vary from one program to another. Many of them are of the same type found on forward mortgages: interest charges, origination fees, and whatever third-party closing costs (title search and insurance, surveys, inspections, document and recording fees, and property taxes) are required in your area.

Two other costs unique to some reverse mortgages are the monthly servicing fee, which can cost up to $35 per month, and a reverse mortgage insurance premium, which can cost up to 2.5 percent of the home's value at closing (this premium is just 0.5 percent if you take no more than 60 percent of the approved funds).

In addition to the upfront insurance charge paid at closing, there is also an annual mortgage insurance premium of 1.25 percent of your reverse mortgage balance. This ongoing premium accumulates and is owed and paid once your loan ends and is paid back.

TIP

Within the federally insured Home Equity Conversion Mortgage (HECM) program, the costs that may be different from one lender to another are the origination fee, the servicing fee, third-party closing costs, and the interest rate. To get the best deal, compare these specific costs.

With HECM loans, there is a maximum origination fee of 2 percent of the first $200,000 of the home's value and 1 percent of the amount above $200,000 to a maximum fee allowed of $6,000. ***Note:*** Individual lenders may charge lower origination fees at their discretion.

It's difficult to evaluate or compare the true, total cost of reverse mortgages because that amount ultimately depends on the following:

- How long you end up keeping the loan
- The cash advances you receive during the loan
- The interest rate charged on the loan
- Your home's value when the loan is over

You can, however, compare the costs of different reverse mortgages by evaluating each loan's total annual average loan cost, also known as the total annual rate. We give you more information about that in the following section.

What's the total annual rate?

The total annual rate on a reverse mortgage includes all the loan's costs. On any given loan, total annual rates depend on two major factors: time and appreciation.

Total annual average rates are generally greatest in the early years of the loan and decrease over time, for two reasons:

- The initial fees and costs become a smaller part of the total amount owed as years go by.
- The likelihood increases that the rising loan balance will catch up to — and then be limited by — the nonrecourse limit the longer you have the loan.

Total annual rates also depend on changes in a home's value over time. The less appreciation, the greater the likelihood that a rising loan balance will catch up to — and then be limited by — the home's value. On the other hand, when a home appreciates at a robust rate, the loan balance may never catch up to (and be limited by) it.

If you end up living in your home well past your projected life expectancy or your home appreciates at a lower rate than anticipated, you may get a true bargain. But if you die, sell, or move within just a few years, the true cost could be quite high.

When deciding to go with a reverse mortgage, you simply can't avoid the fundamental risk that the true cost could end up being quite high. You just have to understand the risk in general, assess the potential range of total rates on a specific loan, and decide whether the risk is worth the benefits you expect to get from the loan.

Just remember, total annual rates aren't really comparable to the interest rates quoted on forward mortgages because

- Total annual rates include all the costs.
- Reverse mortgages require no monthly repayments.
- Reverse mortgages can provide an open-ended monthly income guarantee or a guaranteed credit line (which may grow larger).
- You can never owe more than your home's worth, even if its net value is less than what your loan balance would otherwise have been.

How do reverse mortgages affect your government-sponsored benefits?

Social Security and Medicare benefits aren't affected by reverse mortgages. But Supplemental Security Income (SSI) and Medicaid are different. Reverse mortgages will affect these and other public benefit programs under certain circumstances:

- Because they don't count as income, loan advances on a reverse mortgage generally don't affect your benefits if you spend them during the calendar month in which you get them. But if you keep an advance past the end of the calendar month (in a checking or savings account, for example), it counts as a *liquid asset.* If your total liquid assets at the end of any month are greater than $2,000 for a single person or $3,000 for a couple, you could lose your eligibility.
- If anyone in the business of selling annuities has tried to sell you on the idea of using proceeds from a reverse mortgage to purchase an annuity, you need to know that annuity advances reduce SSI benefits dollar for dollar and can make you ineligible for Medicaid. So if you're considering an annuity and if you're now receiving — or expect that someday you may qualify for — SSI or Medicaid, check with the SSI, Medicaid, and other program offices in your community. Get specific details on how annuity income affects these benefits.

Shopping for a Reverse Mortgage

Reverse mortgages give you a new retirement financial option that previous generations of homeowners didn't have. These loans can provide an important new source of retirement cash — without requiring you to leave your home or to make loan payments for as long as you live there.

But you have to proceed carefully. What you don't know about reverse mortgages *can* hurt you. The most important — and perhaps surprising — facts you need to understand are these:

- You may get a lot more cash from one reverse mortgage program than from another.
- The true cost of one program may be much greater than the cost of another.
- A program giving you significantly more cash may also cost less than any other.

» To find the program that works best for you, you have to take both of the following into account:
   - How much total cash would be available to you in growing versus flat credit lines
   - The comparative total annual rate on competing loans

» Lenders offering a variety of plans may try to sell you one plan versus another because they make more money on it.

Reverse mortgages are a specialty loan product that requires loan officers to receive training to be eligible to work on a reverse mortgage. Most loan officers (even the best ones with decades of experience) don't work with reverse mortgages. When you decide to apply for a reverse mortgage, ask enough questions to make sure the loan officer has done dozens of reverse mortgages. You don't want a loan officer figuring out reverse mortgages on your loan!

Making major choices

Which reverse mortgage plan — if any — would work the best for you?

» The federally insured Home Equity Conversion Mortgage (HECM) is most likely to provide more cash at a lower cost, especially if you want a credit line, or if you own your home jointly with a spouse or other person. But be aware that $636,150 is the maximum loan limit allowed on a HECM as of 2017.

» Consider shopping the two private reverse mortgage providers — American Advisors Group and Finance of America Reverse Mortgage — especially if you own a higher value property. Private reverse mortgage providers aren't subject to the same regulations and loan limits as HECM providers.

Although HECM may be more likely to provide significantly more cash at a lot lower cost on the credit lines most consumers prefer, the best plan for you depends on your specific situation. So you need to consider *all* your reverse mortgage options. That's especially important if you

» Want a monthly loan advance only

» Live in a home worth substantially more than the average

Later in this chapter (see the section "Deciding Whether You Want a Reverse Mortgage"), we give you additional considerations to ponder when thinking about whether a reverse mortgage is your best option.

Counseling

To get a HECM reverse mortgage, you must complete a counseling session with a HUD-approved counselor. Visit `https://portal.hud.gov/hudportal/HUD?src=/program_offices/housing/sfh/hecm/hecmlist` to find approved counselors in your area or call 800-569-4287. Reverse mortgages can get complicated quickly, and most folks find them challenging to fully understand. So having to complete counseling before committing to a reverse mortgage is a good thing.

Counselors ask ten questions during each session to be sure borrows have an understanding of the basics of reverse mortgages. To "pass" the counseling session, the prospective borrowers must answer at least five of the ten questions correctly. If they can't, they may need to go back for more sessions. Counseling fees are reasonable and typically cost about $125, although they may vary based on the borrowers' financial situation and may even be waived for lower income folks.

Deciding Whether You Want a Reverse Mortgage

Only you can decide what a reverse mortgage is worth to you. The value probably mostly depends on your purpose for the money, such as the following:

- Increasing your monthly income
- Having a cash reserve (credit line account) for irregular or unexpected expenses
- Paying off debt that requires monthly repayments
- Repairing or improving your home
- Getting the services you need to remain independent
- Improving the quality of your life (perhaps fulfilling some of your bucket list items)

One approach is to consider a major alternative: selling your home and moving to a less expensive form of housing. Think about the following questions:

- How much money could you get by selling your home?
- What would it cost you to buy and maintain or rent a new one?

- How much could you safely earn (that is, without exposing yourself to excessive risk) on sale proceeds not used for a new home?
- Could you tolerate living in the same home or even in that separate but all-too-close "Granny flat" with your relatives?

House Selling For Dummies, which Eric coauthored with real estate expert Ray Brown (published by Wiley), can help you think through the issues. If you do decide to sell your home, Eric and Ray's book will help you get top dollar.

Thanks to continued innovation in the mortgage industry, you could sell your current home, buy a different one, and, at the time of purchase, take out a reverse mortgage. To be eligible for a so-called "HECM for Purchase," which enables you to buy a home in part using proceeds from a new reverse mortgage, you generally need to make a significant down payment (50-plus percent of the purchase price), and the reverse mortgage finances the rest. You'd do this in place of of making an all-cash purchase.

5

The Part of Tens

IN THIS PART . . .

Find out what options you have if you're facing foreclosure.

Discover ten mortgage traps to avoid.

» Knowing the best sources for objective information and advice

» Understanding the realities of foreclosure investing

Chapter 14

Ten-Plus "Must-Knows" About Foreclosure

Lenders have a contractual right to take over ownership of a property (foreclose) if the borrower can't make required payments. Even in the best of times, some foreclosures occur, but the number of foreclosures accelerates during soft real estate markets or because of risky loans. From 2006 through 2010, the number of foreclosures increased tremendously as real estate prices declined and numerous borrowers found themselves saddled with high-cost mortgages.

In Las Vegas, home prices plunged by more than 60 percent from early 2006 to 2011 — the greatest percentage decline in home prices of the 50 largest metropolitan areas in the nation. With that incredible decrease in home value, it's easy to understand the record number of home foreclosures because many homeowners who hadn't owned for long found that they were living in homes worth less than the amount they owed on their mortgage.

Having the home in which you're living end up in foreclosure is a nasty, unpleasant experience for most folks. In most instances, homeowners become overextended with their bills or lose some or all of their income(s) and simply can't afford to muster their mortgage payment. Meanwhile, some homeowners whose properties end up in foreclosure aren't in dire financial straits. Instead, they choose to walk away from a property that dropped in value and is worth less than the outstanding mortgage amount. As we note in Chapter 3, either course of action will probably have severe repercussions on your credit score and ability to borrow in the future.

In other cases, overextended investors walk away from multiple properties that declined in value. (This was the major factor in the Las Vegas market crash with more than 40,000 homes being purchased by investors seeking rapid appreciation only to see the market plummet.) Instead of continuing to make payments on property that's worth less than they paid for it, some investors cut and run.

Although we feel sorry for some investors caught up in the pre-2007 frenzy of speculative buying of rental homes, this chapter is really geared to homeowners who may be in danger of losing their home to foreclosure. Some tips also apply to folks attracted to investment opportunities on property in foreclosure. While the number of foreclosures is significantly lower throughout the country since 2010, some homeowners are going to be unable to meet their loan obligations and a short sale or foreclosure is in their future.

Deal with Reality

Just as a lot of folks do when consumer debt (on credit cards and auto loans) gets overwhelming, many people falling behind on their mortgage payments want to run and hide. Mortgage statements and bills go unopened and calls from the lender go unanswered and unreturned. Some folks with excessive credit card bills do the same thing. Sticking your head in the sand when it comes to mortgage payments does you no good. You'll lose your home if you don't take action now.

TIP

The sooner you contact your lender and level with them about your problems, the better. Explain your financial situation, debt burdens, and what you can afford to pay monthly on your mortgage. That said, don't allow any person at a financial institution to berate or verbally abuse you. Find a way to do the best you can. Avail yourself of financial counseling and try negotiating better mortgage terms (we cover both of these topics later in this chapter).

Heed this sage advice from veteran mortgage professional Chris Bruno:

> Whether one is in foreclosure, contemplating foreclosure, or buying a foreclosed property, getting competent professional help early in the process is extremely important for a more favorable outcome. I have seen many people come to me at the 11th hour having never responded to the foreclosure documents from the lender. Needless to say, it's very stressful, and the delay only limited their options and made the whole process much more expensive.

Review Your Spending and Debts

The first step in taking the bull by the horns when you're drowning in mortgage debt is to zoom out to 30,000 feet and look at your entire financial situation. Tabulate all your debts and spending. Identify expenses you can most easily reduce. Although your housing expenses are a significant portion of your total expenditures, they're probably less than the majority of your typical monthly expenses.

Complete the worksheets in Chapter 1 of this book to help you identify ways to reduce your spending and debts, including consumer debts. For detailed assistance with analyzing your spending and debts, see the latest edition of Eric's *Personal Finance For Dummies* (Wiley).

Beware of Foreclosure Scams

Perhaps the only thing worse in the real estate world than falling behind on your payments and entering the foreclosure process is falling prey to the circling vultures trying to take advantage of your hardship and lack of financial knowledge. In the late 2000s, increasing numbers of scoundrels and hucksters made claims that they could stop foreclosure no matter what the situation. After charging fees of $1,000-plus and doing little if anything, in the worst cases, unsuspecting homeowners sign over ownership of their property (and begin making rental payments) to the con artists!

Only make use of counselors approved by the U.S. Department of Housing and Urban Development (HUD). We explain how to find these good guys and gals in the "Make Use of Objective Counseling" section, later in this chapter.

Consider Tapping Other Assets

As long as you're not going to declare bankruptcy (check out the "Understand Bankruptcy" section, later in this chapter), you should make a list of assets you might tap to help meet your mortgage payments. These assets may include bank saving accounts, mutual funds, stocks, bonds, cash value life insurance policy balances, 401(k) plans, unneeded personal property you could sell, and so on. Be sure you fully understand all tax consequences before liquidating any investments to help make mortgage payments.

In the unlikely event that you'll file for bankruptcy protection, don't use the proceeds from your other assets for home payments. The reason: You may be able to protect and keep those other assets if you file for bankruptcy.

Make Use of Objective Counseling

A number of nonprofit organizations offer low-cost or free counseling to homeowners in danger of losing their homes to foreclosure. The best way to find those agencies is to contact the U.S. Department of Housing and Urban Development (HUD) "housing counseling agency locator" at 800-569-4287. Select the option for mortgage delinquency counseling and then enter your five-digit zip code to obtain the name and phone number of approved counseling agencies near you.

Alternatively, you can visit the HUD website (www.hud.gov) and then click the HUD Approved Housing Counseling Agencies link under the Resources tab on the home page. In addition to helpful articles, the website enables you to find multiple area counseling agencies.

Negotiate with Your Lender

Smart lenders don't want your property to end up in foreclosure, especially if the mortgage balance exceeds what the lender could reasonably expect to net (after selling and other expenses) from selling the property. If your current mortgage terms appear to doom you to foreclosure, contact your lender immediately and plead your case to have your loan modified. Sure, the modification will hurt your credit, but it's likely already damaged if you're facing foreclosure. Also, remember that the modified (lower) payments may help you keep your home while you rebuild your credit.

You also may want to see whether you qualify under the specific and limited conditions for borrowers seeking to restructure or refinance homes with low equity, no equity, or *negative equity* (the home is worth less than the loan). You may qualify for a government program, such as the Home Affordable Refinance Program (HARP), that allows homeowners to refinance their loan. Note that these programs are constantly evolving and the terms may change periodically, so you need to continually see whether you qualify. For example, the HARP program started in 2009, but by late 2011, it was modified and referred to as HARP 2.0. Then, President Obama proposed further changes and a revised HARP 3.0, but Congress never approved that proposed program. Our point here is that you'll hear a lot of hype about government programs that will solve all your problems. Be cautious and skeptical, but seek the advice of an objective counselor (as we suggest earlier) as there may genuinely be some help out there for you.

TIP

For ideas on how to customize your current loan terms to help you afford your home, consult with a local HUD-approved counselor, as discussed in the previous section. Most lenders can make your current loan more attractive through a modification (by reducing the interest rate or changing the rate to a fixed-rate from an adjustable, for example) if doing so will keep you out of foreclosure and keep you making monthly payments.

Understand Short Sales

If your home is worth less than the amount you owe on the mortgage(s), it is said to be *underwater* or *upside down*. You may think you can't sell the home because you won't clear enough money to satisfy the lender(s), real estate agents, and closing costs, and therefore foreclosure is the only option. But, thankfully, you can opt for a short sale.

A *short sale* means you can sell your house (avoiding foreclosure) and pay off the lender(s) for less than what they are owed. The lender(s) is getting a payoff that is "short" of what it is owed — hence the name short sale.

The lender has to approve a short sale, but it happens regularly. Why would the lender do this? Because it's easier and less expensive for them than processing a full foreclosure. Why would you do this? Because, compared with foreclosure, it is better for your credit (see the "Consider the Future Impact to Your Credit Report" section later in this chapter.)

Seek Legal and Tax Advice

If you're confronted with or considering foreclosure, talk to an experienced real estate lawyer and tax advisor before you agree to a foreclosure or short sale (see the preceding section). In fact, seek their advice before you even start skipping mortgage payments. There are state and federal laws involved, and you need to know

- If the lender loses money on the foreclosure or short sale, can they come after you for the difference (called a *deficiency judgment*)? This varies from state to state and is a question for the attorney.

» If the lender loses money on the foreclosure or short sale, can the IRS tax you on the amount the lender loses? It may sound crazy, but the IRS may consider the loss that the lender suffers (which they write off) as a taxable benefit to you. It is called *debt relief.* This may or may not apply at the time you're reading this, so find out by asking your tax advisor.

Understand Bankruptcy

To make the best decision you can, consider a range of options. When mortgage and other debt prove overwhelming, bankruptcy is one option you should explore and better understand.

Bankruptcy is usually used to eliminate miscellaneous unsecured revolving debts (like credit cards) so you have more money with which to make mortgage payments and keep the home.

The biggest challenge with considering bankruptcy is finding unbiased sources of information and advice. Some supposed counselors won't discuss or recommend it to you; others, such as bankruptcy attorneys, often have a bias at the other end of the spectrum. Truly independent or the HUD-approved counselors recommended earlier in this chapter are a good starting point.

WARNING

Be careful if the financial counselor or advisor is affiliated with a "credit repair" service or a "bankruptcy mill" because his solutions are almost guaranteed to be the products offered by his own or an affiliated company.

Consider the Future Impact to Your Credit Report

Folks who make little if any effort to find a solution to their housing debt woes and who choose to walk away from a property that's proven to be a loss from an investment perspective often suffer consequences down the road. Before taking this step, think for a moment about the long-term consequences. If you were a lender, how motivated would you be to lend money to someone who threw in the towel without working to find a solution? And if you did lend such a person money, would you give him or her the best loan rates and terms that you give folks with excellent credit histories?

TIP

Roll up your sleeves and work with your lender and talk with counselors to find a solution that will enable you to keep your property. Remember that the lender is best served by having the property occupied by an owner who will continue to properly maintain the home. Use that argument to your advantage because the lender will very likely suffer added costs and expenses (such as insurance) if the home is unoccupied for an extended period of time. Many municipalities are well aware that these vacant homes aren't being properly maintained and are an invitation to squatters and crime. They have passed new laws allowing for significant fines and penalties if these homes become a blight on the neighborhood. Your credit report may still suffer damage, but you can minimize the fallout both now and in the future.

Two of the biggest questions after a foreclosure, short sale, or bankruptcy are

- How long before my credit recovers?
- How long before I can get a mortgage again?

Regarding the first question, most lenders don't want you to know that it only takes two to three years (of effort) to rebuild your credit scores to a level worthy of a new home loan. As far as credit cards, auto loans, and other loans? You can get those very quickly after problems on your credit report.

As for getting a loan to buy another house, different types of loans require different waiting periods before you're eligible to apply for a new mortgage. But the waiting periods are often much less than most people expect. Check out Table 14-1 to understand the various waiting periods.

TABLE 14-1 Required Wait Times before Applying for a New Mortgage

Program	Foreclosure	Bankruptcy	Short Sale
Conventional	7 years from completion	**Chapter 7:** 4 years from discharge/dismissal **Chapter 13:** 2 years from discharge/4 years from dismissal	4 years from completion
FHA	3 years from completion date	**Chapter 7:** 2 years from discharge **Chapter 13:** 1 year of payment period must have elapsed with satisfactory payment performance and permission from the court	No waiting period if * Borrower made all mortgage/installment payments within the month due for 12 months before the short sale, *and* * Made all mortgage/installment payments within the month due for the 12-month period before the date of the loan application for the new mortgage 3 years of waiting from completion date required if borrower was in default at time of sale

(continued)

TABLE 14-1 *(continued)*

Program	Foreclosure	Bankruptcy	Short Sale
VA	2 years from foreclosure date	**Chapter 7:** 2 years from discharge **Chapter 13:** 1 year of payment period must have elapsed with satisfactory payment performance and permission from the court	2 years from completion
USDA	3 years from completion	**Chapter 7:** 3 years from discharge **Chapter 13:** 1 year of payment period must have elapsed with satisfactory payment performance and permission from the court	No waiting period if * Borrower made all mortgage/installment payments within the month due for 12 months before the short sale, *and* * Made all mortgage/installment payments within the month due for the 12-month period before the date of the loan application for the new mortgage

Understand the Realities of Investing in Foreclosed Property

You may be considering purchasing a property that's in some stage of foreclosure. Although earning handsome returns on investing in foreclosed property is an option, make absolutely sure that you know what you're getting into. Doing so isn't as easy as some real estate investing cheerleaders may lead you to think.

Often, property that ends up in foreclosure has physical problems. So if you rush to buy without *thoroughly* inspecting a property inside and out, you could end up with more trouble and costs than you expected.

Although a proven way for savvy real estate entrepreneurs to build their empire, investing in foreclosures is for sophisticated, experienced investors only. Finding and buying a good property at an attractive price (including the realistic or actual costs for repairs, renovations, upgrades, plus holding and marketing costs) takes a lot of homework and patience. See the latest edition of our book *Real Estate Investing For Dummies* (Wiley) for more details.

» Using the 2 percent rule to help you, not hold you back

» Being careful about mortgage brokers

Chapter 15
Ten Mortgage No-Nos

Experience is the name everyone gives to their mistakes.

— OSCAR WILDE

Learning from other people's mistakes is infinitely better than learning from your own.

— ERIC AND ROBERT

Mortgage misadventures don't have to happen. Fortunately for you, dear reader, each and every one of the expensive errors in this chapter is easily avoidable. Knowledge *is* power. As you boldly venture forth into the treacherous world of real estate lending, remember our coaching. Armed with your wealth of knowledge, and this book as a handy reference guide, you are truly powerful.

Don't Let Lenders Tell You What You Can Afford

Unless you're richer than Warren Buffet, you could inadvertently overextend yourself when you get a mortgage. How? By taking on more debt than you can comfortably handle. Just because a lender says you qualify for a certain loan amount doesn't mean you should blithely bound into debt for that much money.

Don't commit to a mortgage larger than you can comfortably afford. This lesson was painfully apparent from 2006 through 2010, thanks to a housing slump and a sharply higher rate of foreclosures. But even during good economic times and strong housing markets, foreclosures happen and often are the result of folks being overextended (see Chapter 14 for more info about foreclosures).

Even the best of lenders can't tell you how much you can prudently afford to borrow because they don't know all the nuances of your personal financial situation. They can tell you only how big a financial risk they're willing to take on you.

TIP

Realistically evaluate your present and future financial goals. Estimate how your living expenses will change when buying a given home. Don't fudge the numbers so they come out the way you want them to. You'll hurt only yourself if you underestimate expenses and overestimate income. Carefully read Chapter 1 for more help.

Never Confuse Loan Prequalification with Preapproval

Why waste weeks or even months of your valuable time looking at property you may want to purchase only to belatedly discover that no lending institution other than a pawnshop or a loan shark will give you a loan? Instead of rushing out to gawk at property, smart folks start the home-buying process by determining whether lenders consider them creditworthy and how much they can borrow in dollars and cents.

Getting prequalified for a mortgage isn't tough. Heck, even bankrupt arsonists can get themselves prequalified. Robert's dog (Maddison Griswold) once got a letter indicating that she was prequalified for a home loan! And therein lies the problem. As we note in Chapter 2, loan prequalification entails nothing more than a perfunctory perusal of your finances. In terms of overall effectiveness, it ranks with attempting to raise the water level of the Pacific Ocean by melting the ice cubes from your freezer in it.

Loan preapproval, conversely, is extremely thorough. With your permission, a lender independently verifies financial facts such as your income and expenses, your assets and liabilities, the amount of cash you have for a down payment, and your credit history, including your credit score. If you pass the lender's inspection, you get a letter stating that you've been preapproved for a mortgage — the next best thing to having a line of credit at your disposal. You *know* how much you can borrow.

There's another excellent reason to get preapproved: Credit reports sometimes contain inaccurate information. Left uncorrected, that misinformation may adversely affect a borrower's credit score and make it difficult to qualify for the lowest possible interest rate. If you find errors on your credit report during the preapproval process, you have time to correct them before they cost you money. See Chapter 3 for the details on credit reports.

TIP

With a preapproval in your hands, you also have a delightful advantage over buyers who haven't been preapproved for a loan if you find yourself in a multiple-offer situation. This does happen now that the real estate market has rebounded in most areas of the country, and it's even a strong seller's market in some areas. Because those other people never bothered to authenticate their creditworthiness, the sellers don't know whether they're serious buyers or just tire kickers. You, on the other hand, have written verification that you're a financially qualified buyer. As a result, your offer will be given the attention and respect it so richly deserves.

Avoid Loans with Prepayment Penalties

Suppose that you loaned a couple of pals $2,500. They faithfully promised they'd repay you in a year. So you were overjoyed when you got the money back in six months.

Sad to say, that's not the reaction of certain mortgage lenders. Believe it or not, if your loan has a prepayment penalty, lenders have the right to charge you thousands of dollars for repaying your mortgage before it's due.

Chapter 4 explains how to determine whether the lender can impose a prepayment penalty on a loan you're considering. Don't despair if your present mortgage happens to have a prepayment penalty. As we explain in Chapter 4, you may be able to prepay some of the outstanding loan balance without penalty as long as you time the additional principal payments correctly or keep your payments under a previously specified amount of money, usually 20 percent of the original loan amount.

Don't Reflexively Grab a Fixed-Rate Mortgage

FRM, ARM, GPM, VRM, HELOC, HECM, IOU. The alphabet soup of loans sloshing around in today's financial market would give anyone a mortgage migraine. No matter how complicated they sound, all these loans fall into one of two basic classifications — fixed rate or adjustable rate. At times, a fixed-rate loan is decidedly better than an adjustable-rate mortgage (ARM) and vice versa.

Some people, however, opt for fixed-rate mortgages because these mortgages have been around longer than ARMs and because they're easier to understand. Unfortunately, that means some people are using the wrong criteria to select their mortgages.

Chapter 5 shows how to use the answers to three simple questions to decide whether a fixed-rate mortgage or an ARM is likely the best loan for you. You'll discover that everything boils down to determining how long you plan to keep the loan, how much financial risk you can accept, and how much money you want to borrow.

TIP

If you intend to keep your loan three to ten years, your best financing option may be a hybrid loan of five to ten years, which combines the stability of a fixed-rate mortgage with the lower initial interest rate of an ARM. Most folks don't even know such a loan exists. Now *you* do.

Steer Clear of Toxic 100 Percent Home Equity Loans

Equity is the difference between what your property is worth in today's market and how much you currently owe on it. Suppose, for example, that your house was just appraised for $200,000, and your outstanding loan balance is $120,000. You have $80,000 of equity in your home. Isn't it great to be a homeowner?

You can use a home equity loan (HELOC), which we discuss in Chapter 6, to free up some of that equity for other purposes. Home equity loans can be excellent financial tools when used prudently.

Used imprudently, however, home equity loans are a fast track to ruin. The most shocking example of this is an equity loan for 100 percent (or more, we kid you not) of your home's value. (Before the housing market downturn of the late 2000s scared lenders and regulators silly, we were appalled to see 125 percent home equity loans.) Just like buyers in the years prior to the 2008 financial crisis, lenders thought that the only direction home values went was up! So they foolishly offered loan products that were based on that cornerstone of illogical financial planning.

Homeowners typically get a 100 percent home equity loan to relieve the oppressive burden of high monthly payments on their credit card debt. After getting a 100 percent home equity loan, however, many of these folks blithely run up more credit card bills and eventually find themselves even deeper in the credit abyss.

WARNING

Getting a 100 percent home equity loan to consolidate credit card debt isn't a panacea. If you simply stretch out repayment of debt instead of addressing the underlying problem of credit mismanagement, you'll ultimately pay even more in total interest charges. Worse yet, you'll convert unsecured credit card debt into mortgage debt. That puts your home in jeopardy of foreclosure if you fail to make the scheduled monthly loan payments.

If you consult with an independent HUD-approved financial counselor or advisor (as we suggest in Chapter 14) who advises that you take out a HELOC to pay off that expensive, non-deductible consumer and credit card debt, also follow our advice to cut up those same credit cards and convert to using only debit cards for your day-to-day spending. That way, you'll at least be limited to the balance in your account (unless you foolishly use any of that expensive debit card overdraft protection sold to you by your favorite lender).

Watch Out for Mortgage Brokers with Hidden Agendas

Early on in your quest for the elusive *best* mortgage, you'll have to decide whether you'd rather shop for a loan yourself by contacting lenders directly or use a mortgage broker to shop for you. Mortgage brokers don't lend their own money. They act as intermediaries for direct lenders such as banks and other lending institutions that ultimately provide the funds for your mortgage.

Thousands of lenders out there would love to help you get financing. Many of them are mediocre, a few are good, and an even smaller number are great. Chapter 7 is filled with techniques you can use to isolate the best from the rest.

WARNING

If your broker wants you to get a risky mortgage, such as a balloon loan (see Chapter 6) or a negative amortization ARM (covered next), watch out. The mortgage broker may be sacrificing your best interests to get a bigger commission. Good mortgage brokers concentrate on finding the best loan for you rather than generating the largest possible commission for themselves.

Shun Negative Amortization Mortgages

Good adjustable-rate mortgages, as we note in Chapter 5, adjust both the interest rate and the monthly loan payment at exactly the same time. Avoid ARMs that limit how much the monthly loan payment can increase without similarly limiting interest rate increases. This scenario can lead to *negative amortization*, a dreadful situation in which your loan balance gets larger rather than smaller each month.

Negative amortization occurs whenever your monthly loan payment is too small to pay all the loan's current monthly interest charges. The unpaid portion of interest is *added* to your loan balance. Every month that you have negative amortization, your loan grows larger by the amount of unpaid interest *plus* interest charges on your previous unpaid interest. Imagine making monthly payments but still owing more than you originally borrowed! This should be completely illogical to you and a strong indication that you're living beyond your means.

WARNING

Negative amortization has the potential to be a personal financial neutron bomb. It can financially destroy the borrower without harming the property. If you're offered an ARM with negative amortization, emphatically say, "NO!"

Don't Let the 2 Percent Rule Bully You When Refinancing

A well-intentioned friend may advise you that there absolutely, positively, without fail, must be *at least* a 2 percentage point differential between your present mortgage's interest rate and the new loan's rate before refinancing makes economic sense. The 2 percent rule is nothing more than a quick way to determine how fast you'll recover the cost of refinancing.

With a 2 percentage point spread between your old loan's interest rate and the new mortgage rate, you'll most likely recover all your refinancing costs in less than two years. However, if you don't intend to sell your home within the next few years, an interest rate differential smaller than 2 percent is fine. Getting your refinancing costs back will just take you a little longer. If you plan to stay in your property for many years, and mortgage rates have dropped at least 0.5 percent since you bought your home, you owe it to yourself to at least investigate the economics of refinancing. For more information, see Chapter 11.

Don't Assume That All Reverse Mortgages Are the Same or Bad

Homeowners 62 years of age or older can convert a portion of their home's equity into cash without having to sell the property or repay a loan each month. Eligibility for these home equity conversion mortgage programs (HECM) is based on such things as your age, your home's value, and the amount of your existing mortgage debt. You won't be disqualified, however, if you don't have a high income. On the contrary, many home equity conversion programs are specifically intended for low- to moderate-income folks.

These unusual loan programs are referred to as reverse mortgages, because they operate like a standard mortgage in reverse. Instead of borrowing a lump sum of money that you have to repay monthly, the lender sends you monthly payments. Each monthly payment you get converts some of your home's equity into cash. Yes, you're reducing your home equity to the extent that the cash you receive is less than any home price appreciation that may occur during the life of the reverse mortgage. But you can possibly tap the equity in your home, and if home prices rise sufficiently over time, your heirs may not see a significant reduction in their inheritance. That's called a *win-win*.

WARNING

Reverse mortgages offer eligible homeowners a source of retirement cash. But what you don't know about reverse mortgages can cost you big bucks. For instance, you may be able to get considerably more cash from one program than another. Worse yet, the true cost of various reverse mortgage programs differs significantly from lender to lender — and even among an assortment of programs offered by the same lender. *Proceed with extreme caution.* That said, don't incorrectly assume that a reverse mortgage lender can boot you out of your home against your will.

Avoid Mortgage Life Insurance

Soon after moving into your new home or refinancing your mortgage, you'll get several million junk mail solicitations for *optional* mortgage life insurance policies ghoulishly offering to pay off your loan if you kick the bucket. We strongly urge you not to purchase either mortgage life insurance or mortgage disability insurance. There's no correlation between your loan amount and how much life or disability insurance you need to protect your dependents. What's more, these policies tend to be grossly overpriced for the amount of insurance they offer.

TIP

Shop for insurance wisely. Low-cost, high-quality term life insurance and long-term disability insurance are far better solutions to fill the gaps in your insurance coverage.

6 Appendixes

IN THIS PART . . .

Estimate your monthly mortgage payments using the loan amortization tables.

Use the remaining balance tables to find out how much of your loan remains unpaid as the mortgage is amortized.

Refer to the glossary when you run across a term you're unfamiliar with.

Appendix A

Loan Amortization Table

In Chapter 3, we discuss the four basic components of loans:

- **Principal:** Money you borrow
- **Interest:** Percentage lenders charge you to use their money
- **Term:** Amount of time before your loan comes due
- **Amortization:** Loan payments comprised of principal and interest

By using the nifty tables in this appendix, you can estimate mortgage payments for the most frequently used loan terms ranging from 5 to 30 years and interest rates covering the spectrum from a lusciously low 3 percent all the way up to 18 percent. The amounts shown in these tables indicate how much you'd pay each month to fully repay a $100,000 loan by the end of the indicated term. You can, however, use the tables to calculate the monthly payment for any loan amount by using the following formula:

$$\text{Monthly loan payment} = \frac{\text{your loan amount}}{\$100{,}000} \times \text{payment shown in the table}$$

Example #1: If you get a $250,000, 30-year mortgage at 8.25 percent interest, your monthly principal and interest payment will be

$$\frac{\$250{,}000}{\$100{,}000} \times \$751.21 = \$1{,}878.18\,/\,\text{mo.}$$

Example #2: If you get a $60,000, 20-year mortgage at 12 percent interest, your monthly principal and interest payment will be

$$\frac{\$60{,}000}{\$100{,}000} \times \$1{,}101.09 = \$660.65\,/\,\text{mo.}$$

Monthly Payment to Amortize a Loan of $100,000

Interest Rate	5 Years	7 Years	10 Years	15 Years	20 Years	25 Years	30 Years
3.000%	$1,796.86	$1,321.33	$965.60	$690.58	$554.59	$474.21	$421.60
3.125%	$1,802.43	$1,326.97	$971.38	$696.60	$560.87	$480.73	$428.37
3.250%	$1,808.00	$1,332.62	$977.19	$702.66	$567.19	$487.31	$435.20
3.375%	$1,813.57	$1,338.29	$983.01	$708.75	$573.55	$493.94	$442.09
3.500%	$1,819.17	$1,343.98	$988.85	$714.88	$579.95	$500.62	$449.04
3.625%	$1,824.77	$1,349.68	$994.72	$721.03	$586.40	$507.35	$456.05
3.750%	$1,830.39	$1,355.40	$1,000.61	$727.22	$592.88	$514.13	$463.11
3.875%	$1,836.01	$1,361.13	$1,006.52	$733.44	$599.41	$520.95	$470.23
4.000%	$1,841.65	$1,366.88	$1,012.45	$739.68	$605.98	$527.83	$477.41
4.125%	$1,847.29	$1,372.64	$1,018.40	$745.96	$612.58	$534.76	$484.64
4.250%	$1,852.95	$1,378.41	$1,024.37	$752.27	$619.23	$541.73	$491.93
4.375%	$1,858.62	$1,384.21	$1,030.36	$758.62	$625.92	$548.76	$499.28
4.500%	$1,864.30	$1,390.01	$1,036.38	$764.99	$632.64	$555.83	$506.68
4.625%	$1,869.99	$1,395.83	$1,042.42	$771.39	$639.41	$562.95	$514.14
4.750%	$1,875.69	$1,401.67	$1,048.47	$777.83	$646.22	$570.11	$521.64
4.875%	$1,881.40	$1,407.52	$1,054.55	$784.29	$653.07	$577.33	$529.20
5.000%	$1,887.12	$1,413.39	$1,060.66	$790.79	$659.96	$584.59	$536.82
5.125%	$1,892.86	$1,419.27	$1,066.78	$797.32	$666.88	$591.90	$544.49
5.250%	$1,898.60	$1,425.17	$1,072.92	$803.88	$673.84	$599.25	$552.20
5.375%	$1,904.35	$1,431.08	$1,079.08	$810.47	$680.85	$606.65	$559.97
5.500%	$1,910.12	$1,437.00	$1,085.26	$817.08	$687.89	$614.09	$567.79
5.625%	$1,915.89	$1,442.94	$1,091.47	$823.73	$694.57	$621.57	$575.66
5.750%	$1,921.68	$1,448.90	$1,097.69	$830.41	$702.08	$629.11	$583.57
5.875%	$1,927.47	$1,454.87	$1,103.94	$837.12	$709.24	$636.68	$591.54
6.000%	$1,933.28	$1,460.86	$1,110.21	$843.86	$716.43	$644.30	$599.55
6.125%	$1,939.10	$1,466.86	$1,116.49	$850.62	$723.66	$651.96	$607.61

Monthly Payment to Amortize a Loan of $100,000

Interest Rate	5 Years	7 Years	10 Years	15 Years	20 Years	25 Years	30 Years
6.250%	$1,944.93	$1,472.87	$1,122.80	$857.42	$730.93	$659.67	$615.72
6.375%	$1,950.77	$1,478.90	$1,129.13	$864.25	$738.23	$667.42	$623.87
6.500%	$1,956.61	$1,484.94	$1,135.48	$871.11	$745.57	$675.21	$632.07
6.625%	$1,962.48	$1,491.00	$1,141.85	$877.99	$752.95	$683.04	$640.31
6.750%	$1,968.35	$1,497.08	$1,148.24	$884.91	$760.36	$690.91	$648.60
6.875%	$1,974.23	$1,503.16	$1,154.65	$891.85	$767.81	$698.83	$656.93
7.000%	$1,980.12	$1,509.27	$1,161.08	$898.83	$775.30	$706.78	$665.30
7.125%	$1,986.02	$1,515.39	$1,167.54	$905.83	$782.82	$714.77	$673.72
7.250%	$1,991.94	$1,521.52	$1,174.01	$912.86	$790.38	$722.81	$682.18
7.375%	$1,997.86	$1,527.67	$1,180.50	$919.92	$797.97	$730.88	$690.68
7.500%	$2,003.79	$1,533.83	$1,187.02	$927.01	$805.59	$738.99	$699.21
7.625%	$2,009.74	$1,540.00	$1,193.55	$934.13	$813.25	$747.14	$707.79
7.750%	$2,015.70	$1,546.20	$1,200.11	$941.28	$820.95	$755.33	$716.41
7.875%	$2,021.66	$1,552.40	$1,206.68	$948.45	$828.68	$763.55	$725.07
8.000%	$2,027.64	$1,558.62	$1,213.28	$955.65	$836.44	$771.82	$733.76
8.125%	$2,033.63	$1,564.86	$1,219.89	$962.88	$844.24	$780.12	$742.50
8.250%	$2,039.63	$1,571.11	$1,226.53	$970.14	$852.07	$788.45	$751.27
8.375%	$2,045.63	$1,577.37	$1,233.18	$977.43	$859.93	$796.82	$760.07
8.500%	$2,051.65	$1,583.65	$1,239.86	$984.74	$867.82	$805.23	$768.91
8.625%	$2,057.68	$1,589.94	$1,246.55	$992.08	$875.75	$813.67	$777.79
8.750%	$2,063.72	$1,596.25	$1,253.27	$999.45	$883.71	$822.14	$786.70
8.875%	$2,069.77	$1,602.57	$1,260.00	$1,006.84	$891.70	$830.65	$795.64
9.000%	$2,075.84	$1,608.91	$1,266.76	$1,014.27	$899.73	$839.20	$804.62
9.125%	$2,081.91	$1,615.26	$1,273.53	$1,021.72	$907.78	$847.77	$813.63
9.250%	$2,087.99	$1,621.62	$1,280.33	$1,029.19	$915.87	$856.38	$822.68
9.375%	$2,094.08	$1,628.00	$1,287.14	$1,036.70	$923.98	$865.02	$831.75

Monthly Payment to Amortize a Loan of $100,000

Interest Rate	5 Years	7 Years	10 Years	15 Years	20 Years	25 Years	30 Years
9.500%	$2,100.19	$1,634.40	$1,293.98	$1,044.22	$932.13	$873.70	$840.85
9.625%	$2,106.30	$1,640.81	$1,300.83	$1,051.78	$940.31	$882.40	$849.99
9.750%	$2,112.42	$1,647.23	$1,307.70	$1,059.36	$948.52	$891.14	$859.15
9.875%	$2,118.56	$1,653.67	$1,314.60	$1,066.97	$956.75	$899.90	$868.35
10.000%	$2,124.70	$1,660.12	$1,321.51	$1,074.61	$965.02	$908.70	$877.57
10.125%	$2,130.86	$1,666.58	$1,328.44	$1,082.27	$973.32	$917.53	$886.82
10.250%	$2,137.03	$1,673.06	$1,335.39	$1,089.95	$981.64	$926.38	$896.10
10.375%	$2,143.20	$1,679.56	$1,342.36	$1,097.66	$990.00	$935.27	$905.41
10.500%	$2,149.39	$1,686.07	$1,349.35	$1,105.40	$998.38	$944.18	$914.74
10.625%	$2,155.59	$1,692.59	$1,356.36	$1,113.16	$1,006.79	$953.12	$924.10
10.750%	$2,161.80	$1,699.13	$1,363.39	$1,120.95	$1,015.23	$962.09	$933.48
10.875%	$2,168.01	$1,705.68	$1,370.43	$1,128.76	$1,023.70	$971.09	$942.89
11.000%	$2,174.24	$1,712.24	$1,377.50	$1,136.60	$1,032.19	$980.11	$952.32
11.125%	$2,180.48	$1,718.82	$1,384.59	$1,144.46	$1,040.71	$989.16	$961.78
11.250%	$2,186.73	$1,725.42	$1,391.69	$1,152.34	$1,049.26	$998.24	$971.26
11.375%	$2,192.99	$1,732.02	$1,398.81	$1,160.26	$1,057.83	$1,007.34	$980.77
11.500%	$2,199.26	$1,738.65	$1,405.95	$1,168.19	$1,066.43	$1,016.47	$990.29
11.625%	$2,205.54	$1,745.28	$1,413.12	$1,176.15	$1,075.06	$1,025.62	$999.84
11.750%	$2,211.83	$1,751.93	$1,420.29	$1,184.13	$1,083.71	$1,034.80	$1,009.41
11.875%	$2,218.13	$1,758.60	$1,427.49	$1,192.14	$1,092.38	$1,044.00	$1,019.00
12.000%	$2,224.44	$1,765.27	$1,434.71	$1,200.17	$1,101.09	$1,053.22	$1,028.61
12.125%	$2,230.77	$1,771.97	$1,441.94	$1,208.22	$1,109.81	$1,062.47	$1,038.24
12.250%	$2,237.10	$1,778.67	$1,449.20	$1,216.30	$1,118.56	$1,071.74	$1,047.90
12.375%	$2,243.44	$1,785.39	$1,456.47	$1,224.40	$1,127.34	$1,081.04	$1,057.57
12.500%	$2,249.79	$1,792.12	$1,463.76	$1,232.52	$1,136.14	$1,090.35	$1,067.26
12.625%	$2,256.16	$1,798.87	$1,471.07	$1,240.67	$1,144.96	$1,099.69	$1,076.97

Monthly Payment to Amortize a Loan of $100,000

Interest Rate	5 Years	7 Years	10 Years	15 Years	20 Years	25 Years	30 Years
12.750%	$2,262.53	$1,805.63	$1,478.40	$1,248.84	$1,153.81	$1,109.05	$1,086.69
12.875%	$2,268.91	$1,812.41	$1,485.74	$1,257.03	$1,162.68	$1,118.43	$1,096.44
13.000%	$2,275.31	$1,819.20	$1,493.11	$1,265.24	$1,171.58	$1,127.84	$1,106.20
13.125%	$2,281.71	$1,826.00	$1,500.49	$1,273.48	$1,180.49	$1,137.26	$1,115.98
13.250%	$2,288.13	$1,832.82	$1,507.89	$1,281.74	$1,189.43	$1,146.70	$1,125.77
13.375%	$2,294.55	$1,839.65	$1,515.31	$1,290.02	$1,198.39	$1,156.16	$1,135.58
13.500%	$2,300.98	$1,846.49	$1,522.74	$1,298.32	$1,207.37	$1,165.64	$1,145.41
13.625%	$2,307.43	$1,853.35	$1,530.20	$1,306.64	$1,216.38	$1,175.15	$1,155.25
13.750%	$2,313.88	$1,860.22	$1,537.67	$1,314.99	$1,225.41	$1,184.67	$1,165.11
13.875%	$2,320.35	$1,867.10	$1,545.16	$1,323.35	$1,234.45	$1,194.20	$1,174.98
14.000%	$2,326.83	$1,874.00	$1,552.66	$1,331.74	$1,243.52	$1,203.76	$1,184.87
14.125%	$2,333.31	$1,880.91	$1,560.19	$1,340.15	$1,252.61	$1,213.34	$1,194.77
14.250%	$2,339.81	$1,887.84	$1,567.73	$1,348.58	$1,261.72	$1,222.93	$1,204.69
14.375%	$2,346.31	$1,894.78	$1,575.29	$1,357.03	$1,270.85	$1,232.54	$1,214.61
14.500%	$2,352.83	$1,901.73	$1,582.87	$1,365.50	$1,280.00	$1,242.16	$1,224.56
14.625%	$2,359.35	$1,908.70	$1,590.46	$1,373.99	$1,289.17	$1,251.81	$1,234.51
14.750%	$2,365.89	$1,915.68	$1,598.07	$1,382.50	$1,298.36	$1,261.46	$1,244.48
14.875%	$2,372.44	$1,922.67	$1,605.70	$1,391.04	$1,307.56	$1,271.14	$1,254.45
15.000%	$2,378.99	$1,929.68	$1,613.35	$1,399.59	$1,316.79	$1,280.83	$1,264.44
15.125%	$2,285.56	$1,936.70	$1,621.01	$1,408.16	$1,326.03	$1,290.54	$1,274.45
15.250%	$2,392.14	$1,943.73	$1,628.69	$1,416.75	$1,335.30	$1,300.26	$1,284.46
15.375%	$2,398.72	$1,950.77	$1,636.39	$1,425.36	$1,344.58	$1,309.99	$1,294.48
15.500%	$2,405.32	$1,957.83	$1,644.11	$1,433.99	$1,353.88	$1,319.75	$1,304.52
15.625%	$2,411.93	$1,964.91	$1,651.84	$1,442.64	$1,363.20	$1,329.51	$1,314.56
15.750%	$2,418.54	$1,971.99	$1,659.58	$1,451.31	$1,372.53	$1,339.29	$1,324.62
15.875%	$2,425.17	$1,979.09	$1,667.35	$1,459.99	$1,381.89	$1,349.08	$1,334.68

Monthly Payment to Amortize a Loan of $100,000

Interest Rate	5 Years	7 Years	10 Years	15 Years	20 Years	25 Years	30 Years
16.000%	$2,431.81	$1,986.21	$1,675.13	$1,468.70	$1,391.26	$1,358.89	$1,344.76
16.125%	$2,438.45	$1,993.33	$1,682.93	$1,477.43	$1,400.64	$1,368.71	$1,354.84
16.250%	$2,445.11	$2,000.47	$1,690.74	$1,486.17	$1,410.05	$1,378.54	$1,364.93
16.375%	$2,451.78	$2,007.62	$1,698.58	$1,494.93	$1,419.46	$1,388.39	$1,375.04
16.500%	$2,458.45	$2,014.79	$1,706.42	$1,503.71	$1,428.90	$1,398.24	$1,385.15
16.625%	$2,465.14	$2,021.97	$1,714.29	$1,512.51	$1,438.35	$1,408.11	$1,395.27
16.750%	$2,471.84	$2,029.16	$1,722.17	$1,521.32	$1,447.82	$1,418.00	$1,405.40
16.875%	$2,478.54	$2,036.36	$1,730.06	$1,530.15	$1,457.30	$1,427.89	$1,415.53
17.000%	$2,485.26	$2,043.58	$1,737.98	$1,539.00	$1,466.80	$1,437.80	$1,425.68
17.125%	$2,491.98	$2,050.81	$1,745.91	$1,547.87	$1,476.31	$1,447.71	$1,435.83
17.250%	$2,498.72	$2,058.05	$1,753.85	$1,556.76	$1,485.84	$1,457.64	$1,445.99
17.375%	$2,505.47	$2,065.31	$1,761.81	$1,565.66	$1,495.38	$1,467.58	$1,456.15
17.500%	$2,512.22	$2,072.58	$1,769.79	$1,574.58	$1,504.94	$1,477.53	$1,466.33
17.625%	$2,518.99	$2,079.86	$1,777.78	$1,583.51	$1,514.51	$1,487.49	$1,476.51
17.750%	$2,525.76	$2,087.16	$1,785.79	$1,592.47	$1,524.10	$1,497.46	$1,486.69
17.875%	$2,532.55	$2,094.46	$1,793.81	$1,601.44	$1,533.70	$1,507.44	$1,496.89
18.000%	$2,539.34	$2,101.78	$1,801.85	$1,610.42	$1,543.31	$1,517.43	$1,507.09

Appendix B

Remaining Balance Tables

The tables in Appendix A help you figure out how much you'd need to pay each month to *amortize* (repay) a mortgage. The tables in this appendix, conversely, show how much of your loan remains unpaid as the mortgage is amortized.

A remaining principal balance is shown as a percentage of the original mortgage amount. For example, the number 23.58 indicates that 23.58 percent of the money you originally borrowed still remains to be paid. Remaining balance tables are wonderfully straightforward. Here's how to use them:

1. **Find the table that matches your loan's interest rate.**
2. **Locate the column on that table for your loan's original term.**
3. **Read down the loan term column until you find the remaining balance percentage for your loan's approximate age as noted by the "# of Years Paid on Loan" column on the left side of the table.**
4. **Multiply your original loan amount by that percentage to get the *estimated* remaining loan balance.**

   If you absolutely must know the precise remaining balance to the penny, ask your friendly lender.

Example #1: If you obtained a $250,000, 30-year mortgage at 8.25 percent interest 15 years ago, your estimated remaining principal balance is $\$250{,}000 \times 77.44\% = \$193{,}600$. You may find this astonishing because you're halfway through the loan's 30-year term. As you can see by glancing down the term column, most of your payment consists of interest during the mortgage's early years. At 8.25 percent interest, for example, you pay off only 0.8 percent of principal in the loan's first year. You'll take more than 20 years to repay half of the original loan balance — and well under 10 years to pay off the other half, because more of your monthly payment is principal and less is interest as time goes by.

Example #2: If you obtained a $60,000, 20-year mortgage at 12 percent interest 5 years ago, your estimated remaining principal balance is $\$60{,}000 \times 91.74\% = \$55{,}044$.

Remaining Principal Balance as a Percentage of Original Loan Amount

# of Years Paid on Loan	Interest Rate: 3.000						
	Original Term:						
	5 Years	7 Years	10 Years	15 Years	20 Years	25 Years	30 Years
1	81.18	86.96	91.29	94.63	96.29	97.27	97.91
2	61.78	73.53	82.32	89.11	92.47	94.46	95.76
3	41.80	59.69	73.07	83.42	88.54	91.56	93.54
4	21.21	45.43	63.55	77.56	84.48	88.58	91.25
5	0.00	30.74	53.74	71.51	80.30	85.50	88.90
6		15.60	43.62	65.29	76.00	82.33	86.48
7		0.00	33.20	58.87	71.56	79.07	83.98
8			22.46	52.26	66.99	75.70	81.40
9			11.40	45.45	62.28	72.24	78.75
10			0.00	38.43	57.43	68.66	76.01
11				31.19	52.43	64.98	73.20
12				23.74	47.28	61.19	70.29
13				16.06	41.97	57.28	67.30
14				8.15	36.50	53.25	64.22
15				0.00	30.84	49.11	61.05
20					0.00	26.39	43.66
25						0.00	23.46
30							0.00

# of Years Paid on Loan	Interest Rate: 3.250						
	Original Term:						
	5 Years	7 Years	10 Years	15 Years	20 Years	25 Years	30 Years
1	81.27	87.06	91.39	94.74	96.39	97.36	97.99
2	61.93	73.70	82.50	89.30	92.66	94.63	95.92
3	41.95	59.90	73.32	83.69	88.80	91.82	93.79
4	21.31	45.65	63.84	77.89	84.83	88.91	91.58
5	0.00	30.92	54.04	71.90	80.72	85.91	89.30
6		15.71	43.92	65.72	76.47	82.81	86.95
7		0.00	33.47	59.32	72.08	79.61	84.51
8			22.67	52.72	67.55	76.30	82.00
9			11.52	45.90	62.87	72.88	79.41
10			0.00	38.86	58.04	69.35	76.72
11				31.58	53.04	65.70	73.95
12				24.07	47.89	61.93	71.09
13				16.30	42.56	58.02	68.14
14				8.28	37.05	54.02	65.08
15				0.00	31.37	49.86	61.93
20					0.00	26.95	44.53
25						0.00	24.07
30							0.00

Remaining Principal Balance as a Percentage of Original Loan Amount

Interest Rate: 3.500

# of Years Paid on Loan	Original Term: 5 Years	7 Years	10 Years	15 Years	20 Years	25 Years	30 Years
1	81.37	87.16	91.49	94.83	96.48	97.45	98.08
2	62.08	73.87	82.69	89.49	92.84	94.81	96.09
3	42.10	60.11	73.57	83.96	89.07	92.08	94.03
4	21.42	45.86	64.13	78.22	85.16	89.25	91.90
5	0.00	31.10	54.35	72.29	81.12	86.32	89.69
6		15.82	44.23	66.14	76.93	83.28	87.41
7		0.00	33.74	59.78	72.60	80.14	85.04
8			22.88	53.19	68.11	76.88	82.59
9			11.64	46.36	63.46	73.51	80.05
10			0.00	39.29	58.64	70.02	77.42
11				31.97	53.66	66.41	74.70
12				24.39	48.49	62.67	71.88
13				16.54	43.15	58.79	68.96
14				8.41	37.61	54.78	65.94
15				0.00	31.88	50.62	62.81
20					0.00	27.51	45.41
25						0.00	24.68
30							0.00

Interest Rate: 3.750

# of Years Paid on Loan	Original Term: 5 Years	7 Years	10 Years	15 Years	20 Years	25 Years	30 Years
1	81.46	87.26	91.59	94.93	96.57	97.53	98.16
2	62.23	74.04	82.87	89.68	93.02	94.98	96.25
3	42.25	60.32	73.82	84.22	89.33	92.32	94.27
4	21.52	46.08	64.42	78.55	85.50	89.57	92.91
5	0.00	31.29	54.66	72.67	81.52	86.71	90.07
6		15.93	44.53	66.57	77.39	83.74	87.85
7		0.00	34.01	60.23	73.11	80.66	85.55
8			23.10	53.65	68.66	77.46	83.16
9			11.76	46.82	64.04	74.14	80.68
10			0.00	39.73	59.25	70.69	78.11
11				32.36	54.27	67.11	75.43
12				24.72	49.10	63.40	72.66
13				16.78	43.74	59.54	69.78
14				8.55	38.17	55.53	66.78
15				0.00	32.39	51.38	63.68
20					0.00	28.08	46.28
25						0.00	25.30
30							0.00

Remaining Principal Balance as a Percentage of Original Loan Amount

	Interest Rate: 4.000						
# of Years	Original Term:						
Paid on Loan	5 Years	7 Years	10 Years	15 Years	20 Years	25 Years	30 Years
1	81.46	87.26	91.69	95.03	96.66	97.62	98.23
2	62.37	74.22	83.06	89.86	93.19	95.14	96.40
3	42.41	60.53	74.07	84.48	89.58	92.57	94.49
4	21.62	46.29	64.71	78.88	85.83	89.89	92.51
5	0.00	31.47	54.97	73.05	81.92	87.10	90.44
6		16.05	44.84	66.99	77.85	84.20	88.29
7		0.00	34.29	60.68	73.62	81.18	86.05
8			23.31	54.11	69.21	78.03	83.73
9			11.89	47.27	64.62	74.76	81.30
10			0.00	40.16	59.85	71.35	78.78
11				32.75	54.88	67.81	76.15
12				25.05	49.71	64.12	73.42
13				17.03	44.33	60.28	70.58
14				8.68	38.73	56.29	67.62
15				0.00	32.90	52.13	64.54
20					0.00	28.66	47.15
25						0.00	25.92
30							0.00

	Interest Rate: 4.250						
# of Years	Original Term:						
Paid on Loan	5 Years	7 Years	10 Years	15 Years	20 Years	25 Years	30 Years
1	81.66	87.46	91.79	95.12	96.75	97.70	98.31
2	62.52	74.39	83.24	90.04	93.37	95.31	96.55
3	42.56	60.74	74.31	84.74	89.84	92.81	94.72
4	21.73	46.51	65.00	79.21	86.15	90.20	92.80
5	0.00	31.66	55.28	73.43	82.31	87.48	90.80
6		16.16	45.14	67.41	78.30	84.64	88.72
7		0.00	34.56	61.13	74.12	81.68	86.54
8			23.52	54.57	69.75	78.59	84.28
9			12.01	47.73	65.20	75.37	81.91
10			0.00	40.59	60.44	72.01	79.44
11				33.15	55.49	68.50	76.86
12				25.38	50.32	64.84	74.17
13				17.27	44.92	61.02	71.37
14				8.82	39.29	57.04	68.44
15				0.00	33.41	52.88	65.39
20					0.00	29.23	48.02
25						0.00	26.54
30							0.00

Remaining Principal Balance as a Percentage of Original Loan Amount

# of Years Paid on Loan	Interest Rate: 4.500 Original Term: 5 Years	7 Years	10 Years	15 Years	20 Years	25 Years	30 Years
1	81.75	87.56	91.89	95.22	96.84	97.78	98.38
2	62.67	74.55	83.42	90.22	93.54	95.46	96.69
3	42.71	60.95	74.55	84.99	90.08	93.04	94.93
4	21.83	46.72	65.28	79.53	86.47	90.50	93.08
5	0.00	31.84	55.59	73.81	82.69	87.85	91.15
6		16.28	45.44	67.83	78.74	85.08	89.13
7		0.00	34.84	61.57	74.61	82.18	87.02
8			23.74	55.03	70.29	79.15	84.81
9			12.13	48.19	65.77	75.97	82.50
10			0.00	41.03	61.04	72.65	80.08
11				33.54	56.09	69.18	77.56
12				25.71	50.92	65.55	74.91
13				17.52	45.51	61.75	72.15
14				8.96	39.85	57.78	69.25
15				0.00	33.93	53.63	66.23
20					0.00	29.81	48.88
25						0.00	27.17
30							0.00

# of Years Paid on Loan	Interest Rate: 4.750 Original Term: 5 Years	7 Years	10 Years	15 Years	20 Years	25 Years	30 Years
1	81.84	87.66	91.99	95.31	96.92	97.86	98.45
2	62.81	74.72	83.60	90.40	93.70	95.62	96.83
3	42.86	61.16	74.80	85.25	90.33	93.27	95.14
4	21.93	46.94	65.57	79.85	86.79	90.80	93.36
5	0.00	32.03	55.89	74.18	83.08	88.22	91.49
6		16.39	45.75	68.24	79.18	85.51	89.54
7		0.00	35.11	62.02	75.10	82.67	87.49
8			23.95	55.49	70.82	79.69	85.34
9			12.26	48.64	66.33	76.57	83.08
10			0.00	41.46	61.63	73.29	80.72
11				33.94	56.70	69.86	78.24
12				26.05	51.52	66.26	75.64
13				17.77	46.10	62.48	72.91
14				9.09	40.41	58.52	70.06
15				0.00	34.45	54.37	67.06
20					0.00	30.39	49.75
25						0.00	27.81
30							0.00

Remaining Principal Balance as a Percentage of Original Loan Amount

# of Years Paid on Loan	Interest Rate: 5.000 Original Term: 5 Years	7 Years	10 Years	15 Years	20 Years	25 Years	30 Years
1	81.94	87.76	92.09	95.41	97.01	97.94	98.52
2	62.97	74.90	83.78	90.58	93.87	95.77	96.97
3	43.01	61.37	75.04	85.50	90.57	93.49	95.34
4	22.04	47.16	65.86	80.17	87.10	91.10	93.63
5	0.00	32.22	56.20	74.56	83.45	88.58	91.83
6		16.51	46.06	68.66	79.62	85.93	89.94
7		0.00	35.39	62.46	75.59	83.15	87.95
8			24.18	55.95	71.36	80.23	85.85
9			12.39	49.10	66.90	77.16	83.65
10			0.00	41.90	62.22	73.92	81.34
11				34.34	57.30	70.53	78.91
12				26.39	52.13	66.96	76.36
13				18.03	46.69	63.21	73.67
14				9.24	40.98	59.26	70.85
15				0.00	34.97	55.12	67.88
20					0.00	30.98	50.61
25						0.00	28.45
30							0.00

# of Years Paid on Loan	Interest Rate: 5.250 Original Term: 5 Years	7 Years	10 Years	15 Years	20 Years	25 Years	30 Years
1	82.04	87.86	92.19	95.50	97.09	98.01	98.59
2	63.11	75.06	83.96	90.75	94.03	95.92	97.10
3	43.17	61.58	75.28	85.75	90.81	93.71	95.54
4	22.15	47.37	66.14	80.48	87.41	91.38	93.89
5	0.00	32.40	56.51	74.92	83.82	88.93	92.15
6		16.63	46.36	69.07	80.05	86.35	90.32
7		0.00	35.66	62.90	76.07	83.62	88.39
8			24.39	56.41	71.88	80.75	86.35
9			12.52	49.56	67.46	77.73	84.21
10			0.00	42.34	62.80	74.54	81.95
11				34.74	57.90	71.19	79.57
12				26.72	52.73	67.65	77.06
13				18.28	47.28	63.92	74.41
14				9.38	41.54	59.99	71.63
15				0.00	35.49	55.85	68.69
20					0.00	31.56	51.47
25						0.00	29.08
30							0.00

Remaining Principal Balance as a Percentage of Original Loan Amount

	Interest Rate: 5.500						
# of Years	Original Term:						
Paid on Loan	5 Years	7 Years	10 Years	15 Years	20 Years	25 Years	30 Years
1	82.13	87.96	92.28	95.58	97.17	98.08	98.65
2	63.26	75.23	84.13	90.92	94.19	96.06	97.23
3	43.32	61.79	75.52	85.99	91.04	93.92	95.73
4	22.25	47.59	66.43	80.79	87.71	91.66	94.14
5	0.00	32.59	56.82	75.29	84.19	89.27	92.46
6		16.74	46.66	69.48	80.47	86.75	90.69
7		0.00	35.94	63.34	76.54	84.09	88.82
8			24.61	56.86	72.40	81.27	86.84
9			12.64	50.01	68.01	78.30	84.75
10			0.00	42.78	63.38	75.16	82.54
11				35.13	58.49	71.84	80.21
12				27.06	53.33	68.33	77.75
13				18.53	47.87	64.63	75.14
14				9.52	42.10	60.72	72.39
15				0.00	36.01	56.58	69.49
20					0.00	32.15	52.32
25						0.00	29.73
30							0.00

	Interest Rate: 5.750						
# of Years	Original Term:						
Paid on Loan	5 Years	7 Years	10 Years	15 Years	20 Years	25 Years	30 Years
1	82.23	88.05	92.38	95.67	97.25	98.15	98.71
2	63.40	75.40	84.31	91.09	94.34	96.20	97.35
3	43.47	62.00	75.76	86.23	91.26	94.12	95.91
4	22.36	47.80	66.71	81.09	88.00	91.93	94.38
5	0.00	32.77	57.12	75.65	84.55	89.61	92.76
6		16.86	46.97	69.89	80.89	87.14	91.05
7		0.00	36.22	63.78	77.01	84.54	89.23
8			24.83	57.31	72.91	81.78	87.31
9			12.77	50.47	68.56	78.85	85.28
10			0.00	43.21	63.96	75.76	83.12
11				35.53	59.09	72.48	80.84
12				27.40	53.92	69.01	78.42
13				18.78	48.46	65.33	75.86
14				9.66	42.67	61.44	73.15
15				0.00	36.53	57.31	70.28
20					0.00	32.74	53.16
25						0.00	30.37
30							0.00

Remaining Principal Balance as a Percentage of Original Loan Amount

# of Years Paid on Loan	Interest Rate: 6.000			Original Term:			
	5 Years	7 Years	10 Years	15 Years	20 Years	25 Years	30 Years
1	82.32	88.15	92.47	95.76	97.33	98.22	98.77
2	63.55	75.56	84.48	91.26	94.50	96.33	97.47
3	43.62	62.20	76.00	86.47	91.49	94.32	96.08
4	22.46	48.02	66.99	81.40	88.29	92.19	94.61
5	0.00	32.96	57.43	76.01	84.90	89.93	93.05
6		16.97	47.27	70.29	81.30	87.53	91.40
7		0.00	36.49	64.21	77.48	84.98	89.64
8			25.05	57.76	73.42	82.28	87.77
9			12.90	50.92	69.11	79.40	85.79
10			0.00	43.65	64.53	76.35	83.69
11				35.93	59.67	73.11	81.45
12				27.74	54.52	69.68	79.08
13				19.04	49.04	66.02	76.56
14				9.80	43.23	62.15	73.89
15				0.00	37.06	58.03	71.05
20					0.00	33.33	54.00
25						0.00	31.01
30							0.00

# of Years Paid on Loan	Interest Rate: 6.250			Original Term:			
	5 Years	7 Years	10 Years	15 Years	20 Years	25 Years	30 Years
1	82.41	88.24	92.57	95.84	97.41	98.29	98.83
2	63.69	75.73	84.65	91.42	94.64	96.46	97.58
3	43.77	62.41	76.23	86.71	91.70	94.52	96.25
4	22.57	48.23	67.27	81.70	88.58	92.45	94.84
5	0.00	33.15	57.73	76.36	85.25	90.25	93.34
6		17.09	47.58	70.69	81.70	87.91	91.74
7		0.00	36.77	64.65	77.93	85.42	90.03
8			25.27	58.21	73.92	82.76	88.22
9			13.03	51.37	69.65	79.94	86.29
10			0.00	44.09	65.10	76.94	84.24
11				36.33	60.26	73.74	82.05
12				28.08	55.11	70.33	79.73
13				19.30	49.63	66.71	77.25
14				9.95	43.79	62.86	74.61
15				0.00	37.58	58.75	71.81
20					0.00	33.92	54.84
25						0.00	31.66
30							0.00

Remaining Principal Balance as a Percentage of Original Loan Amount

# of Years Paid on Loan	Interest Rate: 6.500 Original Term: 5 Years	7 Years	10 Years	15 Years	20 Years	25 Years	30 Years
1	82.51	88.34	92.66	95.93	97.48	98.35	98.88
2	63.84	75.89	84.82	91.58	94.79	96.59	97.69
3	43.92	62.62	76.47	86.94	91.92	94.71	96.42
4	22.67	48.45	67.55	82.00	88.86	92.70	95.06
5	0.00	33.33	58.03	76.72	85.59	90.56	93.61
6		17.21	47.88	71.08	82.10	88.28	92.07
7		0.00	37.05	65.07	78.38	85.84	90.42
8			25.49	58.66	74.41	83.24	88.66
9			13.16	51.82	70.18	80.47	86.78
10			0.00	44.52	65.66	77.51	84.78
11				36.73	60.84	74.35	82.64
12				28.42	55.70	70.99	80.36
13				19.56	50.21	67.39	77.93
14				10.09	44.35	63.56	75.33
15				0.00	38.11	59.46	72.56
20					0.00	34.51	55.67
25						0.00	32.30
30							0.00

# of Years Paid on Loan	Interest Rate: 6.750 Original Term: 5 Years	7 Years	10 Years	15 Years	20 Years	25 Years	30 Years
1	82.60	88.43	92.75	96.01	97.55	98.41	98.93
2	63.98	76.06	84.99	91.74	94.93	96.71	97.79
3	44.07	62.82	76.70	87.17	92.13	94.89	96.57
4	22.78	48.66	67.83	82.29	89.13	92.95	95.27
5	0.00	33.52	58.34	77.07	85.93	90.87	93.88
6		17.32	48.18	71.48	82.50	88.64	92.38
7		0.00	37.33	65.50	78.83	86.26	90.79
8			25.71	59.11	74.91	83.71	89.08
9			13.29	52.27	70.71	80.99	87.25
10			0.00	44.96	66.22	78.08	85.30
11				37.13	61.42	74.96	83.21
12				28.77	56.28	71.63	80.98
13				19.81	50.79	68.06	78.59
14				10.24	44.91	64.25	76.03
15				0.00	38.63	60.17	73.30
20					0.00	35.10	56.49
25						0.00	32.95
30							0.00

Remaining Principal Balance as a Percentage of Original Loan Amount

# of Years Paid on Loan	Interest Rate: 7.000			Original Term:			
	5 Years	7 Years	10 Years	15 Years	20 Years	25 Years	30 Years
1	82.69	88.53	92.84	96.09	97.62	98.47	98.98
2	64.13	76.22	85.16	91.90	95.07	96.83	97.89
3	44.23	63.03	76.93	87.40	92.33	95.07	96.73
4	22.88	48.88	68.10	82.58	89.40	93.18	95.47
5	0.00	33.71	58.64	77.41	86.26	91.16	94.13
6		17.44	48.49	71.87	82.88	88.99	92.69
7		0.00	37.60	65.93	79.27	86.67	91.15
8			25.93	59.55	75.39	84.17	89.49
9			13.42	52.72	71.23	81.50	87.72
10			0.00	45.39	66.77	78.63	85.81
11				37.54	61.99	75.56	83.77
12				29.11	56.87	72.26	81.58
13				20.08	51.37	68.73	79.23
14				10.39	45.47	64.94	76.72
15				0.00	39.15	60.87	74.02
20					0.00	35.69	57.30
25						0.00	33.60
30							0.00

# of Years Paid on Loan	Interest Rate: 7.250			Original Term:			
	5 Years	7 Years	10 Years	15 Years	20 Years	25 Years	30 Years
1	82.78	88.62	92.93	96.17	97.69	98.53	99.03
2	64.27	76.38	85.33	92.05	95.21	96.95	97.99
3	44.38	63.23	77.16	87.63	92.54	95.24	96.87
4	22.99	49.09	68.38	82.87	89.67	93.42	95.67
5	0.00	33.90	58.94	77.76	86.58	91.45	94.38
6		17.56	48.79	72.26	83.27	89.34	92.99
7		0.00	37.88	66.35	79.70	87.07	91.50
8			26.16	60.00	75.87	84.63	89.89
9			13.55	53.17	71.75	82.00	88.17
10			0.00	45.83	67.32	79.18	86.31
11				37.94	62.56	76.15	84.32
12				29.46	57.45	72.89	82.17
13				20.34	51.95	69.38	79.87
14				10.54	46.03	65.62	77.39
15				0.00	39.68	61.57	74.73
20					0.00	36.29	58.11
25						0.00	34.25
30							0.00

Remaining Principal Balance as a Percentage of Original Loan Amount

# of Years Paid on Loan	Interest Rate: 7.500		Original Term:				
	5 Years	7 Years	10 Years	15 Years	20 Years	25 Years	30 Years
1	82.87	88.71	93.02	96.25	97.76	98.58	99.08
2	64.42	76.55	85.50	92.21	95.34	97.06	98.08
3	44.53	63.44	77.39	87.85	92.73	95.41	97.01
4	23.10	49.31	68.65	83.15	89.93	93.64	95.86
5	0.00	34.09	59.24	78.10	86.90	91.73	94.62
6		17.68	49.09	72.64	83.64	89.67	93.28
7		0.00	38.16	66.77	80.13	87.46	91.83
8			26.38	60.44	76.34	85.07	90.28
9			13.68	53.62	72.26	82.49	88.60
10			0.00	46.26	67.87	79.72	86.79
11				38.34	63.13	76.73	84.85
12				29.80	58.02	73.50	82.75
13				20.60	52.52	70.03	80.49
14				10.69	46.59	66.29	78.05
15				0.00	40.20	62.26	75.43
20					0.00	36.88	58.91
25						0.00	34.89
30							0.00

# of Years Paid on Loan	Interest Rate: 7.750		Original Term:				
	5 Years	7 Years	10 Years	15 Years	20 Years	25 Years	30 Years
1	82.96	88.80	93.11	96.33	97.82	98.64	99.12
2	64.56	76.71	85.66	92.36	95.47	97.17	98.17
3	44.68	63.64	77.62	88.07	92.93	95.58	97.15
4	23.20	49.52	68.93	83.44	90.18	93.86	96.04
5	0.00	34.27	59.54	78.43	87.22	92.01	94.85
6		17.80	49.40	73.03	84.01	90.00	93.56
7		0.00	38.44	67.19	80.55	87.84	92.16
8			26.60	60.88	76.81	85.50	90.65
9			13.81	54.06	72.77	82.97	89.03
10			0.00	46.70	68.41	80.25	87.27
11				38.74	63.69	77.30	85.37
12				30.15	58.60	74.11	83.31
13				20.86	53.09	70.67	81.10
14				10.84	47.15	66.95	78.70
15				0.00	40.73	62.94	76.11
20					0.00	37.47	59.70
25						0.00	35.54
30							0.00

Remaining Principal Balance as a Percentage of Original Loan Amount

	Interest Rate: 8.000						
# of Years				Original Term:			
Paid on Loan	5 Years	7 Years	10 Years	15 Years	20 Years	25 Years	30 Years
1	83.06	88.90	93.19	96.40	97.89	98.69	99.16
2	64.71	76.87	85.82	92.51	95.60	97.27	98.26
3	44.83	63.84	77.84	88.29	93.12	95.74	97.28
4	23.31	49.74	69.20	83.72	90.43	94.07	96.22
5	0.00	34.46	59.84	78.77	87.53	92.27	95.07
6		17.92	49.70	73.41	84.38	90.32	93.83
7		0.00	38.72	67.60	80.97	88.21	92.48
8			26.83	61.31	77.27	85.92	91.02
9			13.95	54.51	73.27	83.45	89.44
10			0.00	47.13	68.94	80.76	87.72
11				39.15	64.25	77.86	85.87
12				30.50	59.17	74.71	83.86
13				21.13	53.67	71.30	81.69
14				10.99	47.71	67.61	79.33
15				0.00	41.25	63.61	76.78
20					0.00	38.06	60.48
25						0.00	36.19
30							0.00

	Interest Rate: 8.250						
# of Years				Original Term:			
Paid on Loan	5 Years	7 Years	10 Years	15 Years	20 Years	25 Years	30 Years
1	83.15	88.99	93.28	96.48	97.95	98.74	99.21
2	64.85	77.03	85.99	92.65	95.72	97.38	98.34
3	44.98	64.05	78.07	88.50	93.30	95.89	97.41
4	23.42	49.95	69.47	83.99	90.68	94.28	96.39
5	0.00	34.65	60.13	79.10	87.83	92.53	95.28
6		18.04	50.00	73.78	84.73	90.64	94.09
7		0.00	39.00	68.01	81.38	88.58	92.78
8			27.05	61.75	77.73	86.34	91.37
9			14.08	54.95	73.77	83.91	89.84
10			0.00	47.56	69.47	81.27	88.17
11				39.55	64.80	78.41	86.36
12				30.85	59.74	75.30	84.40
13				21.40	54.23	71.93	82.27
14				11.14	48.26	68.26	79.95
15				0.00	41.78	64.28	77.44
20					0.00	38.66	61.25
25						0.00	36.83
30							0.00

Remaining Principal Balance as a Percentage of Original Loan Amount

# of Years Paid on Loan	Interest Rate: 8.500		Original Term:				
	5 Years	7 Years	10 Years	15 Years	20 Years	25 Years	30 Years
1	83.24	89.08	93.37	96.55	98.01	98.79	99.24
2	64.99	77.19	86.15	92.80	95.84	97.47	98.42
3	45.14	64.25	78.29	88.71	93.49	96.04	97.53
4	23.52	50.17	69.74	84.26	90.92	94.48	96.55
5	0.00	34.84	60.43	79.42	88.13	92.79	95.49
6		18.16	50.30	74.16	85.09	90.94	94.34
7		0.00	39.28	68.42	81.78	88.93	93.08
8			27.28	62.18	78.18	86.74	91.71
9			14.22	55.39	74.26	84.36	90.22
10			0.00	48.00	69.99	81.77	88.60
11				39.95	65.35	78.95	86.84
12				31.19	60.30	75.88	84.92
13				21.66	54.80	72.54	82.83
14				11.29	48.81	68.90	80.56
15				0.00	42.30	64.95	78.08
20					0.00	39.25	62.02
25						0.00	37.48
30							0.00

# of Years Paid on Loan	Interest Rate: 8.750		Original Term:				
	5 Years	7 Years	10 Years	15 Years	20 Years	25 Years	30 Years
1	83.33	89.17	93.45	96.62	98.07	98.84	99.28
2	65.14	77.35	86.31	92.94	95.96	97.57	98.50
3	45.29	64.45	78.51	88.92	93.66	96.19	97.64
4	23.63	50.38	70.01	84.53	91.16	94.68	96.71
5	0.00	35.03	60.73	79.75	88.42	93.03	95.69
6		18.28	50.60	74.53	85.43	91.24	94.58
7		0.00	39.56	68.83	82.18	89.28	93.36
8			27.50	62.61	78.62	87.14	92.04
9			14.35	55.83	74.74	84.81	90.60
10			0.00	48.43	70.51	82.26	89.02
11				40.35	65.90	79.48	87.30
12				31.54	60.86	76.45	85.43
13				21.93	55.36	73.14	83.38
14				11.44	49.36	69.54	81.15
15				0.00	42.82	65.60	78.71
20					0.00	39.84	62.77
25						0.00	38.12
30							0.00

Remaining Principal Balance as a Percentage of Original Loan Amount

	Interest Rate: 9.000						
# of Years				Original Term:			
Paid on Loan	5 Years	7 Years	10 Years	15 Years	20 Years	25 Years	30 Years
1	83.42	89.26	93.54	96.69	98.13	98.88	99.32
2	65.28	77.51	86.47	93.08	96.08	97.66	98.57
3	45.44	64.65	78.73	89.12	93.84	96.33	97.75
4	23.74	50.60	70.28	84.80	91.39	94.87	96.86
5	0.00	35.22	61.02	80.07	88.71	93.27	95.88
6		18.40	50.90	74.89	85.77	91.53	94.81
7		0.00	39.84	69.23	82.57	89.62	93.64
8			27.73	63.04	79.06	87.53	92.36
9			14.49	56.27	75.22	85.24	90.96
10			0.00	48.86	71.03	82.74	89.43
11				40.76	66.44	80.00	87.75
12				31.90	61.41	77.01	85.92
13				22.20	55.92	73.74	83.92
14				11.60	49.91	70.16	81.73
15				0.00	43.34	66.25	79.33
20					0.00	40.43	63.52
25						0.00	38.76
30							0.00

	Interest Rate: 9.250						
# of Years				Original Term:			
Paid on Loan	5 Years	7 Years	10 Years	15 Years	20 Years	25 Years	30 Years
1	83.51	89.35	93.62	96.76	98.18	98.93	99.35
2	65.42	77.66	86.62	93.22	96.19	97.75	98.64
3	45.59	64.85	78.95	89.33	94.01	96.47	97.86
4	23.84	50.81	70.54	85.06	91.61	95.05	97.00
5	0.00	35.41	61.32	80.39	88.99	93.51	96.06
6		18.52	51.21	75.26	86.11	91.81	95.04
7		0.00	40.12	69.63	82.95	89.94	93.91
8			27.96	63.47	79.49	87.90	92.67
9			14.62	56.71	75.70	85.66	91.31
10			0.00	49.29	71.53	83.21	89.82
11				41.16	66.97	80.52	88.19
12				32.25	61.97	77.57	86.40
13				22.47	56.48	74.33	84.44
14				11.75	50.46	70.78	82.29
15				0.00	43.86	66.89	79.93
20					0.00	41.01	64.26
25						0.00	39.40
30							0.00

Remaining Principal Balance as a Percentage of Original Loan Amount

# of Years Paid on Loan	Interest Rate: 9.500						
	Original Term:						
	5 Years	7 Years	10 Years	15 Years	20 Years	25 Years	30 Years
1	83.60	89.44	93.70	96.83	98.24	98.97	99.38
2	65.56	77.82	86.78	93.35	96.30	97.84	98.71
3	45.74	65.06	79.17	89.53	94.18	96.60	97.96
4	23.95	51.02	70.81	85.32	91.84	95.23	97.14
5	0.00	35.60	61.61	80.70	89.27	93.73	96.24
6		18.64	51.51	75.62	86.44	92.08	95.25
7		0.00	40.40	70.03	83.33	90.27	94.16
8			28.18	63.89	79.92	88.27	92.97
9			14.76	57.14	76.16	86.08	91.65
10			0.00	49.72	72.04	83.67	90.21
11				41.56	67.50	81.02	88.62
12				32.60	62.51	78.11	86.87
13				22.74	57.03	74.91	84.95
14				11.91	51.01	71.39	82.84
15				0.00	44.38	67.52	80.52
20					0.00	41.60	64.98
25						0.00	40.04
30							0.00

# of Years Paid on Loan	Interest Rate: 9.750						
	Original Term:						
	5 Years	7 Years	10 Years	15 Years	20 Years	25 Years	30 Years
1	83.68	89.52	93.78	96.90	98.29	99.01	99.41
2	65.71	77.98	86.94	93.49	96.41	97.93	98.77
3	45.89	65.26	79.39	89.72	94.34	96.73	98.06
4	24.06	51.24	71.07	85.58	92.05	95.41	97.27
5	0.00	35.79	61.91	81.01	89.54	93.95	96.41
6		18.76	51.81	75.97	86.76	92.35	95.46
7		0.00	40.68	70.43	83.71	90.58	94.41
8			28.41	64.31	80.34	88.63	93.26
9			14.89	57.57	76.62	86.49	91.98
10			0.00	50.15	72.53	84.12	90.58
11				41.97	68.02	81.51	89.03
12				32.95	63.06	78.64	87.33
13				23.01	57.58	75.48	85.45
14				12.07	51.55	71.99	83.38
15				0.00	44.90	68.15	81.10
20					0.00	42.19	65.70
25						0.00	40.67
30							0.00

Remaining Principal Balance as a Percentage of Original Loan Amount

	Interest Rate: 10.000						
# of Years				Original Term:			
Paid on Loan	5 Years	7 Years	10 Years	15 Years	20 Years	25 Years	30 Years
1	83.77	89.61	93.87	96.97	98.35	99.05	99.44
2	65.85	78.13	87.09	93.62	96.52	98.01	98.83
3	46.04	65.46	79.60	89.92	94.50	96.85	98.15
4	24.17	51.45	71.33	85.83	92.27	95.57	97.40
5	0.00	35.98	62.20	81.32	89.80	94.16	96.57
6		18.88	52.10	76.33	87.08	92.61	95.66
7		0.00	40.96	70.82	84.07	90.88	94.65
8			28.64	64.73	80.75	88.98	93.53
9			15.03	58.01	77.08	86.88	92.30
10			0.00	50.58	73.02	84.56	90.94
11				42.37	68.54	82.00	89.43
12				33.30	63.60	79.17	87.77
13				23.29	58.13	76.04	85.93
14				12.22	52.09	72.58	83.91
15				0.00	45.42	68.76	81.66
20					0.00	42.77	66.41
25						0.00	41.30
30							0.00

	Interest Rate: 10.250						
# of Years				Original Term:			
Paid on Loan	5 Years	7 Years	10 Years	15 Years	20 Years	25 Years	30 Years
1	83.86	89.70	93.95	97.03	98.40	99.09	99.47
2	65.99	78.29	87.24	93.75	96.62	98.09	98.89
3	46.20	65.65	79.82	90.11	94.65	96.97	98.24
4	24.28	51.66	71.59	86.08	92.48	95.74	97.52
5	0.00	36.17	62.49	81.62	90.06	94.37	96.73
6		19.01	52.40	76.68	87.39	92.86	95.85
7		0.00	41.24	71.21	84.43	91.18	94.88
8			28.87	65.15	81.16	89.33	93.80
9			15.17	58.44	77.53	87.27	92.61
10			0.00	51.00	73.51	84.99	91.29
11				42.77	69.06	82.47	89.82
12				33.66	64.13	79.68	88.20
13				23.56	58.67	76.59	86.41
14				12.38	52.63	73.16	84.42
15				0.00	45.94	69.37	82.21
20					0.00	43.35	67.10
25						0.00	41.93
30							0.00

Remaining Principal Balance as a Percentage of Original Loan Amount

# of Years Paid on Loan	Interest Rate: 10.500 Original Term: 5 Years	7 Years	10 Years	15 Years	20 Years	25 Years	30 Years
1	83.95	89.78	94.03	97.10	98.45	99.13	99.50
2	66.13	78.44	87.39	93.88	96.72	98.16	98.94
3	46.35	65.85	80.03	90.30	94.81	97.09	98.33
4	24.38	51.88	71.85	86.33	92.68	95.90	97.64
5	0.00	36.36	62.78	81.92	90.32	94.57	96.88
6		19.13	52.70	77.03	87.70	93.10	96.04
7		0.00	41.52	71.59	84.79	91.47	95.10
8			29.10	65.56	81.56	89.66	94.06
9			15.31	58.86	77.97	87.65	92.90
10			0.00	51.43	73.99	85.42	91.62
11				43.17	69.57	82.94	90.20
12				34.01	64.66	80.19	88.62
13				23.84	59.21	77.13	86.86
14				12.54	53.16	73.74	84.91
15				0.00	46.45	69.97	82.75
20					0.00	43.93	67.79
25						0.00	42.56
30							0.00

# of Years Paid on Loan	Interest Rate: 10.750 Original Term: 5 Years	7 Years	10 Years	15 Years	20 Years	25 Years	30 Years
1	84.04	89.87	94.10	97.16	98.49	99.16	99.53
2	66.27	78.60	87.54	94.00	96.82	98.23	99.00
3	46.50	66.05	80.24	90.49	94.95	97.20	98.41
4	24.49	52.09	72.11	86.57	92.88	96.05	97.75
5	0.00	36.55	63.07	82.22	90.57	94.77	97.03
6		19.25	53.00	77.37	88.00	93.34	96.22
7		0.00	41.80	71.98	85.14	91.75	95.31
8			29.33	65.97	81.95	89.98	94.31
9			15.45	59.29	78.41	88.02	93.19
10			0.00	51.85	74.46	85.83	91.95
11				43.58	70.07	83.39	90.56
12				34.36	65.19	80.68	89.02
13				24.11	59.75	77.66	87.31
14				12.70	53.70	74.30	85.40
15				0.00	46.96	70.57	83.28
20					0.00	44.50	68.47
25						0.00	43.18
30							0.00

Remaining Principal Balance as a Percentage of Original Loan Amount

# of Years Paid on Loan	Interest Rate: 11.000						
	Original Term:						
	5 Years	7 Years	10 Years	15 Years	20 Years	25 Years	30 Years
1	84.12	89.96	94.18	97.22	98.54	99.20	99.55
2	66.41	78.75	87.69	94.13	96.91	98.31	99.05
3	46.65	66.25	80.45	90.67	95.10	97.31	98.49
4	24.60	52.30	72.37	86.81	93.07	96.20	97.86
5	0.00	36.74	63.36	82.51	90.81	94.95	97.16
6		19.37	53.30	77.71	88.29	93.57	96.39
7		0.00	42.08	72.36	85.48	92.03	95.52
8			29.56	66.38	82.34	90.30	94.55
9			15.59	59.71	78.84	88.38	93.47
10			0.00	52.28	74.93	86.23	92.26
11				43.98	70.57	83.84	90.92
12				34.72	65.71	81.17	89.42
13				24.39	60.28	78.19	87.74
14				12.86	54.23	74.86	85.87
15				0.00	47.47	71.15	83.79
20					0.00	45.08	69.13
25						0.00	43.80
30							0.00

# of Years Paid on Loan	Interest Rate: 11.250						
	Original Term:						
	5 Years	7 Years	10 Years	15 Years	20 Years	25 Years	30 Years
1	84.21	90.04	94.26	97.28	98.59	99.23	99.57
2	66.55	78.90	87.84	94.25	97.01	98.37	99.10
3	46.80	66.45	80.66	90.85	95.24	97.41	98.56
4	24.71	52.51	72.63	87.05	93.26	96.34	97.97
5	0.00	36.93	63.64	82.80	91.05	95.14	97.30
6		19.50	53.59	78.05	88.58	93.79	96.55
7		0.00	42.36	72.73	85.82	92.29	95.72
8			29.79	66.79	82.72	90.61	94.78
9			15.73	60.14	79.26	88.73	93.74
10			0.00	52.70	75.39	86.63	92.57
11				44.38	71.07	84.27	91.26
12				35.07	66.23	81.64	89.80
13				24.66	60.81	78.70	88.16
14				13.02	54.76	75.41	86.33
15				0.00	47.98	71.73	84.29
20					0.00	45.65	69.79
25						0.00	44.42
30							0.00

Remaining Principal Balance as a Percentage of Original Loan Amount

Interest Rate: 11.500

# of Years Paid on Loan	Original Term: 5 Years	7 Years	10 Years	15 Years	20 Years	25 Years	30 Years
1	84.30	90.13	94.34	97.34	98.63	99.26	99.60
2	66.69	79.06	87.99	94.37	97.10	98.44	99.14
3	46.95	66.64	80.86	91.03	95.38	97.51	98.63
4	24.82	52.72	72.88	87.29	93.45	96.48	98.06
5	0.00	37.12	63.93	83.09	91.29	95.32	97.42
6		19.62	53.89	78.38	88.87	94.01	96.71
7		0.00	42.64	73.11	86.15	92.55	95.90
8			30.02	67.19	83.10	90.91	95.00
9			15.87	60.56	79.68	89.07	93.99
10			0.00	53.12	75.85	87.01	92.86
11				44.78	71.55	84.70	91.59
12				35.43	66.74	82.11	90.17
13				24.94	61.34	79.21	88.57
14				13.18	55.28	75.95	86.78
15				0.00	48.49	72.30	84.77
20					0.00	46.22	70.44
25						0.00	45.03
30							0.00

Interest Rate: 11.750

# of Years Paid on Loan	Original Term: 5 Years	7 Years	10 Years	15 Years	20 Years	25 Years	30 Years
1	84.38	90.21	94.41	97.40	98.68	99.30	99.62
2	66.83	79.21	88.13	94.49	97.19	98.50	99.19
3	47.10	66.84	81.07	91.20	95.51	97.61	98.70
4	24.93	52.94	73.13	87.52	93.63	96.61	98.16
5	0.00	37.31	64.21	83.37	91.52	95.49	97.55
6		19.74	54.19	78.71	89.14	94.22	96.86
7		0.00	42.92	73.48	86.47	92.80	96.09
8			30.25	67.59	83.47	91.20	95.22
9			16.01	60.97	80.09	89.41	94.24
10			0.00	53.54	76.30	87.39	93.14
11				45.18	72.04	85.12	91.91
12				35.78	67.25	82.57	90.52
13				25.22	61.86	79.70	88.97
14				13.35	55.80	76.48	87.21
15				0.00	49.00	72.86	85.24
20					0.00	46.78	71.07
25						0.00	45.64
30							0.00

Remaining Principal Balance as a Percentage of Original Loan Amount

# of Years Paid on Loan	Interest Rate: 12.000			Original Term:			
	5 Years	7 Years	10 Years	15 Years	20 Years	25 Years	30 Years
1	84.47	90.29	94.49	97.46	98.72	99.32	99.64
2	66.97	79.36	88.27	94.60	97.27	98.56	99.23
3	47.25	67.03	81.27	91.38	95.65	97.71	98.77
4	25.04	53.15	73.39	87.75	93.81	96.74	98.25
5	0.00	37.50	64.50	83.65	91.74	95.65	97.66
6		19.87	54.48	79.04	89.42	94.43	97.00
7		0.00	43.20	73.84	86.79	93.05	96.26
8			30.48	67.99	83.83	91.49	95.42
9			16.15	61.39	80.50	89.73	94.48
10			0.00	53.95	76.75	87.76	93.42
11				45.58	72.52	85.53	92.22
12				36.13	67.75	83.02	90.87
13				25.50	62.37	80.19	89.35
14				13.51	56.32	77.00	87.64
15				0.00	49.50	73.41	85.71
20					0.00	47.35	71.69
25						0.00	46.24
30							0.00

# of Years Paid on Loan	Interest Rate: 12.250			Original Term:			
	5 Years	7 Years	10 Years	15 Years	20 Years	25 Years	30 Years
1	84.56	90.38	94.56	97.52	98.76	99.35	99.66
2	67.11	79.51	88.42	94.71	97.36	98.62	99.27
3	47.41	67.23	81.48	91.55	95.77	97.80	98.83
4	25.15	53.36	73.64	87.97	93.99	96.87	98.33
5	0.00	37.69	64.78	83.93	91.96	95.81	97.77
6		19.99	54.78	79.36	89.68	94.63	97.14
7		0.00	43.48	74.21	87.10	93.28	96.43
8			30.71	68.38	84.19	91.76	95.62
9			16.29	61.80	80.90	90.05	94.71
10			0.00	54.37	77.19	88.12	93.68
11				45.97	72.99	85.93	92.52
12				36.49	68.24	83.46	91.21
13				25.77	62.89	80.67	89.72
14				13.67	56.84	77.52	88.05
15				0.00	50.00	73.95	86.15
20					0.00	47.91	72.31
25						0.00	46.84
30							0.00

Remaining Principal Balance as a Percentage of Original Loan Amount

# of Years Paid on Loan	Interest Rate: 12.500						
	Original Term:						
	5 Years	7 Years	10 Years	15 Years	20 Years	25 Years	30 Years
1	84.64	90.46	94.63	97.57	98.80	99.38	99.67
2	67.25	79.66	88.56	94.83	97.44	98.68	99.31
3	47.56	67.42	81.68	91.72	95.90	97.89	98.89
4	25.26	53.57	73.89	88.19	94.16	96.99	98.42
5	0.00	37.88	65.06	84.20	92.18	95.97	97.88
6		20.12	55.07	79.68	89.94	94.82	97.28
7		0.00	43.75	74.57	87.41	93.51	96.59
8			30.94	68.77	84.54	92.03	95.81
9			16.43	62.21	81.30	90.36	94.93
10			0.00	54.78	77.62	88.47	93.94
11				46.37	73.45	86.32	92.81
12				36.84	68.74	83.89	91.53
13				26.05	63.40	81.14	90.08
14				13.84	57.35	78.02	88.45
15				0.00	50.50	74.49	86.59
20					0.00	48.46	72.91
25						0.00	47.44
30							0.00

# of Years Paid on Loan	Interest Rate: 12.750						
	Original Term:						
	5 Years	7 Years	10 Years	15 Years	20 Years	25 Years	30 Years
1	84.73	90.54	94.71	97.63	98.84	99.41	99.69
2	67.39	79.81	88.70	94.94	97.52	98.73	99.34
3	47.71	67.62	81.88	91.88	96.02	97.97	98.95
4	25.36	53.78	74.13	88.41	94.32	97.10	98.50
5	0.00	38.07	65.34	84.47	92.39	96.12	97.98
6		20.24	55.36	80.00	90.20	95.00	97.40
7		0.00	44.03	74.93	87.71	93.74	96.74
8			31.17	69.16	84.89	92.30	96.00
9			16.57	62.62	81.68	90.66	95.15
10			0.00	55.20	78.04	88.81	94.18
11				46.77	73.91	86.70	93.09
12				37.20	69.22	84.31	91.85
13				26.33	63.90	81.60	90.44
14				14.00	57.86	78.51	88.83
15				0.00	51.00	75.02	87.02
20					0.00	49.02	73.50
25						0.00	48.03
30							0.00

Remaining Principal Balance as a Percentage of Original Loan Amount

# of Years Paid on Loan	Interest Rate: 13.000			Original Term:			
	5 Years	7 Years	10 Years	15 Years	20 Years	25 Years	30 Years
1	84.81	90.62	94.78	97.68	98.88	99.43	99.71
2	67.53	79.95	88.84	95.04	97.60	98.79	99.38
3	47.86	67.81	82.08	92.04	96.14	98.05	99.00
4	25.47	53.99	74.38	88.63	94.48	97.22	98.57
5	0.00	38.27	65.62	84.74	92.60	96.27	98.08
6		20.37	55.66	80.31	90.45	95.18	97.53
7		0.00	44.31	75.28	88.01	93.95	96.89
8			31.41	69.55	85.23	92.55	96.17
9			16.72	63.03	82.07	90.96	95.35
10			0.00	55.61	78.47	89.14	94.42
11				47.16	74.37	87.07	93.36
12				37.55	69.71	84.72	92.15
13				26.61	64.40	82.05	90.78
14				14.17	58.36	79.00	89.21
15				0.00	51.49	75.54	87.43
20					0.00	49.57	74.09
25						0.00	48.62
30							0.00

# of Years Paid on Loan	Interest Rate: 13.250			Original Term:			
	5 Years	7 Years	10 Years	15 Years	20 Years	25 Years	30 Years
1	84.90	90.71	94.85	97.73	98.91	99.46	99.72
2	67.67	80.10	88.97	95.15	97.67	98.84	99.41
3	48.01	68.00	82.27	92.20	96.26	98.13	99.05
4	25.58	54.20	74.62	88.84	94.64	97.33	98.64
5	0.00	38.46	65.90	85.00	92.80	96.41	98.18
6		20.49	55.95	80.62	90.70	95.36	97.64
7		0.00	44.59	75.63	88.30	94.16	97.03
8			31.64	69.93	85.56	92.80	96.34
9			16.86	63.43	82.44	91.24	95.55
10			0.00	56.02	78.88	89.46	94.65
11				47.56	74.82	87.44	93.62
12				37.90	70.18	85.13	92.44
13				26.89	64.90	82.49	91.10
14				14.33	58.86	79.48	89.58
15				0.00	51.98	76.05	87.83
20					0.00	50.12	74.66
25						0.00	49.20
30							0.00

Remaining Principal Balance as a Percentage of Original Loan Amount

	Interest Rate: 13.500						
# of Years				Original Term:			
Paid on Loan	5 Years	7 Years	10 Years	15 Years	20 Years	25 Years	30 Years
1	84.98	90.79	94.92	97.79	98.95	99.48	99.74
2	67.81	80.25	89.11	95.26	97.74	98.89	99.44
3	48.16	68.20	82.47	92.36	96.37	98.21	99.10
4	25.69	54.41	74.87	89.05	94.80	97.43	98.71
5	0.00	38.65	66.18	85.26	93.00	96.54	98.26
6		20.62	56.24	80.93	90.94	95.53	97.75
7		0.00	44.87	75.98	88.58	94.37	97.17
8			31.87	70.31	85.89	93.04	96.50
9			17.00	63.83	82.81	91.52	95.74
10			0.00	56.42	79.29	89.78	94.87
11				47.95	75.26	87.79	93.87
12				38.26	70.66	85.52	92.73
13				27.17	65.39	82.92	91.42
14				14.50	59.36	79.95	89.93
15				0.00	52.47	76.55	88.22
20					0.00	50.66	75.22
25						0.00	49.78
30							0.00

	Interest Rate: 13.750						
# of Years				Original Term:			
Paid on Loan	5 Years	7 Years	10 Years	15 Years	20 Years	25 Years	30 Years
1	85.07	90.87	94.99	97.84	98.98	99.50	99.75
2	67.94	80.39	89.25	95.36	97.82	98.93	99.47
3	48.31	68.39	82.66	92.51	96.48	98.28	99.15
4	25.80	54.62	75.11	89.26	94.95	97.53	98.78
5	0.00	38.84	66.45	85.52	93.19	96.68	98.35
6		20.75	56.53	81.23	91.17	95.69	97.86
7		0.00	45.15	76.32	88.86	94.56	97.30
8			32.11	70.69	86.21	93.27	96.66
9			17.15	64.23	83.17	91.79	95.92
10			0.00	56.83	79.69	90.09	95.08
11				48.34	75.70	88.14	94.11
12				38.61	71.12	85.91	93.00
13				27.46	65.87	83.35	91.73
14				14.66	59.86	80.41	90.27
15				0.00	52.96	77.04	88.60
20					0.00	51.20	75.77
25						0.00	50.35
30							0.00

Remaining Principal Balance as a Percentage of Original Loan Amount

Interest Rate: 14.000							
# of Years	Original Term:						
Paid on Loan	5 Years	7 Years	10 Years	15 Years	20 Years	25 Years	30 Years
1	85.15	90.95	95.06	97.89	99.02	99.53	99.77
2	68.08	80.54	89.38	95.46	97.89	98.98	99.50
3	48.46	68.58	82.85	92.67	96.59	98.35	99.19
4	25.91	54.83	75.35	89.46	95.09	97.63	98.84
5	0.00	39.03	66.73	85.77	93.38	96.80	98.43
6		20.87	56.82	81.53	91.40	95.85	97.96
7		0.00	45.43	76.66	89.13	94.76	97.43
8			32.34	71.06	86.53	93.50	96.81
9			17.29	64.63	83.53	92.05	96.10
10			0.00	57.23	80.09	90.39	95.28
11				48.73	76.13	88.48	94.35
12				38.97	71.58	86.28	93.27
13				27.74	66.36	83.76	92.03
14				14.83	60.35	80.86	90.61
15				0.00	53.44	77.53	88.97
20					0.00	51.73	76.31
25						0.00	50.92
30							0.00

Interest Rate: 14.250							
# of Years	Original Term:						
Paid on Loan	5 Years	7 Years	10 Years	15 Years	20 Years	25 Years	30 Years
1	85.23	91.02	95.13	97.94	99.05	99.55	99.78
2	68.22	80.68	89.51	95.56	97.95	99.02	99.53
3	48.61	68.77	83.04	92.82	96.69	98.42	99.23
4	26.03	55.04	75.59	89.66	95.24	97.73	98.90
5	0.00	39.22	67.00	86.02	93.56	96.93	98.51
6		21.00	57.11	81.83	91.63	96.00	98.06
7		0.00	45.71	77.00	89.40	94.94	97.55
8			32.57	71.44	86.84	93.72	96.95
9			17.44	65.02	83.88	92.31	96.27
10			0.00	57.64	80.48	90.68	95.48
11				49.12	76.56	88.81	94.57
12				39.32	72.04	86.65	93.53
13				28.02	66.83	84.17	92.32
14				15.00	60.84	81.31	90.93
15				0.00	53.92	78.01	89.33
20					0.00	52.27	76.84
25						0.00	51.49
30							0.00

Remaining Principal Balance as a Percentage of Original Loan Amount

	Interest Rate: 14.500						
# of Years				Original Term:			
Paid on Loan	5 Years	7 Years	10 Years	15 Years	20 Years	25 Years	30 Years
1	85.32	91.10	95.19	97.98	99.08	99.57	99.79
2	68.35	80.83	89.64	95.65	98.02	99.06	99.55
3	48.76	68.96	83.23	92.96	96.79	98.49	99.27
4	26.14	55.25	75.83	89.86	95.37	97.82	98.95
5	0.00	39.41	67.28	86.27	93.74	97.04	98.58
6		21.13	57.40	82.12	91.85	96.15	98.15
7		0.00	45.99	77.33	89.66	95.12	97.66
8			32.81	71.80	87.14	93.93	97.09
9			17.58	65.42	84.23	92.56	96.43
10			0.00	58.04	80.87	90.97	95.67
11				49.51	76.98	89.13	94.79
12				39.67	72.49	87.01	93.77
13				28.30	67.31	84.57	92.60
14				15.17	61.32	81.74	91.24
15				0.00	54.40	78.48	89.68
20					0.00	52.79	77.36
25						0.00	52.05
30							0.00

	Interest Rate: 14.750						
# of Years				Original Term:			
Paid on Loan	5 Years	7 Years	10 Years	15 Years	20 Years	25 Years	30 Years
1	85.40	91.18	95.26	98.03	99.11	99.59	99.80
2	68.49	80.97	89.77	95.75	98.08	99.10	99.58
3	48.91	69.15	83.42	93.11	96.89	98.55	99.31
4	26.25	55.46	76.06	90.05	95.51	97.90	99.01
5	0.00	39.61	67.55	86.51	93.91	97.16	98.65
6		21.25	57.68	82.41	92.06	96.30	98.24
7		0.00	46.26	77.66	89.92	95.30	97.77
8			33.04	72.17	87.44	94.14	97.22
9			17.73	65.80	84.57	92.80	96.59
10			0.00	58.43	81.24	91.24	95.85
11				49.90	77.39	89.45	95.00
12				40.02	72.94	87.37	94.01
13				28.58	67.78	84.96	92.87
14				15.34	61.80	82.17	91.55
15				0.00	54.88	78.94	90.02
20					0.00	53.32	77.87
25						0.00	52.60
30							0.00

Remaining Principal Balance as a Percentage of Original Loan Amount

	Interest Rate: 15.000						
# of Years				Original Term:			
Paid on Loan	5 Years	7 Years	10 Years	15 Years	20 Years	25 Years	30 Years
1	85.48	91.26	95.33	98.08	99.14	99.60	99.81
2	68.63	81.11	89.90	95.84	98.14	99.14	99.60
3	49.06	69.34	83.61	93.25	96.99	98.61	99.35
4	26.36	55.67	76.30	90.24	95.64	97.99	99.06
5	0.00	39.80	67.82	86.75	94.08	97.27	98.72
6		21.38	57.97	82.70	92.27	96.43	98.33
7		0.00	46.54	77.99	90.17	95.46	97.87
8			33.27	72.53	87.73	94.34	97.35
9			17.87	66.19	84.90	93.03	96.74
10			0.00	58.83	81.62	91.51	96.02
11				50.29	77.80	89.75	95.20
12				40.37	73.38	87.71	94.24
13				28.87	68.24	85.34	93.13
14				15.51	62.27	82.59	91.84
15				0.00	55.35	79.39	90.34
20					0.00	53.84	78.37
25						0.00	53.15
30							0.00

Appendix C

Glossary

The difference between the almost-right word and the right word is really a large matter — it's the difference between the lightning bug and the lightning.

—MARK TWAIN

Terms that appear in *italics* within the definitions are defined elsewhere in this glossary.

acceleration clause: A mortgage contract provision that gives the lender the right to demand payment of the entire outstanding balance if you miss a monthly payment, sell the property, or otherwise fail to perform as promised under the terms of your mortgage. (See also *due-on-sale clause.*)

adjustable-rate mortgage (ARM): A mortgage whose *interest rate* and monthly payments vary throughout its life. ARMs typically start with an unusually low interest rate (see *teaser rate*) that gradually rises over time. If the overall level of interest rates drops, as measured by a variety of different indexes (see *index*), the interest rate of an ARM generally follows suit. Similarly, if interest rates rise, so does a mortgage's interest rate and monthly payment. The amount that the interest can fluctuate is limited by *caps* (see *periodic cap* and *life cap*). Before you agree to an adjustable-rate mortgage, be sure you can afford the highest payments that would result if the interest rate on your mortgage increased to the maximum allowed.

adjustment period or adjustment frequency: How often the *interest rate* for an *adjustable-rate mortgage* changes. Some adjustable-rate mortgages change every month, but one or two adjustments per year is more typical. The less frequently your loan rate shifts, the less financial uncertainty you may have. But if you opt for less frequent adjustments in your mortgage rate, you'll probably have a higher *teaser rate* or initial interest rate. (The initial interest rate is also called the "start rate.")

amortization: Lender jargon for the process of gradually paying down a debt, usually by making monthly payments throughout the loan's term. In the early years of a mortgage, most of the monthly payment goes toward payment of interest and little toward reducing the loan balance.

annual percentage rate (APR): A figure that states the total yearly cost of a mortgage as expressed by the actual rate of interest paid. The APR includes the base *interest rate, points,* and any other add-on loan fees and costs. As a result, the APR is invariably higher than the rate of interest that the lender quotes for the mortgage but gives a more accurate picture of the likely cost of the loan. Keep in mind, however, that most mortgages aren't held for their full 15- or 30-year terms, so the effective annual percentage rate is higher than the quoted APR because the points and loan fees are spread out over fewer years.

annuity: A monthly cash advance for life from an insurance company.

appraisal: A professional opinion about the market value of the house you want to buy (or already own if you're *refinancing* your loan). You must pay for the mortgage lender to hire an appraiser, because this opinion helps protect the lender from lending you money on a home that's not worth enough (in the event that you *default* on the loan and the lender must *foreclose* on the property). For typical homes, the appraisal fee is several hundred dollars.

appreciation: The increase of a property's value.

ARM indexes: See *certificates of deposit, treasury bills, the 11th District Cost of Funds Index (COFI),* and *The London Interbank Offered Rate Index (LIBOR).*

assessed value: The value of a property (according to the local county tax assessor) for the purpose of determining *property taxes.*

assumable mortgage: Allows future buyers of a home to take over the remaining loan balance of a mortgage. If you need to sell your house but *interest rates* are high, having an assumable mortgage may be handy. You may be able to offer the buyer your assumable loan at a lower interest rate than the current going interest rate. Assumable, *fixed-rate mortgages* are virtually extinct these days because lenders realize that they lose a great deal of money on these types of mortgages when interest rates skyrocket. Some *adjustable-rate mortgages* are assumable.

balloon loans: Loans that require level payments, just as a 15- or 30-year *fixed-rate mortgage* does, but well before their *maturity* date (typically three to ten years after the start date), the full remaining balance of the loan becomes due and payable. Although balloon loans can save you money because they charge a lower rate of interest relative to fixed-rate loans, balloon loans are dangerous. Being able to *refinance* a loan is never a sure thing. Thus, we're not fans of balloon loans.

bridge loan: A loan that enables you to borrow against the *equity* that is tied up in your old home until it sells. These loans can help if you find yourself in the generally inadvisable situation of having to close on a new home before you have sold your old one. Bridge loans are expensive compared to other alternatives, such as using a *cash reserve,* borrowing from family, or using the proceeds from the sale of your current home. In most cases, you need the bridge loan for only a few months to tide you over until you sell your house. Thus, the loan fees can represent a high cost (about 10 percent of the loan amount) for such a short-term loan.

cap: One of two different types of limits for *adjustable-rate mortgages.* The *life cap* limits the highest or lowest *interest rate* that is allowed over the entire life of a mortgage. The *periodic cap* limits the amount that an interest rate can change in one *adjustment period.* A one-year ARM, for example, may have a start rate of 5 percent with a plus or minus 2 percent periodic adjustment cap and a 6 percent life cap. On a worst-case basis, the loan's *interest rate* would be 7 percent in the second year, 9 percent in the third year, and 11 percent (5 percent start rate plus the 6 percent life cap) forevermore, starting with the fourth year.

cash reserve: A sufficient amount of cash left over after closing on a mortgage loan to make the first two mortgage payments or to cover a financial emergency. This amount is required by most mortgage lenders. If you're a seller who's thinking of extending credit to buyers, you'd also be wise to insist that they have adequate cash reserves.

certificates of deposit (CDs): An interest-bearing bank investment that locks an investor in for a specific period of time. Adjustable-rate mortgages are sometimes tied (indexed) to the average interest rate banks are paying on certificates of deposit (CDs). CDs tend to move rapidly with overall changes in interest rates. However, CD rates tend to move up a bit more slowly when rates rise, because profit-minded bankers take their sweet time to pay more interest to depositors. Conversely, CD rates tend to come down quickly when rates decline so bankers can maintain their profits.

closing costs: Costs that generally total from 2 to 5 percent of a home's purchase price and are completely independent of (and in addition to) the *down payment.* Closing costs include such expenses as *points* (also called the loan *origination fee*), an *appraisal* fee, a *credit report* fee, mortgage interest for the period between the closing date and the first loan payment, *homeowners insurance* premium, *title insurance,* prorated *property tax,* and recording and transferring charges. When you're finally ready to buy your dream home, don't forget that you must have enough cash to pay all these costs to complete the purchase.

condominiums: Housing units contained within a larger development area in which residents own their actual units and a share of everything else in the development (lobby, parking areas, land, and the like, which are known as common areas).

conforming loans: Mortgages that fall within *Fannie Mae* and *Freddie Mac's* loan limits. If you borrow less than this amount, you'll get a lower interest rate than on so-called nonconforming or *jumbo loans.*

contingencies: Conditions contained in almost all home-purchase offers. Sellers or buyers must meet or waive all their respective contingencies before the deal can be closed. These conditions are related to such factors as the buyer's review and approval of property inspections or the buyer's ability to obtain the mortgage financing specified in the contract. If you're a homebuyer, make absolutely certain that your offer contains a loan contingency.

convertible adjustable-rate mortgages: Loans that (unlike conventional *adjustable-rate mortgages*) give you the opportunity to convert to a *fixed-rate mortgage,* usually between the 13th and 60th month of the loan. For this privilege, convertible adjustable-rate mortgage loans have a higher rate of interest than conventional adjustable-rate mortgages, and a conversion fee (which can range from a few hundred dollars to 1 percent or so of the remaining loan balance) is charged. Additionally, if you choose to convert your ARM to a fixed-rate mortgage, you'll probably pay a slightly higher rate than you can get by shopping around for the best rates available at the time you convert.

cooperatives (co-ops): Apartment buildings where residents own a share of a corporation whose main asset is the building they live in. Cooperative apartments are generally harder to finance and harder to sell than condominiums.

cosigner: A friend or relative who comes to a borrower's rescue by cosigning (which literally means being indebted for) a mortgage. If you have a checkered past in the credit world, you may need help securing a mortgage, even though you're currently financially stable. A cosigner can't improve your *credit report* but can improve your chances of getting a mortgage. Cosigners should be aware, however, that cosigning for your loan will adversely affect their future creditworthiness, because your loan becomes what is known as a contingent liability against their borrowing power.

credit line: A credit account that permits a *reverse mortgage* borrower to control the timing and amount of the loan advances (also known as a "line of credit").

credit report: A report that documents your history of repaying debt. It's the main report lenders use to determine your creditworthiness. You must pay for this report, which is used to determine your ability to handle all forms of credit and to pay off loans in a timely fashion. If you're a seller who's providing financing for buyers, get their permission to obtain a credit report on them.

debt-to-income ratio: Measures your future monthly housing expenses, which include your proposed mortgage payment (debt), property tax, and insurance in relation to your monthly income. Mortgage lenders generally figure that you shouldn't spend more than about 40 percent of your monthly income on housing costs.

deed: The document that conveys title to real property. Before you receive the deed to your new home, the *escrow* holder must receive the payoff for the old loan on the property, your new mortgage financing, and your payments for the *down payment* and *closing costs.* The title insurance company must also show that the seller holds clear and legal title to the property for which title is being conveyed.

deed in lieu of foreclosure: Instead of *foreclosure,* which is generally costly and time consuming for all parties, a deed in lieu of foreclosure is a voluntarily entered agreement whereby the borrower conveys ownership of the property in *default* to the lender to satisfy outstanding debt on that property.

deed of trust: A security instrument that transfers title to property to a third person (the *trustee*) as a guarantee you'll repay a debt. Like a mortgage, a deed of trust makes real property security for money you borrow.

default: Status that is most often caused by failure to make monthly mortgage payments on time. You're officially in default when you've missed two or more monthly payments. Default also refers to other violations of mortgage terms such as trying to pass your loan on to another buyer when the property is sold, which triggers the loan's *due-on-sale clause.* Default can lead to *foreclosure* on your house.

delinquency: Status that occurs when the mortgage lender doesn't receive a monthly mortgage payment by the due date. At first a borrower is delinquent; then he or she is in *default.*

depreciation: Decrease in a property's value (the reverse of *appreciation*).

down payment: The part of the purchase price that the buyer pays in cash, upfront, and does not finance with a mortgage. Generally, the larger the down payment, the better the deal you can get on a mortgage. You can usually qualify for the best available mortgage programs with a down payment of 20 percent of the property's value.

due-on-sale clause: A mortgage clause that entitles the lender to demand full payment of all money due on a loan when the borrower sells or transfers title to the property.

earthquake insurance: Either an earthquake insurance rider on a homeowners policy or a separate policy that pays to repair or rebuild a home if it's damaged in an earthquake. Some lenders insist that borrowers obtain earthquake insurance. Even if your mortgage lender doesn't, we strongly recommend that you get earthquake insurance if you live in an area with earthquake risk.

11th District Cost of Funds Index (COFI): An adjustable-rate mortgage (ARM) index that tracks the weighted average cost of savings, borrowings, and advances for Federal Home Loan Bank Board member banks located in California, Arizona, and Nevada (the 11th District). Because the COFI is a moving average of interest rates that bankers have paid depositors over recent months, it tends to be a relatively stable, slower moving ARM index.

encumbrance: A right or interest someone else holds in a homeowner's property that affects its title or limits its use. A mortgage, for example, is a money encumbrance that affects a home's title by making it security for repayment of the loan.

equity: In the real estate world, equity refers to the difference between the market value of a home and the amount the borrower owes on it. For example, if your home is worth $200,000 and you have an outstanding mortgage of $140,000, your equity is $60,000.

escrow: The holding of important documents and money related to the purchase/sale of real estate by a neutral third party (the escrow officer) prior to the close of the transaction. After the seller accepts an offer, the buyer doesn't immediately move into the house. A period when *contingencies* have to be met or waived exists. During this period, the escrow service holds the *down payment* and other buyer and seller documents related to the sale. "Closing escrow" means that the deal is completed. Among other duties, the escrow officer makes sure the previous mortgage is paid off and the loan is funded.

Fannie Mae: See *Federal National Mortgage Association.*

Federal Home Loan Mortgage Corporation (FHLMC): One of the best-known institutions in the secondary mortgage market. Also known as Freddie Mac, the FHLMC buys mortgages from banks and other mortgage-lending institutions and, in turn, sells these mortgages to investors. These loan investments are considered safe because Freddie Mac buys mortgages only from companies that conform to its stringent mortgage regulations, and Freddie Mac guarantees the repayment of *principal* and interest on the mortgages that it sells.

Federal Housing Administration mortgage (FHA): Mortgages that are generally targeted to people with low incomes. The main advantage of these mortgages is that they require a small *down payment* (usually 5 percent or less of a home's purchase price). FHA mortgages also offer competitive *interest rates* — typically 0.5 to 1 percent below the interest rates on other mortgages. The downside is that, with an FHA mortgage, the buyer must purchase mortgage default insurance (see *private mortgage insurance*).

Federal National Mortgage Association (FNMA): One of the best-known institutions in the secondary mortgage market. Also known as Fannie Mae, the FNMA buys mortgages from banks and other mortgage-lending institutions and, in turn, sells them to investors. These loan investments are considered safe because Fannie Mae buys mortgages only from companies that conform to its stringent mortgage regulations, and Fannie Mae guarantees the repayment of *principal* and interest on the loans that it sells.

fixed-rate mortgage: A mortgage that allows you to lock in an *interest rate* for the entire term (generally 15 or 30 years) of the mortgage. Your mortgage payment will be the same amount every month. Compare fixed-rate mortgages with *adjustable-rate mortgages.*

fixed-term reverse mortgage: A *reverse mortgage* that becomes due and payable on a specific date.

flood insurance: Insurance that homebuyers in federally designated flood areas must purchase to obtain a mortgage. If there's even a remote chance that your area may flood, having flood insurance is prudent.

foreclosure: The legal process by which a lender takes possession of and sells property in an attempt to satisfy mortgage indebtedness. When you *default* on a loan and the lender deems that you're incapable of making payments, you may lose your home to foreclosure. Being in default, however, doesn't necessarily lead to foreclosure. Some lenders are lenient (and smart enough to realize that foreclosure is costly for them). They'll help you work out a solution if they see that you can remedy your problems.

formula: The way to calculate interest rate revisions for *adjustable-rate mortgages.* Add the ARM's *margin* to the *index* to get the adjusted *interest rate* (margin + index = interest rate).

Freddie Mac: See *Federal Home Loan Mortgage Corporation.*

graduated-payment mortgage: A rare loan specifying monthly payments that increase by a predetermined formula (for example, a 3 percent increase each year for seven years, after which time payments no longer fluctuate).

home equity: The market value of a home minus any debt against it.

home equity conversion: The *reverse mortgage* process of turning home equity into cash without having to sell or rent the home or make regular loan repayments.

Home Equity Conversion Mortgage (HECM): The *reverse mortgage* program insured by the *Federal Housing Administration (FHA).*

home equity loan: Technical jargon for a type of *second mortgage* that allows you to borrow against the *equity* in your house. If used wisely, a home equity loan can help people pay off high-interest, non-tax-deductible consumer debt or meet other short-term needs, such as payments on a remodeling project.

homeowners insurance: A policy that protects what is probably your most valuable asset — your home. Mortgage lenders will always require that you have this coverage before funding your loan. "Dwelling coverage" covers the cost to rebuild a house. The liability insurance portion of this policy protects you against accidents that occur on your property. The personal property coverage pays to replace your lost worldly possessions.

hybrid loans: Loans that combine features of *fixed-rate* and *adjustable-rate mortgages.* The initial *interest rate* for a hybrid loan may be fixed at the same rate for the first three to ten years of the loan (as opposed to only 6 to 12 months for a standard adjustable-rate mortgage); then the interest rate adjusts biannually or annually. The longer the interest rate remains the same, the higher the initial interest rate will be. These loans are best for people who plan to own their house for a short time (fewer than ten years) and who don't like the volatility of a typical adjustable-rate mortgage.

index: A measure of the overall level of market *interest rates* that the lender uses as a reference to calculate the specific interest rate on an adjustable-rate loan. The index plus the *margin* determines the interest rate on an *adjustable-rate mortgage.* One index used on some mortgages is the six-month treasury bill. For example, if the going rate for these treasury bills is 4 percent and the margin is 2.5 percent, your interest rate would be 6.5 percent. Other common indexes used are the *certificates of deposit* index, *11th District Cost of Funds index,* and *LIBOR index.*

interest rate: Interest charges generally accrued as a percentage of the amount borrowed. The interest rate is usually quoted in percent per year. (Interest is the amount lenders charge you to use their money.)

jumbo loans: Mortgages that exceed the *Fannie Mae* and *Freddie Mac* maximum permissible *conforming loan* amounts (also called *jumbo conforming* or *nonconforming loans*). You pay a higher interest rate for nonconformity. The higher the loan amount, the more it hurts the lender if you *default* on your loan. Lenders generally require more than the usual 20 percent down on jumbo loans.

late charge: A lender fee charged if a mortgage payment is received late. Late charges can be as much as 5 percent of your mortgage payment, so be sure to get your loan payments in on time.

lien: A legal claim against a property for the purpose of securing payment for work performed and money owed on account of loans, judgments, or claims. Liens are *encumbrances* that must be paid off before a property can be sold or title can transfer to a subsequent buyer. The liens that are a matter of public record on a property for sale appear on a property's preliminary report.

life cap: The limit that determines the maximum amount your *adjustable-rate mortgage* interest rate and monthly payment can fluctuate up or down during the duration of the loan. The life cap is different from the *periodic cap* that limits the extent to which your interest rate can change up or down in any one *adjustment period.*

lifetime advances: On a *reverse mortgage,* fixed monthly loan advances for the rest of a borrower's life.

loan advances: Payments made to a *reverse mortgage* borrower or to another party on behalf of a borrower.

lock-in: A mortgage lender's written commitment to guarantee a specified *interest rate* to the mortgage borrower provided that the loan is closed within a set period of time. The lock-in should specify the number of *points* to be paid at closing. For the privilege of locking in the rate in advance of the closing of a loan, you may pay a slight interest rate premium.

London Interbank Offered Rate Index (LIBOR): An *adjustable-rate mortgage* (ARM) index. It's an average of the interest rates that major international banks charge each other to borrow U.S. dollars in the London money market. Relative to other ARM indexes, LIBOR responds rapidly to changes in interest rates. This international interest-rate index is used on some mortgages because foreign investors buy American mortgages as investments.

lump sum: A single loan advance at closing of particular *reverse mortgage* loans.

margin: The amount that's added to the *index* to calculate the *interest rate* for an *adjustable-rate mortgage.* Most loans have margins around 2.5 percent. Unlike the index (which constantly moves up and down), the margin never changes over the life of the loan.

maturity: When a loan becomes due and payable.

mortgage: A word used by lenders to describe a formidable stack of legal documents borrowers must sign to get the money they need to *refinance* or buy *real property.* Ordinary folks of the nonlender variety generally refer to a home loan as a mortgage.

mortgage broker: A person who can help you obtain a mortgage. Mortgage brokers buy mortgages wholesale from lenders, mark the mortgages up (typically from 0.5 to 1 percent), and sell them to buyers. A good mortgage broker is most helpful for people who don't want to shop around on their own for a mortgage or for people who have blemishes on their *credit reports.*

mortgage life insurance: Insurance guaranteeing that the lender will receive its money in the dismal event that the borrower meets an untimely demise. Those who sell this insurance will try to convince you that you need this insurance to protect your dependents and loved ones. Don't waste your money — mortgage life insurance is relatively expensive compared to low-cost, high-quality term life insurance.

negative amortization: Occurs when an outstanding mortgage balance increases despite the fact that the borrower is making the required monthly payments. Negative amortization occurs with *adjustable-rate mortgages* that *cap* the increase in the monthly loan payment but don't cap the *interest rate.* Therefore, the monthly payments don't cover all the interest that the borrower actually owes. We strongly recommend you avoid loans with this feature.

nonconforming loans: See *jumbo loans.*

nonrecourse mortgage: A loan in which a lender can use only the value of the home as security for repayment of the mortgage in the event of a loan *default.*

origination: The administrative process of setting up a mortgage, including the preparation of documents.

origination fee: See *points.*

periodic cap: The limit on the amount that the *interest rate* of an *adjustable-rate mortgage* can change up or down in one *adjustment period.* See also *cap.*

points: Interest charges paid upfront when a borrower closes on a loan. Also known as a loan's origination fee, points are actually a percentage of the total loan amount (one point is equal to 1 percent of the loan amount). For a $100,000 loan, one point costs $1,000. Generally speaking, the more points a loan has, the lower its *interest rate* should be. All the points paid on a purchase mortgage are deductible in the year they're paid. If you *refinance* your mortgage, however, the points you pay at the time that you refinance must be *amortized* (spread out) over the life of the loan. If you get a 30-year mortgage when you refinance, for example, you can deduct only one-thirtieth of the points on your taxes each year.

preapproval: A process — far more rigorous than *prequalification* — that mortgage lenders use to determine how much money they'd lend you based on a thorough review of your financial situation. Getting a preapproval letter strengthens your negotiating position when you're buying a home, because it shows the sellers your seriousness and creditworthiness.

prepayment: The payment of extra principal on a mortgage — in other words, making higher than minimum loan payments to pay off a mortgage faster than is required by the lender.

prepayment penalty: A fee that discourages borrowers from making additional payments on their mortgage loan principal to pay the loan off faster. We highly urge you to avoid mortgages that penalize prepayment.

prequalification: An informal process whereby lenders, based entirely on the information you disclose about your financial situation, provide an opinion about the amount of money you may be able to borrow. This assessment is neither binding nor necessarily accurate, because the lenders haven't verified any of your financial information.

principal: The amount borrowed for a loan. If you borrow $100,000, your principal is $100,000. Each monthly mortgage payment consists of a portion of principal that must be repaid plus the *interest* that the lender is charging you for the use of the money. During the early years of your mortgage, your loan payment is primarily interest.

private mortgage insurance (PMI): Insurance that protects the lender in case a borrower defaults on a mortgage. If your *down payment* is less than 20 percent of your home's purchase price, you'll likely need to purchase private mortgage insurance (also known as "mortgage default insurance"). The smaller the down payment, the more likely a homebuyer is to *default* on a loan. Private mortgage insurance can add hundreds of dollars per year to your loan costs. After the *equity* in your property increases to 20 percent, you no longer need the insurance. Don't confuse this insurance with *mortgage life insurance.*

promissory note: This note is the evidence of your debt, an IOU that specifies exactly how much money you borrowed as well as the terms and conditions under which you promise to repay it.

property tax: Yearly tax (paid by the owner) assessed on a home. Property tax annually averages 1 to 2 percent of a home's value, but property tax rates vary widely throughout this great land.

real property: Dirt. Plain old terra firma and any buildings such as homes, garages, tool sheds, barns, or other structures permanently attached to the land.

reconveyance: The conveyance back to a property owner of legal title held by a trustee according to terms of a *deed of trust*. A deed of reconveyance is usually recorded when the loan has been repaid as constructive proof that the debt is satisfied.

refinance: Lending industry jargon for taking out a new mortgage loan (usually at a lower *interest rate*) to pay off an existing mortgage (generally at a higher interest rate). Refinancing (also called a refi) isn't automatic, nor is refinancing guaranteed. Refinancing can also be an expensive hassle. Carefully weigh the costs and benefits of refinancing.

reverse annuity mortgage: A *reverse mortgage* in which a lump sum is used to purchase an *annuity.*

reverse mortgage: A loan that enables elderly homeowners, who typically are low on cash, to tap into their home's *equity* without selling their home or moving from it. Specifically, a lending institution makes a check out to the homeowners each month; the homeowners then use the proceeds any way they wish. This money is really a loan against the value of a home. Because the money is a loan, it's tax-free when the homeowners receive it. These loans are *nonrecourse.* The downsides of these loans are that they deplete estate equity, the fees and *interest rates* tend to be on the high side, and some require repayment within a certain number of years.

second mortgage: A mortgage that ranks after a first mortgage in priority of recording. In the event of a *foreclosure,* the proceeds from the sale of the home are used to pay off the loans in the order in which they were recorded. You can have a third (or even a fourth) mortgage, but the further down the line the mortgage is, the higher the risk of *default* — hence, the higher *interest rate* on the mortgage. See also *home equity loan.*

short sale: Done with a property in *default,* to keep it from *foreclosure.* The lender agrees to accept the proceeds from selling the property as fully satisfying outstanding debt even though the amount of that debt exceeds the sale proceeds.

Supplemental Security Income (SSI): A federal government program providing monthly cash benefits to low-income persons aged 65 and over, blind, or disabled.

tax deductible: Payments that you may deduct against your federal and state taxable income. The interest portion of mortgage payments, loan *points,* and *property taxes* are tax deductible.

teaser rate: The attractively low interest rate that most *adjustable-rate mortgages* start with. This rate is also known as the initial interest rate. Don't be sucked into a mortgage because it has a low teaser rate. Look at the mortgage's *formula* (index + margin = interest rate) for a more reliable method of estimating the loan's future interest rate — the interest rate that will apply after the loan is "fully indexed."

tenure advances: Fixed monthly *reverse mortgage* loan advances for as long as a borrower lives in a home.

term: In a mortgage plan, the amount of time (typically 15 or 30 years) a lender gives a borrower to repay the loan.

term advances: Fixed monthly *reverse mortgage* loan advances for a specific period of time.

title insurance: Insurance that covers the legal fees and expenses necessary to defend your title against claims that may be made against your ownership of the property. The extent of your coverage depends on whether you have an owner's standard coverage or extended-coverage title insurance policy. To get a mortgage, you also have to buy a lender's title insurance policy to protect your lender against title risks.

treasury bills (T-bills): Short-term U.S.-government bonds. Some ARM indexes are based on the interest rate that the government pays on the pile of federal debt. The most commonly used government interest rate indexes for ARMs are for six-month and twelve-month treasury bills. The treasury bill indexes tend to respond quickly to market changes in interest rates.

VA loans: Loans made by the Department of Veterans Affairs (formerly the Veterans Administration). These *mortgages* help eligible people (those on active duty; qualified unmarried, former spouses of veterans; and veterans of the American military services) buy primary residences. The rules to obtain these mortgages are less stringent in certain respects than are the rules for conventional mortgages. VA loans require no *down payment* as long as the appraised value of the house is below a certain threshold level, and the *interest rate* on VA loans typically falls 0.5 to 1 percent below the rate currently being charged on conventional loans.

Index

Numerics

A

D

E

F

G

H

M

N

Q

R

S

T

U

V

W

About the Authors

Eric Tyson, MBA, is a bestselling author and syndicated columnist. Through his counseling, writing, and teaching, he equips people to manage their personal finances better. Eric is a former management consultant to Fortune 500 financial service firms, has successfully invested in real estate securities for more than three decades, and has started and managed several businesses.

Eric earned his bachelor's degree in economics at Yale and an MBA at the Stanford Graduate School of Business. Despite these handicaps to clear thinking, he had the good sense to start his own company, which took an innovative approach to teaching people of all economic means about investing and money.

An accomplished freelance personal finance writer, Eric is the author of the national bestsellers *Personal Finance For Dummies* and *Investing For Dummies*, coauthor of *Home Buying For Dummies*, and was an award-winning columnist for the *San Francisco Examiner*. His work has been featured and quoted in hundreds of national and local publications, including *Newsweek*, the *Wall Street Journal*, *Forbes*, *Kiplinger's Personal Finance Magazine*, the *Los Angeles Times*, and *Bottom Line/Personal*; and on Fox, NBC's *Today Show*, ABC, CNBC, PBS's *Nightly Business Report*, CNN, CBS national radio, Bloomberg Business Radio, and Business Radio Network. He's also been a featured speaker at a White House conference on retirement planning.

He's on the web at `www.erictyson.com`.

Robert S. Griswold, MSBA, is a successful real estate investor, expert witness, and hands-on landlord/property manager with a large portfolio of residential and commercial rental income properties. He uses print and broadcast journalism to bring his many years of experience to his readers, listeners, and viewers.

He is the author of *Property Management For Dummies* and *Property Management Kit For Dummies* and for 15 years was the real estate expert for NBC San Diego, with a regular on-air live-caller segment. Robert was the host of a live weekly radio talk show, *Real Estate Today!*, for nearly 15 years, and he's also the columnist for the syndicated "Rental Roundtable" and "Rental Forum" columns. These popular features are published in dozens of major newspapers throughout the country, and Robert has been recognized twice as the number-one real estate broadcast journalist in the nation by the National Association of Real Estate Editors.

Robert's educational background includes having earned a BS and two master's degrees in finance and business economics, real estate finance, international finance, real estate and urban land economics, and real estate development, all from the Marshall School of Business at the University of Southern California. His real estate investing and managing professional designations include the

CRE (Counselor of Real Estate), the CPM (Certified Property Manager), the CCIM (Certified Commercial Investment Member), the ARM (Accredited Residential Manager), the GRI (Graduate, REALTOR Institute), the CCAM (Certified Community Association Manager), and the PCAM (Professional Community Association Manager).

Robert has been retained on more than 2,000 legal matters as an expert in the standard of care, custom, and practice for all aspects of real estate ownership and management in both state and federal cases throughout the country. He is the president of Griswold Real Estate Management, Inc., managing residential, commercial, retail, and industrial properties throughout California and Nevada.

On a personal level, Robert enjoys travel (particularly cruises), sports, and family activities. He truly enjoys real estate and tries to keep life in perspective through humor!

Dedication

This book is hereby and irrevocably dedicated to my family and friends, as well as to my counseling clients and customers, who ultimately have taught me everything I know about how to explain financial terms and strategies so all of us may benefit. —Eric Tyson

I want to thank God for giving me any and all abilities I may have to assist others with their real estate investments and financing decisions. This book is dedicated to my heroic and brave son Michael Griswold, who (although he has lost his eyesight) is successfully battling Stage IV brain melanoma. With God's love and Michael's incredible faith and determination, he has defied all the odds to make medical history. Of course, we want to thank our family, friends, medical professionals, and caregivers on "Team Michael" for their never-ending efforts and support. We are truly blessed to have a medical team led by Dr. Gregory A. Daniels and Dr. Scott A. Godfrey, who never gave up on Michael and are a key factor in his amazing and successful battle to date against one of the most deadly cancers of all. —Robert Griswold

Authors' Acknowledgments

We offer our heartfelt thanks and appreciation to the many good people at Wiley, including Tracy Boggier for going to bat for this book, Vicki Adang for her fine project management skills, and Jennette ElNaggar for her helpful editing suggestions.

We also wish to express our deepest thanks and appreciation to our friends and colleagues.

Publisher's Acknowledgments

Senior Acquisitions Editor: Tracy Boggier

Development Editor: Victoria M. Adang

Copy Editor: Jennette ElNaggar

Technical Editors: Randy Johnson, Larry Wallace

Production Editor: Magesh Elangovan

Cover Photo: © Ever/iStockphoto